D0153801

COMPASSIONATE AUTHORITY

COMPASSIONATE AUTHORITY

Democracy and the Representation of Women

KATHLEEN B. JONES

ROUTLEDGE

NEW YORK   LONDON

Published in 1993 by

Routledge
An imprint of Routledge, Chapman and Hall, Inc.
29 West 35th Street
New York, NY 10001

Published in Great Britain by

Routledge
11 New Fetter Lane
London EC4P 4EE

Jones, Kathleen B., 1949–
    Compassionate authority : democracy and the representation of
women / by Kathleen B. Jones.
        p. cm.
    Includes bibliographical references (p.   ) and index.
    ISBN 0-415-90643-1—ISBN 0-415-90644-X
    1. Women in politics. 2. Sex role—Political aspects.
3. Authority. 4. Sovereignty. 5. Feminist theory. I. Title.
HQ1236.J66   1992
305.42—dc20   92-24356
                                                          CIP

ISBN 0-415-90643-1 (HB)
ISBN 0-415-90644-X (PB)

In Memory of Betty A. Nesvold
1922–1992

Contents

Preface

The concept of authority has received extensive treatment in the literature of political theory, but very little direct discussion of it is to be found in feminist circles. Feminists seem to talk all around the problem of authority without ever seriously questioning whether what we have come to mean by the concept is consistent with feminist politics. Our efforts have been directed more at investigating how to remove the remaining obstacles to women's being in authority, or how to integrate women into politics, than inquiring about whether women's entering the field of authority as gendered subjects would challenge the terms of authority itself.

This book aims to break some of the silences in our discourse about politics by considering the question of the democratization of authority from a different angle: what if democratization means not only the assimilation of actual women into existing political structures, but, simultaneously, requires the critical recognition of representations of sexual difference as the basis for a different perspective on authority? Put differently, I wonder whether an iconoclastic exploration of the symbolic history of gender might provide a way to reconceptualize authority, and women's relation to it, in ways that depend upon neither the negation of women's distinctive gender characteristics nor the uncritical affirmation of gender differences.

My strategy will be iconoclastic. I intend to challenge certain sacred precepts—such as building theory from women's experiences—that have become "taken for granted" in feminist theory. I think that iconoclasm is important if we are to begin to engage in what Wendy Brown recently called "public conversations with one another." Iconoclasm may mean the shattering of sacred images, old as well as new, but it also permits the reconstruction of other portraits of a feminist polity that are more "women-friendly."

Despite my sympathy for the postmodernist project, with its suspicion of essentialist categories, I admit my own reluctance to jettison "women" as an important subject of feminist theory. To treat women as a dispensable category seems tragic in 1992. It's 1992, and political structures continue to be securing the wealth of a few through the construction of an "integrated circuit" of exploited labor. (Haraway, in Nicholson, 207) This integrated circuit is formed most often through women's labor, connecting segregated tinder boxes of communities in the police states of the inner cities of the United States to the sweat shops of Export Processing Zones in Hong Kong; Colon, Panama; and Guadalajara, Mexico. The mark of the integrated circuit is stamped in the label of our designer clothes, bought on sale at Macy's, descarded, and sold again at a local yard sale to raise money for women's organizations in Central America.

In 1992 we need to begin to take responsibility for our lives, and for the ways that each of us contributes to the maintenance of the integrated circuit. Yet, as Cherríe Moraga reminds us, it is "much easier to rank oppressions and set up a hierarchy, rather than to take responsibility for our own lives." (1984, 58) We get into ranking oppressions when we confuse authority with sovereignty. We need to break with this practice and begin to engage in dialogue in a reconstructed, democratic public space about what kinds of meaningful collective life we envision within which diversity can flourish. Yet we also need to admit that some of our conversations will have to deal with the painful questions of not only how we will facilitate the building of inclusive communities, but whether and how we can make judgments about excluding some from a polity friendly to women. It will be with regard to this last-named enterprise that what I have called compassionate authority will find its most serious political challenge. Will compassionate authority be resilient enough to establish political solidarity and to recognize, as Hannah Arendt argued, the dignity of the strong as well as the weak?

This book has been many years in development. I have benefitted from having unusually supportive colleagues as well as loving friends. Many of the people I have to thank will recognize parts of conversations and papers in these pages. Others will probably be surprised to see the final form to which some ongoing exchanges have ultimately led. I am grateful to the Department of Women's Studies at San Diego State University for my academic home and for providing me with the opportunity to present portions of the manuscript at various faculty colloquia over the years. Special thanks to Stanford University's Institute for Research on Women and Gender, especially to my dear friend Sherri Matteo, and to the University of California at Berkeley's Beatrice Bain Research Group for their hospitable environments and for exciting dialogue during my 1988 sabbatical semester.

Richard Flathman deserves my appreciation for his long-standing support of all the different directions in which the ideas in this book have gone. I owe thanks, too, to William Connolly and all the participants in the 1984 National Endowment for the Humanities seminar at University of Massachusetts, Amherst for inspiration. There I met Kathy Ferguson, who remains one of my most important feminist "buddies." Her comments and criticisms over the years have helped shape my thinking in many ways. I am enormously grateful to Jean Bethke Elshtain, whose humor and intellect have always been a support to me, and whose willingness to read portions of this manuscript under duress has been constant.

I am indebted to many other colleagues and friends who have taken the time to read and comment on my work in its various incarnations. They include Terence Ball, Nancie Caraway, Melinda Cuthbert, Mildred Dickeman, Virginia Held, Julie Hemker, Jane Jaquette, Evelyn Fox Keller, Howard Kushner, Ellen Lewin, Tracy Strong, Paul Thomas, and Françoise Vergès. Thanks are due also to Cecelia Cancellaro for her support of this project, and to the two reviewers for Routledge for their insightful suggestions.

I have had the good fortune of directing National Endowment for the Humanities Summer Seminars for School Teachers on topics realted to this book in 1988, 1989, and 1992. To each of those groups of dedicated scholar-teachers I am grateful for dialogue that helped bring my ideas to completion. But to my 1992 colleagues Deborah Alade, Kathy Barron, Debby Bodie, Herb Brodsky, Colleen Duggan, Liz Goldstein, Lexy Green, Vicky Greenbaum, Deb Hall, Ranjinie Jayawardana, Liz La Porte, Sarah Peterson, Judy Sisson, Sydney Spiegel, and Jainie Thrailkill who painstakingly read the manuscript in its entirety in page proof, thanks for your enthusiasm and support.

Those who have been closest to me have borne most of the burden of the ups and downs of this book. To my father and stepmother, Edward and Caroline Jones, thanks for your love and support. To my friend Ashley Phillips, thanks for the support, never-failing conversation, and dedication to the women's movement. To my colleague, friend, ex-commuting buddy, and my son's photography hero, Lynda Koolish, thanks for being there. To my students at San Diego State University and at the University of California, Berkeley, much appreciation for many inspiring and challenging classroom-and-beyond experiences. To Paul Thomas, thanks for the love and the tolerance of my travels, intellectual and otherwise. To my sons, Jed and Ari, and to George, thanks for your sacrifices of planes unbuilt, books unread, movies unseen, and conversations attenuated. To my friend and co-survivor, Françoise Vergès, *merci plus que je dit. To Co-Madres* and to *Mujeres por la Dignidad y la Vida: Venceremos*! Finally, to Amy, thanks for the rainbows in my soul.

I have dedicated this book to the memory of my friend and colleague Betty A. Nesvold. She paved the way for so many of us women in political science. Thanks, Betty, for helping us to begin and to finish. We miss you.

Introduction: Feminist Paradoxes and the Trouble with Authority

I began this book some years ago trying to understand the relationship between women and authority. Then I assumed that women's exclusion from authority was what needed explaining. Exploring theories ranging from Marxism to feminist psychoanalytic theory, I became interested in the ways that the internalization of codes of femininity and masculinity contributed to a basic organization of society around the pivot of gender-based divisions of responsibility and privilege. My intention then was to "examine the connections between these divisions [of responsibility and privilege] and the problem of the democratization of authority." I concluded that it was important to conceptualize the dynamics of authority relations more broadly than traditional political theory had considered, especially by recognizing the internal connections between patterns of authority in the public realm and the social organization of gender. Making the exercise of political authority more democratic, I argued, would depend upon "changes in the private sphere." (Jones 1980, 2, 38) Yet the more I explored the literature on authority, with its predilection to conflate authority with command, the more I concluded that the concept and practice of authority was what needed to change. I shifted my analysis from inquiring into those conditions that would enhance women's being in authority, women's being enabled to command, to asking whether the dominant conceptualization of authority as commanding sovereignty represented a gendered-masculine practice as normative; I began to explore alternative concepts and practices of authority.

This book has become an extended reflection on the paradox of my writing about authority. I am a member of a group, namely women, generally not having been recognized as having any—that is, authority in the public sense. The paradox of being a woman writing about authority has been doubled by another within recent feminist theory

1

itself: the effort to integrate women into public life as equals while still claiming that what matters is that *women,* not genderless and sexless persons, will become more fully present in public life. The paradox is reflected in contemporary feminist efforts to reconcile the argument that gender should not be used to structure and enforce anyone's assignment to a social or political place, with the claim that gender, as symbolic category, might remain significant to and productive of the rethinking and restructuring of political reality and authority.

This paradoxical endorsement in feminist theory of both equality and difference implies that were different women integrated into public life, and were the sets of interests connected historically and symbolically with women's experiences to become part of political thinking, then the practice of politics and authority would be transformed. Such an argument followed from the claim of feminist standpoint theorists that because women's knowledge and experiences were distinctive, the conceptualization and practice of authority would have to be reconfigured in order to accommodate women's epistemological and existential perspectives on authority within the discourse of political analysis and political action.

Feminist political theory became engaged with the question of how the incorporation of different women's political values and interests would decenter the hegemony of androcentric constructions of political theory and political action. So engaged, feminists became involved with the project of rebuilding knowledge of politics from the ground up, focusing theoretical efforts on producing more representative narratives of women's lives, and on the basis of these, on constructing more inclusive theories and practices of politics.

There were political interests behind this project, but however flawed and biased it was, the intention was to build a more inclusive theory and to work for a more democratic world. At the same time, post-structuralism began to have considerable influence in contemporary theory. By deconstructing the validity of such basic categories of feminist analysis as "women," "exploitation," "liberation," "gender," and "patriarchy," post-structuralism challenged the possibility of realizing modernist epistemological projects either to build general theories of women's experiences or to create more complete political narratives. (Weed, 1989, x)

Because of their own criticism of the dream of objectivity and their defense of context-bound epistemologies, many feminist theorists, myself among them, have been sympathetic to post-structuralist methodologies. Yet feminist theory's contemporary deployment of a post-Enlightenment strategy of deconstructing truth claims in the name of the endless plurality of discourse has, ironically, gained ascendancy at precisely the moment when women's studies scholarship has been producing works whose reinterpretations of classical texts, or rereadings of women's experiences and values, have been hailed as authoritative, and in many disciplines, regarded as the basis for transforming the curriculum. This has led some feminists to become suspicious of postmodernist politics. As Nancy Hartsock has written:

> Why is it exactly at the moment when so many of us who have been silenced begin to demand the right to name ourselves, to act as subjects rather than objects of history, that just then the concept of subjecthood becomes 'problematic'? *Just when we are forming our own theories of the world, uncertainty emerges about whether the world can be adequately theorized?* (1987, 196 emphasis added; cf. Miller 1986, 104–06)

So here is another paradox: contemporary feminists have contributed to the rejection of authority while continuing to demand the status of the authoritative for their own narratives including, ironically, the narratives of post-structuralists. In this light, some feminists' claims that the "quest for mastery . . . is a phallocentric one" become either overdrawn or disingenuous. (Modleski 1986, 127–8) Feminist discourse, including post-structuralist feminist theory, becomes trapped by the appeal of sovereign authority.[1]

It is possible to resolve these paradoxes only if we confront directly the problem of what authority has been understood to be. In political theory the discourse on authority has depended heavily on sexual dichotomies which structure, among other things, the direction in which authority appears to move: from the top down. Faced with an imagery of authority evidently connected to metaphors of domination that are sexually resonant, some feminists have argued for a retreat from authority to a purer state of perfectly consensual harmony. (MacKinnon, 1982) Yet simply to reject authority as inherently tainted is naive and concedes too much to the dominant tradition defining it. Instead of endorsing this quest for utopian *reconciliation,* with its appeal to some "higher," purer, "eternally feminine" harmonics, I urge that we adopt a more contradictory and more difficult theoretical position with respect to the problem of authority.

Feminists should acknowledge their political ambitions to authority while simultaneously engaging in the practice of rethinking authority's nature and effects. This makes a feminist critique of authority an (ironic) imperative. This critique not only might engage with the struggle to "redistribute and democratize *access to and control over* the means of interpretation and communication"; (Fraser 1987, 53, emphasis added) it also could transform radically the *mode* of interpretation and communication. Feminist theory would then be disturbing authority, dislodging the hold of current understandings of what authority is by a different staging of the drama of the authorial project. (Miller 1986)

The sort of transformative project with which I am concerned in this book engages with an interrogation of the characteristics of authority itself. A necessary aspect of this approach is to consider the ways that specific constructions of masculinity and femininity figure in the elaboration of arguments about what authority is and how one recognizes it. Identifying these specific features depends upon deploying some concept of gender. Yet gender is not a stable concept; representations of masculinity and femininity have a history. My interpretation of historical works in this project rests on reading texts in their context while, simultaneously, reading them against the grain. This second level of reading approaches historical texts from the perspective of the present; it risks anachronistic interpretations. The risk can be mitigated by not imputing contemporary intentions to historical actors and texts. Yet contemporary methods of interpretation and strategies of reading, such as psychoanalysis, structuralism, and post-structuralism can be employed fruitfully in considerations of what meanings we make of the past in the present. Such meanings "are obtained from a prior epoch in a manner that indisputably recasts, even violates, the 'truth' of the epoch." (Brown 1988, 17) Since every interpretation is, arguably, a violation of the "truth"—assuming that truth is some timeless, recoverable core— every interpretation is anachronistic in the literal sense of the term: reading backwards. "Reading backwards" enables us to tease out the "warring forces *within the text itself.*" (Johnson 1981, xiv)

Authority has not yet been subjected to feminist analysis. That itself is evidence of the discursive power of modern definitions of authority. We are so used to thinking about authority as some kind of legitimate control exercised over others, some sort of social coordination occupying a space between coercion and persuasion, that an alternative seems unimaginable. (Jones 1987, 156) Feminists are now comfortable with unsettling the traditional understandings of citizenship, power, justice, and other central concepts; yet authority remains threatening and unassailable.

I believe that feminists have resisted addressing the question of authority because we are so ambivalent about it. We want authority; we want to explode it; we want those who have not had authority before to take it for themselves. We include feminists among those who have not had authority before so that we can take it for ourselves. Yet we insist that we will not practice authority in the same way as the dominant class—those who already have authority—has done: monopolizing it and keeping others out.

Such ambivalence has been exacerbated by the realization that, increasingly, much of the contemporary debate among feminists is located within the academy. And this academy, especially in the United States, is becoming more isolated from the larger community that surrounds it, with the risk that the most progressive intellectuals might become the least politically *engagé*. At the same time, within the academy, theory itself has become highly rarified and depoliticized even while it insists most on its being on the politically radical cutting edge. The recovery of feminism's most radical moment is promised to those who embrace the position that both systems of domination and modes of resistance are neither fixed, locatable, nor limitable, but always fluid, circulating, and multiple. But with what political struggles, besides establishing its own hegemony as cultural "authority," is such a radical critique engaged? In the academy we can amuse ourselves by performing for one another, stringing together "always already" plural signifiers in endless daisy chains, but we will still wake up tomorrow in Bush's New World Order, an order where racism, sexism, and economic exploitation are global and pervasive, even if they are not practiced in the same way everywhere. Political radicalism is not a "style" or a "performance" that one can endlessly slip in and out of, never being caught in the same outfit twice, except for those who always already can afford seats at the Opera.

Several other commentators have argued that the "politics" with which post-modernism is most directly concerned is the politics of the academy itself and the struggles for control of hiring, resources, tenure, etc., within that context. The social effects of post-modernist critiques are felt most directly "not in the world of political and economic domination of the Third World by colonial and neocolonial powers, but rather in the academic institutions in which such authors participate." (Sangren 1988, 411) Barbara Christian has written about the politics of what she calls the "takeover in the literary world by Western philosophers from the old literary elite." This "takeover," she contends, reinforces the power of the new elite of the New Criticism so that *"their* way, *their* terms, *their* approaches remained central and became the means by which one defined literary critics." Consequently, many scholars and activists who had been involved in the process of reclaiming the contemporary and past literatures of the Third World and of people of color found themselves distracted from this project, having their energies "diverted into continually discussing the new literary theory." (1990, 339–40) The "new" methods served to reestablish the old politics of class, race, and sex privilege. (Mascia-Lees, Sharpe, and Cohen 1989)

As I write these words, I remain haunted and constrained by the logic of the criticisms I want to unsettle. I am caught by having to respond to the position that I want to critique, thereby authorizing its discursive power to control the terms of debate. Talking about the place of certain theories in "the academy," I am compelled, by the power of those whom the academy recognizes as establishing the terms of the debate, to reply within those terms in order to be heard. I hope to disturb these terms by calling attention to subversive, even potentially liberating, effects of deploying gendered epistemologies "against the grain." This book reflects, in part, on how feminism's promise of a transformative politics and a critical political theory depends upon reconfiguring authority as concept and practice.

Feminism can be represented as an antifoundational discourse, since it has been one of the modern iconoclastic anti-traditions contributing to the further erosion of certain values, once allegedly axiomatic, upon which authority has been grounded. The feminist critique of patriarchalism has shaken the foundation of a particular form of authority in public and private life. Carole Pateman's critique of the "sexual contract," for example, exposed the patriarchal underpinnings of modern liberal ideas about authority derived from consent. She argued that the foundation of modern contractarian exchanges of obedience for protection was rooted in a "fraternal patriarchy" which granted to men as men sexual rights over women; "rights" which were nonetheless defined as non-political. Under these terms, women were excluded as parties to the social contract. (1988)

At the same time, other feminists have argued not so much against authority per se as against women's being denied access to it. Susan Okin and Zillah Eisenstein, for instance, have called attention to those conditions of the organization of the sexual division of labor which have consigned women to the private sphere and which have limited women's ability to develop those talents and psychological attributes associated with being in authority. (Okin 1980, 1990;

Eisenstein, 1980) Their critique suggests that if modernity has killed authority, the feminist quest for the liberation and self-determination of women reflects a desire to resurrect authority and make it more accessible to women.

Still other feminists implicitly have confused authority with domination and have tended to associate authority in almost any form with the practices of masters, dominators, predators, and patriarchs. Accepting a position safely "outside" authority, they have called for the development of an alternative vision of politics and community untainted and unsullied by modes of authority and domination characteristic of the "malestream." Both Catherine MacKinnon and Andrea Dworkin, for instance, identify the essence of masculinity with the will to power and domination. Their solution to the problem is to eschew authority altogether while, at the same time, claiming their position is the correct feminist position. (MacKinnon, 1982)

In all of these cases, the assumption has been that the current understanding of authority as social control is incontrovertible. But resistance to questioning the nature and practice of authority is a serious mistake and has created a significant gap in the expanding literature in feminist political theory. Without questioning the practice and meaning of authority, feminists cannot develop a coherent vision of alternatives for building political community—alternatives both to the "illusory community" of capitalistic social relationships based on exchange, as well as to the artificial equality and vapid community of liberal contractarianism. Unless we address directly the question of authority, which is the question of founding a meaningful common life, then we remain silent about the most basic political questions: How do we make sense of public life? How do we act rightfully, and not just act?

POST-STRUCTURALIST FEMINISM, AUTHORITY IN THE ACADEMY, AND FEMINIST POLITICS

The current post-structuralist turn in feminist theory has compounded resistance to authority. The question "What makes actions rightful?" depends on judgments and, in the discourse of genealogy, judgments are disciplinary by definition. Once one accepts the thesis that every authoritative interpretation of public life opens up certain options for living only by closing down others, the temptation to suspend all judgment and to refuse to speak or to act increases. Who can speak for/as/about whom, who can use the term "woman" knowingly, authoritatively? Every interpretation becomes an imposition, every action a constraint. Doubts about certainty and truth seem to render impossible the articulation of any clear plan of political action.

Doubts and guilt abound. If there can be no generally accepted principles of action, then political theorizing itself becomes suspect, political inertia threatens, and the temptation is strong to retreat into private fantasy. As Richard Rorty put it, commenting on the implications of Derrida's deontological theory, theory is simply dropped "in favor of fantasizing. There is no moral to these fantasies, nor any public (pedagogic or political) use to be made of them." (1989, 125)

Once the secure foundation of the truthfulness of any interpretative claim has been called into question, to speak with authority about gender, about women and men and what sexual differences have represented, becomes both impossible and undesirable. Speaking about gender becomes impossible because skepticism immediately supplants acceptance of any generalizations about gender as even provisionally true. It becomes undesirable to speak about gender because even temporarily fixing categories such as gender, or even provisionally making statements such as "in the interests of women, we should secure reproductive rights," are seen as politically dangerous since they risk reproducing, at the level of theory and strategy, the hegemony of binary oppositions.

The hidden assumption here is that the binary form of gender *must* be subverted if the (what has now, ironically, become the unchallengeable) political goal of feminism is to be reached: the denaturalization of sex and gender, and the unbounded freedom to proliferate multiple identities in an endless series of subversive repetitions. (Butler *Gender Trouble*, 149) If the category "women" can operate as a coherent and stable subject for feminist theory only insofar as gender relations are reified, then, some post-structuralist feminists have argued, feminism becomes impossible the moment it founds itself in that subject.

In this view even the strategic assertion that women are different, even an assertion that insists on reclaiming sexual difference in order not to be disappeared, legitimates the very principle of sexual dimorphism that feminists have argued undergirds patriarchy and the system of sexual exploitation that it institutionalizes. In other words, to say that women are different is to imply that this difference is specifiable, immediately generating the nagging question: "Different from what?" Since the very stability of the sign, "women," excludes whatever experiences cannot be fit neatly into feminist discourse about how to recognize women, the category "women," whether deployed by feminists or anti-feminists, becomes "normative in character and hence exclusionary in principle." (Butler, *Gender Trouble,* 5; Butler in Nicholson, 325)

The implication is that the theoretical authority of "women" as a category in feminist theory can be purchased only at the expense of the liberation of women, whoever they are, from having to be women, whatever that means. Only by abandoning the notion of a "female subject" as the foundational moment of feminist theory, only by dethroning "women" as the subjects of feminist politics can feminist theory return to take up its (proper) project of feminist political theorizing from the (proper) point of departure: the "illimitable *et cetera*" that might lead to the "denaturalization of gender as such." (Butler, *Gender Trouble,* 143, 149)

This move to abandon women as the subjects of feminist theory and politics has deeply troubling political implications. Denaturalization easily slips into denial; the refusal to be given, or even to give one's self, a "name" shades over into fantasies of autogenesis. (Vergès 1991) The fantasies with which feminist post-structuralists in the United States have become mesmerized are imaginative narratives that promise the possibility of escaping the constraints and responsibilities of a specific location in time and place by avoiding being caught in a specifiable corporeality: if I can dress my body up in the costumes of the unexpected, then I can refuse to have a shape limited by the meaning that my body is supposed to have.

The "celebration of heterogeneity and the proliferation of identities" current in feminist theory, (Weed 1989, xx) combined with the assertion that one need never (ought never) accept the limits of identity, have the peculiar effect of negating birth, history, privilege and social responsibility in one breath. Writing about Roland Barthes, Naomi Schor has argued that the denial of sexual difference in the discourse of "pure difference" reflects the "dominant male discourse on sexuality in post-structuralist France." (1989, 48) Jane Gallop has contended that the "wish to escape sexual difference might be but another mode of denying women." (cited in Schor 1989, 49) I would add that the claim that one can resist having an identity for which one is responsible is a claim made from a privileged subject position that denies its own class-, race-, and nation-situatedness.[2] Consider Butler's discussion of the cultural politics of "drag, cross-dressing, and the sexual stylization of butch/femme identities" (*Gender Trouble*, 137) as "playfulness" in the context of the following story reported recently within the *San Francisco Chronicle:*

Transvestite Leaps to Death From Hotel

A transvestite wearing a red leather dress and black stockings jumped to his death from a San Francisco hotel early yesterday. (May 4, 1991, A 12)

Post-structuralist critiques have been pushing feminist theory toward abandoning a category of binary, and presumably reified, gender distinctions, and have been working toward a more complex theory of cultural "identity" as well as toward establishing political practices built on "coalitional strategies that *neither presuppose nor fix their constitutive subjects in their place*." (Butler in Nicholson 1990, 339) Yet power refuses to disappear with the wave of the deconstructionist's magical wand. The political-economic context that remains, fantasies of parodic floating signifiers notwithstanding, is extraordinarily more fixed and materially more powerful than any appeal to the "politics" of parodic performances alone could unsettle. Systems of law, global economic inequalities, the structured disenfranchisement and disempowerment of most women and most men in the world, the consolidation of the influence of the military-industrial complex (as evidenced in the Gulf War) in the super-imperialist New World Order—all of these are working to constitute and to fix very specific subjects in a very confined and inegalitarian geopolitical space. Talking about words will not make this reality go away. For most of the women and men in the world talking about, endless talking about, is all that has been forever. Politics is not the mere effect of discourse.

Those who have felt the state's inscription of rules on their bodies in the form of torture, imprisonment, beatings, disappearings, forced or "accidental" starvation, systematic illiteracy, and the denial of the basic dignity of human survival will not find comfort in a feminist politics built on (parodic) laughter, or what Mas'ud Zavarzadeh called "ludic postmodernism." (1991, chap. 2) To be insisting upon plural subject positions within the global political economic setting of increasingly monopolized wealth, power, and violence seems ironic and politically dangerous. To be urging that we abandon the concept of "sexual difference" and dispense with the idea of "a female subject" in the midst of both a renewed attack on reproductive rights in the

United States and elsewhere and the growth of a global reproductive technologies industry trafficking in the bodies of Third World women becomes self-defeating, suicidal. This industry is designed, in part, to make the human (female) womb obsolete, the pregnant (female) body dispensable. At the same time, this industry's development has had the (perhaps) unintended consequence of more deeply connecting motherhood and femininity by raising the standards for defining any woman's "infertility." These are only some of the material, structural dimensions undergirding the power of binary comparisons. Wishing them away in the name of the fluidity of identity permitted by "gender parody" is a little like celebrating the Halloween Carnival in the Castro district of San Francisco and forgetting about the police guarding the borders. We still cannot "refuse to take a shape for which [we] must take responsibility." (Bordo in Nicholson 1990, 144) And should we want to refuse?

The idea that we can dispense with the "female subject" as focus of feminist theory and politics in favor of some theory and politics founded on the recognition that gender and sex share a "fundamentally phantasmatic status" (Butler, *Gender Trouble,* 147) represents an extremely anti-political and thoroughly liberal position. It is important to remember who is urging this strategy and in what institutional and geopolitical location its manuevers have been given the greatest victory celebrations. Whose interests are reflected in a fascination with "illimitable differences"? Whose body is the body as surface? The current romance with heterogeneity, the desire to be (politically?) engaged with the world under the mark of a sign that says "this is not me," mirrors the representation of the global political economy as an immense shopping mall you can wander through aimlessly and anonymously, as long as you haven't left home without your American Express card.

I am reminded of Marx's observation that money permits the bourgeois to buy everything that he (or she) is not. (*Economic and Philosophic Manuscripts*) Money facilitates exchange and symbolizes the substitutability of something for anything. Having money permits one the fantasy of escaping corporeality and history. It also enables one to ignore the political-economic system of global inequality that constructs differential opportunities to resist "the regulation of sexuality within the reproductive domain." For women, especially women of color, who have had to bear the marks on their bodies of a long history of slavery and rape, the systematic denial of adequate prenatal care, high rates of infant mortality, extraordinary risks of mortality and morbidity from drugs, AIDS, and diseases of poverty, "resistance" could take the form of the demand to be able to *enter,* not to escape, the reproductive domain on more equal terms. (Collins 1991, 135).

If money has been the medium of exchange in capitalist circulation, "difference" has become the medium of exchange in feminist circulation. It may be that "the injunction *to be* a given gender produces necessary failures." (Butler, *Gender Trouble* 145) Yet it is one thing to recognize the ways in which, for instance, the welfare mother has been represented as a failure to be a "good enough mother," and to suggest that this and other such "necessary failures"—the single mother, the lesbian mother, the woman who is never a mother—reveal the vulnerability to subversions of "the injunction *to be* a given gender." It is quite another thing to acknowledge that the welfare mother's "failure," along with the single mother's, lesbian mother's, and the woman who is never a mother's, are much more likely to be internalized by these women (women?) as personal failures instead of being embraced either as subversive practices or as indications of the fallibility of the system of gender to reproduce itself. Unless all of these "failures" become aware of and assert themselves as politically defiant ones, the academic assignment of them to the category of cultural rebel will neither address their immediate needs nor create the foundations for a new politics. In fact, the academic recuperation of the marginalized and the exploited in the interests of a theory that displaces its own interestedness, that is, that fails to turn the critical gaze in its own direction, risks reproducing the dynamics of colonization and the resulting domestication of difference that it claims to want to avoid. Ironically, for all of her deconstructing of the category "women," Butler fails to take on the critique of the category "feminism." What does "feminist politics" mean in the sentence, "feminist politics could do without a 'subject' in the category of women"? (*Gender Trouble,* 142)

The often heated debates about the authoritative status of "women" as a useful analytic category in feminist theory reflect only the most recent expressions of dilemmas surrounding the contested status of canonical, authoritative representations and interpretations of women's experiences. Profound uncertainty remains about whether recognizing sexual differences is strategically possible without solidifying old stereotypes about "women's place." Yet the contemporary prominence of post-structuralism in feminist theory and post-structuralist texts in the university classroom has meant that a whole generation of women's studies students, and budding feminists in other disciplines—most of whom have had no direct experience of the women's movements' earlier political struggles—are reeling from having the epistemological and political foundation of their burgeoning criticisms of sexism, racism, and inequality pulled out from underneath their feet. And this is a generation of American students who have no adult memory of American politics before the age of Reagan. The pedagogical prominence of post-structuralism is occurring within the context of fiscal crises and radical conflicts that are transforming the university into an ever more elitist, exclusionary institution. The danger is that avoiding the question of what authority means contributes, in this charged political context, to the solidification of the power of those structures and institutions whose politics of exclusion we have been trying to transform.

Within this context it seems important to insist that, in the hands of feminists, the strategic deployment of generalizations about women, and the invocation of "classificatory fictions" about gender, are necessary to the feminist political project and are politically distinguishable from the essentializing of women in the hands of patriarchy. As Diana Fuss has argued, there are no "interior values intrinsic to the sign [of women] itself"; instead "political investments" depend upon the "the shifting and determinative discursive relations which produced it." (1989, 20) To say that every statement that includes the noun "women" necessarily repeats the same binary constructions is to give both too much and too little weight to the power of language to limit change. It also is to assume that to assert the authority of gender as a category in feminist theory is, necessarily, to stake a sovereign claim.

If it is necessary to criticize the essentializing effects of constructing an ontology of gender, this critique should not negate the subversive effects of deploying gender "against the grain" of dominant representations of sexual difference. The theoretical construction of categories such as "women" or gender does not, in itself, imply the erasure of any political process whereby, in any individual's or group's life, conscriptions that gender effects can be both willfully and unconsciously reinforced and/or transgressed. Moreover, in order for any critics of the totalizing effects of certain categories to refuse the description reflected in certain terms, such as "women," they must first deploy the category that is being refused: I am a woman, but I am not that name, "woman." Ironically, the move to de-authorize "women" as categorical subject of feminist theory rhetorically masks the re-authorization of a univocal concept of truth—or is the statement that "gender is neither true nor false" not cast as a truth?

ANTI-RACISM AND THE CRITIQUE OF HEGEMONY

Confusion and uncertainty about the categorical necessity of concepts of sexual difference have been compounded by the allegations that mainstream Western feminist scholarship either has ignored non-Western women or analyzed questions of sexual difference from a position which privileges "feminist interests as they have been articulated in the United States and Western Europe." (Mohanty 1984, 337–38) In other words, Western feminists have falsely universalized their analyses of women's exploitation on the basis of ethnocentric and hegemonic readings of non-Western practices and ideas. In place of a complex theory, these critics contend that Western feminists have insisted on the authority of their definition of women "as a singular group on the basis of a shared oppression." The resulting homogenization of women's experiences "erases all marginal and resistant modes of experience." (Mohanty, 1984, 337, 352; Romero 1988; Hammami and Rieker 1988; Ghoussaub 1988; and Spelman 1988) By translating non-Western practices of, for example, suttee into the terms of what Western feminists judge to be exploitative, Western feminists have abrogated the authority of Third World feminists to speak for or represent themselves.[3]

Within Western feminism, feminists of color have argued, similarly, that certain voices have been ignored or marginalized. "I had grown frustrated that the same few women-of-color were asked to read or lecture in universities and classrooms, or to submit work to anthologies and quarterlies." (Anzaldúa, 1990, xvi) Recently, lines dividing the "we" within American feminist theory have been drawn most starkly in terms of color. The claim has been made that by privileging gender as an analytic category, feminist theorists have reproduced the very hegemonic structures of thought that feminism intended to subvert. Much feminist theory, now called "whitefeminism," has been charged with racism. Gloria Anzaldúa, for example, has written that "the people who practice Racism—*everyone who is white in the U.S.*—are victims of their own white ideology and are impoverished by it. . . . Often whitefeminists want to minimize racial difference by taking comfort in the fact that we are all women and/ or lesbians, and suffer similar sexual-gender oppressions. . . . They ["whitefeminists"] seem to want a complete, totalizing identity." She contends that this is because the category "woman" has become hegemonic in "whitefeminism." Even when "they" make some efforts to acknowledge differences, "in the act of pinpointing and dissecting racial, sexual or class 'differences' of women-of-color, whitewomen not only objectify these differences, but also change those differences with their own white, racialized, scrutinizing and alienating gaze." (1990, xix, xxi)

Anzaldúa's powerful and stinging indictment of the exclusionary and colonizing practices of certain forms of feminist discourse has different effects on different readers. I am aware that the legitimacy of my criticism, advanced by a "white feminist," might be dismissed *a priori* because of my race. Yet the force of Anzaldúa's rhetoric depends upon reducing the identity of "whitewomen" to one aspect of their (our) being, namely, their (our) "color." Moreover, her argument assumes that the category "color" exists unproblematically, and that its meaning is apparent and incontrovertible. "Color" becomes an essential category that marks one's cultural heritage automatically. Does the color of one's skin, or the color of the group with which one identifies signify, by itself, one's political position and establish the boundaries of one's feminism? How far does the politics of color take us toward understanding the dynamics of class distinctions between and among women "of color," both within and between nation-states?

If hegemony in feminism is to be resisted, this means resisting old and new forms of hegemony, including the newest forms of hegemony expressed in American feminist theory terms of identity politics. Statements such as Anzaldúa's that "everyone who is white in the U.S." practices racism are not fundamentally different from statements insisting that "all men are sexists." As bell hooks has argued about the latter, not only do such statements silence debate altogether, they preclude thinking about political action in solidarity. They reinforce a peculiarly American approach to political change by transforming critical challenges to the *structures* of inequality into the logic of interest group politics, that is, into demands for one's "fair share" of resources. This approach, as Iris Young has written, obscures the institutional context within which distribution occurs, focusing instead on "the size of portions individuals have." (*Justice and the Politics of Difference,* 18) There is no question that provision of more fairly distributed material and cultural "goods" to those who have been deprived of access is a pressing need. Simultaneously, though, critical focus must remain on the social structures and institutional contexts which frame distribution.

In writing these criticisms, I am aware of the risk of having what I say dismissed by its being read as evidence of a basic refusal to accept responsibility for the ways that I have benefited from racism, or as the result of a desire to gloss over real differences of privilege among women. I do not deny that, within the context of American feminism, racial privilege continues to structure how knowledge is produced and circulated and to authorize specific forms of feminist theory over others. Acknowledging this fact requires undoing privilege, the first step toward which is realizing the subtle ways that privilege is reproduced by not having to be named as such. This realization is painful for feminists, not only because it shatters the illusion of sisterhood, but also because it assigns primary responsibility for racism to every white person, including feminists who thought they already were beyond racism. I do not refuse either the pain or the responsibility. My efforts here is to call for ways to reestablish dialogue while understanding that dialogue will be both painful and pleasurable if it occurs within the context of an analysis that resists confusing the "accidental" features of one's identity—being white, black, or any color—with a political classificatory system that assigns privileges to one group over another. If the racial subject has been produced politically, then it becomes possible to disaffiliate from race privilege, to become "disloyal to civilization," especially a civilization that uses racism to divide and conquer the relatively powerless and to deny women the pleasure of one another's company and conversation. (hooks and Childers 1990, 60–80; Hirsch and Keller 1990, 2–5; Rich 1979, 275–310; Caraway 1991)

The *strategic* assertion of identity remains necessary to the development of any political movement, even a movement towards "open" coalitions. At the same time, if the assertion of identity is not to become the goal itself, then healthy skepticism about the adequacy of the politics of identity and the limits of nationalism, about the pleasures and dangers of lobbying for access to an existing system of power, and about adversarial organizing is necessary along the way. Instead of such skepticism, we are witnessing the rise of new forms of nationalism and heart-wrenching territorial wars within feminism. Feminists have become captured by the same political discourse that prevents Zionists from ever even listening to the P.L.O., that cuts off dialogue between members of the Ulster Party and the I.R.A. We have established "pass laws" in feminism. We have created intellectual Bantustans. And we accuse each other of these things. Perhaps this was unavoidable. Yet while we remain distracted by these skirmishes, those who have traditionally structured the terms of access to various institutions of power continue to do so.

I do not believe we can, or should, avoid the necessarily difficult and discomforting debates about varieties of exclusionary practices and about racism in the development of feminist theory and practice. Learning to recognize the privilege afforded by various subject positions is essential to unlearning to accept one's privilege. And that includes recognizing how disingenuous it is to think that anti-racism is achieved by a mere nod in the direction of diversity, or through the patronizing practice of supporting efforts at outreach which define women who have been marginalized in feminist circles as women who need to be "saved." (Pratt 1984) Attentive, vigilant criticism of the racist and classist messianism of certain forms of feminism remains an urgent necessity.

Yet it also is imperative to continue to talk about the difference between "*being* white," or "*being* Chicana," or "*being* Black" as a question of skin color and as an effect of "power and politics." In the former case, racism, defined as an automatic by-product of one's color, seems immutable; culture and politics and race are reduced to biological categories. In the latter case, racism is transcendable and undoing racism depends upon those, whites, who would have had greater access to rights and privilege because of skin color working together to undo the structures of privilege, in different ways, with people of color who have been denied rights and privileges. In this sense anti-racism calls upon whites and people of color to unlearn the practices of race privilege; despite the fact that we cannot shed our skin, together we can disengage from the alienated politics of passing and the alienating politics of privilege.

I am concerned, though, that the claimed authority of one person/ group's voice over others, including the (denied) proclamation of the authority of post-structuralism, risks reproducing the very exclusionary politics that it aims to subvert, reinforces the view that authority can only ever consist in "command and control" centers, and freezes the development of feminist politics at the dictatorship stage of the seizure of power. By refusing to reformulate authority, we concede to the terms of the debate about who should/can have authority within the established discursive frame; we concede that authority is about command.

I am equally wary of the hidden anti-feminist political consequences of some versions of post-structuralist feminism, especially because of the continued existence of increasingly more monolithic, though by no means unimpeachable, centers of power. Calling for a plurality of voices with which to contest the meaning of basic political categories of feminism, such as patriarchy, male hegemony, heterosexism, exploitation, liberation, and consciousness, and then requiring that theorists situate these categories within specific cultural and historical locations and consider local possibilities for resistance, is laudable. Yet the implication of certain criticisms has been the claim that the feminist concept of "male domination" itself is disciplinary in the sense that it forces a specific reading of women's experiences—namely, that women are exploited (only by) men. These criticisms suggest that the coherence of feminism as a political theory and a political strategy has been undermined.

Although I applaud the localizing of resistance, because I agree that we cannot await some prior synthesis of our differences in order to object to the system that exists, I am unconvinced that we can, individually or spontaneously, drag the system of sexism to defeat. I remain too horrified by the deadly, pyrotechnic displays of prowess in the Gulf War, and too aware of the recuperation of "difference" in the interests of legitimating the American military as an equal opportunity employer and then lionizing the American military woman as the symbol of liberation, to endorse the kind of coalitional politics that waits to figure out the "shape or meaning of its coalitional assemblage" until after it has already been achieved. (Butler *Gender Trouble,* 15)

"AGAINST THE GRAIN": RECONFIGURING AUTHORITY

Criticisms about the impossibility of avoiding exclusionary practices in theory building have called feminist theory and its authority into question. If any theory's claim that it provides an authoritative reading or interpretation of any experience depends upon excluding from its assumptions about human existence what does not fit its script, then it becomes impossible to avoid the pitfalls of falsely universalizing from limited experiences. Theory is built through discursive generalizations—the representational effects of language—with the attendant tendencies to confuse "word" with "thing." Feminist theory's captivation with the "representation" of women, its effort to make visible what was hidden by patriarchal discourse, finds itself caught no less in this representational fiction. As long as theory is grounded in the search for a more authentic identity—including the "authentic" identity offered by becoming freed from gender—it cannot avoid substituting the experiences of one group—the dominant, the privileged, or even the marginalized— for the experiences of all. "Is it ever legitimate to say 'women' without qualification?" (Hartsock 1987, 189) If the answer is a resounding "No," then perhaps feminists should abandon the attempt to speak authoritatively about women's experiences. That depends, of course, on what is meant by "authoritatively."

It is both controversial and productive to acknowledge that women are "capable not only of participating in . . . [patriarchal] discourse but of occasionally deriving pleasure from it." (Modleski in de Lauretis 1986, 133; Elshtain 1987) At the most basic level, this means acknowledging that we care not only about whether we are "heard," but also whether we are "listened to" in the sense that what we say matters to the shaping of shared purpose that founds public life. One of the tasks of feminist research has been to demonstrate whether and to what extent women's relationship to and participation in patriarchal discourse in its many manifestations, and the pleasures and pains that women might derive from it, exist for anyone and *mean* the same thing for different people. Explorations of this sort have led to the revelation of fissures in the architecture of patriarchal discourse.

The contradictory nature of a patriarchal gender system is expressed in the fact that its reduction of human diversity to codes of sexual dimorphism provides the basis for gender discipline and, simultaneously, creates the conditions for consciousness of that system's own vulnerability to difference. Possibilities exist in any social, discursive order for ironic strategies of resistance to apparently monolithic codes. Contradictions make potential a kind of imitation, a "mimesis" in Luce Irigaray's terms, which enables us to "recover the place of exploitation by discourse, without allowing [ourselves] to be simply reduced to it." (1985, 76) Discursive mimesis can reveal and transgress the limits prescribing certain forms of identity and self-consciousness, certain modes of collective action and patterns of solidarity. Yet it depends on the sign of what it is mocking in order to work its effects. As Linda Zerilli has observed, "mimicry enacts a defamiliarized version of femininity; it is a rhetorical strategy that aims to convert female subordination into an affirmation of the 'feminine' through a parodic mode of speaking/writing." (1991, 261)

Categories of gender and race can be deployed against themselves. The structure and ideology of the women's movements, like the structure and ideology of movements of racial solidarity, have deployed the categories of "Woman" and "Black," or both simultaneously, against the systems of exploitation that sought to contain their meaning. The assertion of sexual difference, along with the assertion of racial difference, are attempts to recuperate what has been excluded by sexist and racist assertions of difference and to defy the limits within which these differences have been located.

Women and men have played with the codes of patriarchy in the past in ways which have called attention to how and whom those codes discipline. Yet it is important to stress that whether their playing subverts the codes or reinforces them depends strongly on the material context and on the staging of the parody and the play, as well as on the subject's intention and the audience's reading and reaction. Discursive mimesis ultimately can be recuperated by the dominant order in order to reinforce the system, thereby containing the more disruptive effects of doubling and masquerade. As Natalie Zemon Davis has noted, both festival and literary inversions of sex roles were replete in preindustrial Europe. Images of disorderly women, of "women on top" were "multivalent image[s] that could operate, first, to widen behavioral options for women within and even outside marriage, and, second, to sanction riot and political disobedience for both men and women in a society that allowed the lower orders few formal means of protest." (1975, 131) Yet when the reversal of roles explored in parody became actual, as was the case with Elizabeth I, when the reversal threatened to displace an original hierarchy and replace it with a different order, the mimesis, whether intentionally or not, frequently provoked hostile resistance to the new system that it augured.

For instance, Martha Vicinus documented how nineteenth-century suffragists' strategy of wearing stylish "womanly" dress, and the importance they saw in projecting an image of femininity "even as women were performing unfeminine acts," triggered violent and sexually symbolic attacks on suffragists by their opponents. When "militants encroached on male space," Vicinus wrote, "they often met with fierce resistance. . . . They could be repeatedly pinched, punched in their breasts, fondled under their skirts, and spat in the face, have their hats pulled off, and suffer other indignities. . . . In order to protect their public space, men were willing to permit, even encourage, the violation of woman's most intimate space—her body." Suffragists adoption of traditional dress was ironic: by calling attention to themselves as women, they highlighted the maleness of public space and exposed the gender system on which that system was constructed. (1985, 264–65; cf. Wheelwright 1989; Jones and Vergès 1991; and Evans 1980)

In recent feminist film theory a critical, mimetic strategy has been used to analyze Hollywood films that appear to reflect the dominant culture's construction of women and the female. Reading these texts "against the grain" has permitted the denaturalization and demystification of the ways that women are positioned in film. Making visible the technical, cultural, and ideological processes of film that constitute certain sets of meanings surrounding "woman" has opened up alternative readings of these dominant codes and provided a way to transform them because counterinterpretations have revealed certain ambiguities that such classic narrative representations of women sought to contain. (Kuhn 1982) By calling attention to the ways that point-of-view shots structure the narrative and suture the viewer into the position of the one who is looking; by dissecting the ways that the camera's voyeurism constructs "the gaze" and fetishizes the female body; and by learning to deconstruct the codes of film, this body of feminist work has disclosed the dominant ideological and discursive operations at work in film, while simultaneously, it has read these texts in ironic ways: as texts with an excess of meaning.

For example, using Hitchcock's films, Tonia Modleski has demonstrated how particular representations of sexuality in this genre "are images of ambiguous sexuality that threaten to destabilize the gender identity of protagonists and viewers alike." (1988, 1) Contrary to the prevalent reading of Hitchcock's films, which has used them "in order to show how women in classic Hollywood cinema are inevitably made into passive objects of male voyeuristic and sadistic impulses," Modleski argues for a more complex reading of Hitchcock's representation of gender, one that uses his films to "reveal some of the difficulties for women in becoming socialized in patriarchy". (1988, 1, 2; cf. Foucault, *Herculine Barbin*)

I want to deploy a similar strategy in the analysis of gender and authority. We can challenge women's exclusion from authority by reading the dominant texts about authority "against the grain." If we examine the dominant texts on authority in modern political theory, from Hobbes through Schaar and Raz, we can locate a similar tension and sexual ambiguity within the gendered order that authority imposes. When political authority is defined as the rightful imposition of order on disorder, or the substitution of an artificial unity for a lived diversity in community, it excludes women and the symbolically female from its practice axiomatically. Women represent disorder. This definition of authority as legitimately imposed order hides other narratives of authority which recognize different practices of meaningfully constructing community. These practices need to be unearthed and reconsidered. Their narratives might be more consistent with authority's etymology. "Authority" derives from *augere* (to augment) and connotes an activity of growth, not decay. In the public arena, authority expresses our connection with others as an augmentation of our selves, rather than an obstacle to self-fulfillment.

The mimetic interpretations of political theory that I describe in this book push beyond limiting the conceptualization of alternatives to the dominant discourse on authority to the choice between complicity with existing structures of authority or abject denial of women's claims to wield authority in any disciplinarian sense. Feminists should resist both sides of these sexist alternatives. (Miller 1986, 115) Resisting this choice provides important space for dissent, leaving open the possibility of different representations of authority and more progressive gender practices.

Two caveats are important. Feminist theorists need to remain alert to "the limits of the canonical economy for thinking through critical political questions of gender [that] become evident when the voices of feminists become submerged in those of the theorists who are invoked, consciously or not, to give women the cultural authority to speak." (Zerilli 1991, 259) If we cannot force the canonical texts into the shape we want them to have for feminist purposes without risking the danger of becoming trapped by their framework or drowning out by the din of their words, then neither can we avoid re-reading these in subversive ways. Instead, we should refuse to locate their meanings in any permanent or ahistorical place. Yet even these resistant readings should not substitute for political action. To confuse either counterhegemonic "readings" of ideology or alternative "writing practices," *disconnected from collective action,* with political transformation risks leaving the dominant system intact. By privileging literate, discursive interventions in the hallowed halls of academe over the "cruder" forms of political intervention in the everyday struggles to survive by millions of ordinary people, progressive intellectual work limits its political strategy and "vision" to producing radically chic texts. Equally telling, this bias betrays its own bourgeois prejudices by its sublime indifference to what Susan Sontag once called "the immediate plight of women."

RETHINKING AUTHORITY

The discourse on authority in modernity has assumed that authority is about command. It has centered on analysis of the establishment of democratic practices of social coordination through the institution of constitutional sovereignty (rule-governed behavior), on descriptions of the characteristics of democratic leadership (authorities), and on explication of purposes of social interaction (the authoritative, or "governing" values) along with justifications of interpretations of the authoritative (the canonical). Whether and how women are represented in relation to these practices and features of authority is connected fundamentally to inquiry into the robustness and meaning of women's presence in politics.

Each of the following chapters is organized around one of these themes of rules, leadership, etc. Yet each chapter is conceived as a mimetic strategy of resistance to the dominant ways these dimensions of authority have been defined. By approaching the field of authority through the lens of gender, I hope to foreground and then to transform the sexual metaphorics and practices which have, until now, enabled us to recognize authority. My aim is not only to argue that women should be included in authority, but that authority itself needs to be reconstructed in order to accommodate what women have been claimed, and have claimed for themselves, to represent.

Chapter 1 considers the effect of conceptualizing authority as sovereignty. Following a close reading of Hobbes, I consider how the practice of authority as sovereignty rests on claims that privilege the connections between authority and masculinity. Chapter 2 considers the practice of recognizing authorities. What sort of body is the body politic? If leadership is marked by certain signs, as Hobbes called them, which enable us to recognize authorities, are different practices of recognition gendered? (Gates 1987, 33) Chapter 3 continues this investigation by exploring the ways that the roles and knowledge held to be authoritative construct masculinity as normative. Chapter 4 explores further the "authoritative" by examining how representations of practices of judgment and willfulness exclude representations of women from them. Then, using the general outlines of modern theories of authority developed in chapters 3 and 4, chapter 4 posits the potentiality for feminist resistance to them. Following Arendt's critique of authority defined as domination, I suggest ways that a concept of "compassionate authority" can provide an alternative to the logic of authority as sovereign imperative control. In chapter 5, I consider whether feminists' excavation of "women's experiences" and cultural vision provides the basis for a different "imaginative geography" that maps our shared humanity onto a transformed polity. Since the authoritative is subject to interpretation, this chapter also explores the problems of language, translation, edition, and transformation of authoritative canons within feminism, both the dominant and the marginal, or "minor," ones. Do feminist incursions into canonicity yield different modes of interpretation? Or does canonicity necessarily depend upon excluding what does not fit the newly legitimated genre? The conclusion synthesizes these arguments into a more general theory of gender, authority, and authorship.

Notes

1. Hammami and Rieker note that, in the Middle East, "[t]he veil like all forms of clothing is a signifier; what it signifies is determined by the social and political context in which it is used." (1988, 93.) This is no less true of the "veiling" of some feminist discourse on power and authority by a language of disavowal. Later I will examine how certain discursive strategies—for example, the deployment of the category of "women's experiences" as the authoritative source of knowledge—veil the quest for sovereign control over representational practices in feminist theory. Whether the interpretation of these signs depends upon the social and political contexts in which they are used, or the intentions of the actors, will also be explored.

2. Butler writes: "Because the articulation of an identity within available cultural terms instates a definition that forecloses in advance the emergence of new identity concepts in and through politically engaged actions, the foundationalist tactic cannot take the transformation or expansion of existing identity concepts as a normative goal. . . . An open coalition will affirm identities that are alternately instituted and relinquished according to the purposes at hand." (*Gender Trouble*, 15–16) The idea that one can discard identity like a change of costume betrays its class and race origins. Compare Butler's cultural politics with Patricia Williams's reflections on the complexity of coming to terms with the imposition of an identity on blacks through slavery while refusing to reduce the identity of blacks to the images constructed through slavery. Williams writes that "claiming for myself a heritage the weft of whose genesis is my own disinheritance is a profoundly troubling paradox. . . . The greatest challenge is to allow the full truth of partializing constructions to be felt for their overwhelming reality—reality that otherwise I might rationally try to avoid facing. In my search for roots, I must assume, not just as history but as an ongoing psychological force that, in the eyes of white culture, irrationality, lack of control and ugliness signify not just the whole slave personality, not just the whole black personality, but me." (1988, 6, 11) Unwilling to discard her past, even the white part of the past that discards her, Williams's strategy is to "look straight at people, particularly white people; not to let them stare me down. . . . To look is to make myself vulnerable; yet not to look is to neutralize that part of myself which is vulnerable." (11–12.)

3. Biddy Martin and Chandra Mohanty have argued more recently that certain critiques of "what is increasingly identified as 'white' or 'Western' feminism unwittingly leave the terms West/East, white/non-white polarities intact; they do so, paradoxically, by starting from the premise that Western feminist discourse is inadequate to or irrelevant to women of color or Third World women. . . . The reproduction of such polarities only serves to concede 'feminism' to the 'West' all over again." (1986, 193.) This critique seems applicable to Mohanty's own work, "Under Western Eyes."

1

Authority as Sovereignty: Gender, the Social Contract and Univocal Rule

FEMINIST THEORY AND THE CONCEPTUALIZATION OF POLITICS

Over the last decade and a half, feminist theorists have produced a large body of scholarship demonstrating gender bias in Western political discourse. Contending that most classical political theories, and many contemporary ones, have assumed that women's exclusion from public life needs no explanation, feminist theorists have charged the tradition of political theory with sexism. Despite the scope and sophistication of this work, there has been no consensus among feminists about what constitutes gender bias, nor about what "including" women in public life means.

Sometimes feminist criticism has taken the approach of cataloguing what classical theorists actually have said about women in their texts, and judging these statements to be misogynistic, has announced the case for gender bias settled. (Okin 1979; Eisenstein 1981) At other times feminist analysis has taken the form of exploring what aspects of social existence, such as reproduction and domestic life, have been assumed to be politically irrelevant and how these assumptions have barred women from equal participation in public life. (Okin 1979, 1990) In other, more rare cases, theorists have provided genealogies of some of the central concepts of political discourse, such as power and citizenship, in order to reveal the host of different, gendered practices and meanings on which the dominant forms of power and citizenship are parasitic, or which they produce as necessary companion practices. In Wendy Brown's words, "the historical relationship between constructions of manhood and constructions of politics emerges through and is traced upon formulations of political foundations, political order, citizenship, action, ra-

26

tionality, freedom and justice." (1988, 4; cf. Hartsock 1983, Elshtain 1981, Elshtain, 1985, and O'Brien 1981)

In a sense these different approaches represent different stages in the development of feminist political theory. In an earlier stage of contemporary feminist theory building, the focus was on analyzing the set of obstacles to women's fuller participation in politics. Theorists such as Susan Okin and Zillah Eisenstein emphasized the significance of the historical, gender-differentiated separation of "public life" from "private life." Okin, for instance, traced women's ultimate exclusion from politics in the theories of Plato, Aristotle, Rousseau, and Mill to the ways that women's nature was defined functionalistically and the family was defined naturalistically. Since women were defined in terms of the reproductive and caretaking functions for which they were assumed to be suited by nature, they were excluded from full participation as citizens. She concluded that as a result of the continued operation of such assumptions in modern law, even today "women, though enfranchised citizens, are handicapped by the fact that neither their socialization nor their training, neither the expectations placed on them nor the opportunities or rewards afforded to them in their adult lives are such as to enable them to achieve economic, social, or political equality with men." (1979, 293)

The solution to women's exclusion from politics lay in reducing the obstacles to women's fuller integration into public life. An essential feature of this integrationist project was the renegotiation of the division of "private" responsibilities between men and women so that more women could "go public." Theorists supporting this approach contended that public policies designed to restructure the family, such as state-supported child-care programs, would lead to the fuller integration of women in politics; the creation of a democratic, sex-egalitarian family would facilitate the creation of the truly democratic society. Only when a concerted effort was made to challenge the patriarchal structure of the state by demanding changes in the organization of the systems of reproduction, production, and distribution—demands not only for legal rights, but also to change the sexual division of labor in the economy and the home that operate to "keep women in their place as secondary wage earners and as mothers" (Eisenstein 1981, 248)—would women's political inequality be ended. Only elliptically, if at all, did such theorists question whether "bringing women in" was the same as transforming the gendered discourse of power, citizenship, and authority. (Okin, 1979, 286)

More recently, Virginia Sapiro has explored the ways that women's private roles—"marriage, motherhood, homemaking and the underlying ideology of privatization"—continue to confine women in a gender-differentiated social structure and to impair women's ability to be fully integrated in politics. Sapiro has pointed out that "privatization breeds political marginality." (Sapiro 1983, 33) Privatization disconnects women from political life by teaching women to be "something other than full citizens." (172) Instead of being socialized for active participation in citizenship, women have been socialized to put home and private virtues ahead of public action. The remedy for this was not only legal reform but, in Sapiro's view, also eliminating "political femininity, privatization." (183) If caretaking—of children, men, and women themselves—was more equitably distributed through resocialization, then women would become capable of political action. Her hope was that a greater degree of democracy would be secured when the inegalitarianism and restrictedness of the private sphere has been superceded. (cf. Okin 1990) Like her predecessors, Sapiro did not address directly the extent to which the existing norms and structures of political life might preclude the incorporation of an egalitarian caretaking ethos into public life. Yet critical investigation of the norms of citizenship and authority, as well as efforts to alter the focus of community life away from zero-sum competition, are imperative if changing the nature of public life is the goal of feminist theory and politics. In Sapiro's work these transformations remained unexplored.

Approaches to reading the great works of political theory in order to discover what various authors have said about women and what place has been assigned to women, reflect a method of interpretation of political discourse that treats gender as a descriptive category; that is, gender is taken to be "a concept associated with the study of things related to women." (Scott 1986, 1057) In contrast, other theorists have attempted to uncover the different ways that representations of gender in the historical discourse of political theory work to structure the nature of politics itself in terms of a discourse of masculinity. Generally, theorists subscribing to this second approach treat gender as a cultural code of representation, as a way to categorize behaviors and practices that are not necessarily connected to sex differences. Societies, Joan Scott has observed, "use [gender] to articulate rules of social relationships, or construct the meaning of experience." (1063) Theorists studying Western discourse from this perspective have contended that the nature of politics has been derived from a particular representation of masculinity as normative. At the same time, representations of femininity have been central to the delineation of the boundaries of public life: the realm of the "feminine" often has been what public life was defined against.

Arlene Saxonhouse, for instance, has argued that although women were excluded from political action, from participation in the polis, they have been considered part of the " 'regime,' that which encompasses the entire set of political, social, economic and religious relationships that characterize any community. . . . An understanding of the female's place in any society is critical for understanding the nature and aims of the political life of that particular community." (1985, 16) Jean Bethke Elshtain has explored how the exclusion of women's activities of caretaking and nurturance narrowed the discourse of politics. (Elshtain 1981) Nancy Hartsock has considered how the particular notions of power that informed Western political thinking reflected a gendered discourse in such a way that "military capacity, civic personality, and masculinity have [become] coextensive." (in Stiehm *Women's Views*, 123) In the history of political thought, the gendered representation of the forces that threaten the political community took the form of a "continuing characterization of threats to the political community as female." (in Stiehm, *Women's Views*, 284)

From a different vantage point, Evelyn Fox Keller's *Reflections on Gender and Science* explored the ways that a particular discourse of science connected knowledge with power and defined power as domination or control over objects, even when the "objects" were human. (1985) This conceptualization of knowledge and understanding of power were linked, in Keller's analysis, to a particular discourse of masculinity and led to the systematic exclusion from the episteme of science "not only of women but of all the values associated with women's work." (1988, 17) Scientific cognition came to be associated with "thinking like a man" regardless of the sex of the person practicing it. The solution to the gendering of science and power as masculine, Keller concluded, was not signalled by the mere entrance of increasing numbers of women into the sciences. The solution lay instead in asking what an alternative discourse of power and knowledge would look like. (1988, 13)

Instead of a merely descriptive usage of gender, these latter feminist theorists have treated gender as a basic linguistic category operating simultaneously as a referent to the actual lived experiences of some women and some men, and as a code of meaning in and through which actual experiences are constructed. In diverse ways they have challenged the gendered discourse of politics and knowledge and have contended that the only way to transform the enterprise of theory radically, and to include what women have represented in the shaping of public life, was to decenter the focus on experiences, activities, and values that represented masculinity. Such a transformative project necessitated the subversion of representations of masculinity as the norm.

If gender operates as a signifier, or mode of representation of the political in certain texts, then we need to interrogate the nature of the political itself. Instead of asking whether women are written about in the canonical texts, we need to explore how the absence of the feminine often has been used to demarcate the space of political action. We need to ask, for instance, why the body generally has been ignored or forgotten or even hidden in most theories of political action. When political action has been described in more physical terms as, for instance, the behavior engaged in by "defenders of the state," we might wonder whether such actions can be seen as political if different sorts of gendered bodies perform them. (Wheelwright 1989; Warner 1981; Jordanova 1976) We might also ask what sort of body the body politic is or can be.

For instance, the terms of the dominant political discourse have structured the conceptualization of citizenship and political participation in a specifically gendered way. (Jones 1990) Aristotle might be taken as paradigmatic. To Aristotle citizens were those who actively participated in ruling. By nature, he argued, women were meant to be ruled. Ontologically they were excluded from citizenship. Yet not all men were capable of ruling. Aristotle argued that all slaves, male and female, were born to be ruled. Being ruled became a gendered category not because only women were included in it, but because the code of being ruled signalled effeminacy. Ruling was a gendered category not because only men were included, but because ruling was the sign of masculinity. Accordingly, women who ruled often have been represented in masculine terms, operating in a masculine context. (Pitkin 1984; Brown 1988; Spelman 1988; Fraser 1989; Warner 1981)

In their various ways Saxonhouse, Elshtain, Hartsock, and Keller have contributed significantly to excavating the gendered discourse of citizenship and of power. Yet none of them has explored systematically the question of authority. Instead, analysis of power has been allowed to stand for analysis of authority, in part because the two terms have been so frequently conflated with one another in the literature about politics. Taking up the relationship between authority and gender remains central to questions about the meaning of democracy and justice that have occupied so much space in feminist narratives of politics. If the struggle for democracy is about much more than having equal access to positions of rulership, posing instead a more radical challenge to the compatibility of relationships of rule and hierarchy in a free society of equal, though different, persons, then conceding the validity of the dominant conceptualization of authority as a system of rule undermines efforts to establish a more radical moment for feminist politics. This more radical moment is represented by the effort to found a public realm not as an escape from, but rooted in, what Hannah Arendt called the earth-boundedness of the "human condition of plurality." (1958, 222) It may be ironic to appropriate Arendt's term as a sign of feminist politics. Her own work had a decidedly anti-feminist tone. Despite that, as I hope to show, Arendt's critique of authority is a uniquely appropriate reconceptualization of authority for postmodern times. Her remarkably fruitful insights can be recuperated for feminist ends. (Dietz in Pateman and Shanley 1991, Elshtain 1985)

ACCESS TO AUTHORITY?

Much feminist theory has focused on the question of democracy from the perspective of enhancing women's participation in politics. It has asked why women should continue to be excluded from politics and decision making. An enormous literature documents the various legal, social, psychological, and economic ways that women have been confined to "second-class citizenship." Most of these works have rested on the claim that until theorists systematically and persistently explore the myriad ways that women, because of the burden of their private roles, have been precluded from full participation in public life, democratic theory will remain biased.

The main feminist approach to democracy has been from the perspective of an inquiry that identifies the obstacles to the complete integration of women in public life and aims to construct the conditions for the greater participation of women, assuming along the way that these conditions are already constructed for men. (Brennan and Pateman 1979) For instance, Nancy Fraser has written that "we are therefore struggling for women's autonomy in the following special sense: a measure of *control over* the means of interpretation and communication sufficient to permit us *to participate on a par with men* in all types of social interaction, including political deliberation and decision-making." (in Benhabib and Cornell 1987, 53, emphasis added) Thus the demand for greater democracy has taken the form of arguments for removing the remaining "procedural and material obstacles" to women's participating in deliberation and decision making "on a par with men" so that women, too, may exercise "control over" the community. Obstacles that rest within the conceptualization of what participation in authority means, limits that reside discursively in definitions of what activities count as practices of authority in the first place, are not addressed in this approach to democratizing politics. Instead, it is assumed that democracy is about "control over" the community exercised by greater numbers of persons.

The assumption that liberal democratic authority remains a kind of "control over" the community despite increases in the number and types of "controllers" links liberalism's apparent shift in thinking about authority—a shift insofar as authority in the liberal tradition is said to be created through the actions of those who will become obligated to it, instead of being instituted from above—with the long tradition of thinking about authority that preceded its modern formulation. In most of Western political philosophy, it has been common to regard authority as a distinctive type of social control or influence. (Peters 1967; Friedman 1973; Kahn 1968) Often the distinction between authority and force becomes blurred. (Friedman 1973) Most theorists, though, have attempted to distinguish authority as a peculiar form of getting people to obey social prescriptions without overtly being coerced into doing so.

Most theorists of authority would agree that some sort of surrender of private judgment—at least in the weak sense of submitting to the judgment of another without making conduct dependent on one's assessment of the merits of the command—is entailed in any concept of authority. The implication is that, in some sense, recognition of authority itself is sufficient for accepting the prescriptions produced by authority systems. Put differently, if authority is defined as a "mutually recognized normative relationship giving the one the right to command and the other the duty to obey," (Friedman 1973) then any justification of authority depends only on clarification of the criteria whereby authority is recognized as such in the first place. One does not have to be persuaded to obey those in authority, nor is one coerced into obeying. One obeys those in authority because they are entitled to obedience. (Oakeshott 1975)

Such a notion of authority appears to separate the obligation to obey from any judgment about the substantive merits of specific acts one is required to perform. (Raz 1975, 1985) Yet the particular act of recognition that establishes authority in the first place can neither originally nor over time be disassociated from the web of common beliefs that constitutes the identity of those in authority, or of those subject to it. Although many political theorists concede that communal beliefs establish the criteria for recognizing authority originally, they still contend that the idea of authority requires that subjects suspend disbelief once a leader's right to rule is established. Yet the conceptual stress on the rationality of deferential obedience hides the ambiguous and contentious ground out of which obedience is constructed. The idea of authority as traditional hierarchy makes sense so long as we accept on faith that the need for an ordered, efficient social system takes precedence over any other form of political, communal existence.

ACCESS AND LIBERAL SOCIAL CONTRACT THEORY

Instead of questioning the identification of authority with a form of social control, most feminists, as we have seen, have urged the removal of the remaining obstacles to women's integration into authority relations. In staking these claims, feminists have been supported by the tradition of social contract theories of authority and the critique of patriarchalism which those theories offered.

Contract theory, with its complement, natural rights theory, promised the theoretical possibility of developing an inclusive authority; one, that is, that provided a logic for the claim that every individual had the equal right to represent herself in authority relations through electoral action. No one could claim the right to subordinate another without her consent. At the same time, feminists have contended that proponents of social contract theory from Hobbes to Rawls have failed to sustain a consistent anti-patriarchalism with regard to women's integration. Some feminists have set themselves the task of exposing this residual patriarchalism and of supporting political strategies that undermine it. (Pateman 1988; Okin 1990)

Despite their critique of the resurgence of what Vogel called "sex guardianship" in seventeenth- and eighteenth-century political thought and legal systems, feminist critics of social contract theories have accepted the general conceptualization of authority in these theories. Authority remains defined as the exercise of sovereign social control by legitimate rulers on behalf of the public's welfare. As a practice, sovereignty claims to be gender neutral; it is represented as a tool of influence disconnected from sexual politics. Anyone can be in authority. Yet whether authority as the practice of sovereignty can include women warrants further investigation.

A deeply problematic side of democratic theory has been downplayed by feminists. This concerns the question of how to reconcile intensive and extensive "participation" of diverse groups in politics with the requirements of authority, of founding a meaningful order. Feminists, like so many other theorists, have finessed this challenge by supporting implicitly the claim that the foundation of democratic authority in consent balances a concern for individual autonomy with the requisites of rule-governed behavior through the convention of consent to duty. As long as we are all, as individuals, equally bound by the terms of the contract, then the participation of the previously excluded in no way compromises the ability of the system to maintain order, that is, to apply the rules fairly. More extensive participation merely increases the number of those whose consent is required and whose obligations are expected to be fulfilled. Of course there may be special burdens that certain groups have previously borne privately, such as domestic responsibilities, which will have to be redistributed in order to secure equal access to participatory opportunities. But if redistribution creates new public claims against the state, or additional private claims against individuals or groups who had been previously "excused" from sharing such responsibilities by virtue of their being members of the privileged sex, race, class, or sexuality, these claims need not compromise the principle of equal subjection to the rules.

Yet there are hidden implications involved in embracing contract theory which should make feminists wary of the kind of authority so established and concerned about whether or not it is compatible with other feminist claims made about the radically disturbing presence of women in politics. Women are not mere numbers; "woman as symbol cannot really be inserted into the public arena," as Genevieve Lloyd has pointedly reminded us, "without creating a major upheaval." (Lloyd 1987, 76) Women's presence in politics represents not just the acknowledgment of another interest group with the right to share in decision making, but the presence of a *particular kind* of group whose bodies, and whose values and senses of obligation, have been characterized in Western discourse as antithetical to public life, and as (again in Lloyd's words) symbolizing "all that war and citizenship are supposed to contain and transcend." (76)

Women's bodies pose a peculiar problem: they can be menstruating bodies; they can be pregnant bodies; lactating bodies. Women's bodies are the bodies from which we all emerge. How would public life and political authority have to be rethought if the menstruating, pregnant, birthing, lactating female body, the dividing and divided body, were taken not as the exception to the rule but as the point of departure? (Vergès 1991; Eisenstein, 1988) "Women's values" often have been expressed in the language of nurturance, compassion, and care-taking, and women's duties identified with the protection of the familial, the particular, and the everyday. (Saxonhouse 1985)[1] It is the *particularity* of women's different interests *as women* that unsettles public order. Recognizing the right of individuals who happen to be women to participate in decision making—making a gender-neutral claim for inclusiveness, and treating sexual difference as accidental and inconsequential—does not unsettle public life because difference has been neutralized. What would happen to the practice of authority if those compassionate concerns associated symbolically with women, those modes of knowledge connected to "intuition, insight, and vision," which conjoin the moral with the aesthetic, the rational with the affective, became directly woven into the fabric of authority? John Schaar has argued that these other modes of knowing can be seen as the basis for the construction of what he has called "humanly significant leadership." Deploying a gendered imagery for this leadership practice—with metaphors he fails to analyze—Schaar contended that the language in which an authority derived from these other modes of knowledge would speak is "suggestive, alluring, pregnant, evocative." (1981, 41) Would this shift make authority more humane, but at the expense of rationality and objectivity? Or would it force us to consider what public deference to universal rules means? Favoring order over what Hannah Arendt called "the calamities of action . . . [that] arise from the human condition of plurality," (1958, 220) elides consideration of the sorts of aesthetic, affective, and cognitive claims that authority silences in the traditional view of it as social control.

FEMINIST THEORY AND CONTRACT THEORY

Being in authority as currently practiced or staying outside authority have been the predominant alternatives explored in contemporary feminist theory. In both cases the conceptualization of authority itself remains unchallenged. As a way toward the alternative conceptualization of authority I suggested earlier, in this chapter I will look backwards to the foundation of arguments made about the factors that exclude women from authority, and construct authority as a form of masculinized mastery.

Feminist theorists such as Carole Pateman have traced the exclusion of women from modern public life in the history of modern political thought to neo-patriarchal assumptions about the terms of the "sexual contract" which, she has contended, undergirds social contract theory and its successors. The construction of a democratic, sexually egalitarian practice requires, Pateman concluded, rethinking the relationships between nature and convention, between domestic life and conventional political life so that women are no longer automatically and "naturally" associated with the former. In this chapter we will descend into the hidden abode of social contract conceptualizations of authority as representative sovereignty. There we will ask: are women present as women in this practice of authority?

Feminist theory falls within the range of democratic social theories which explores the possibility of the empirical realization of a more fully participatory society, that is, one in which individuals are not excluded arbitrarily from sharing in authority. Feminists have argued that women have been among those who have been arbitrarily excluded and made marginal to politics. Feminist research and theory have considered how the structures of sexual, social, political, and economic power continue to interfere with the goal of radically democratizing decision making. The investigation of barriers to equal access is something feminist theory shares with liberal theory. But unlike traditional liberal theory, which generally insisted on the "naturalness" of a separation between private arenas of domestic life and the economy, and public life, feminists have insisted on the contrary. Feminists have documented the internal connections between the articulation of authoritative values in the private realm and the nature and structure of authority in the public realm. Writers such as Pateman, Okin, and others have emphasized the necessity of considering the connections between nonpolitical (i.e., nongovernmental) experience and the development of a participatory authority structure. Consequently, they have been critical of those theories which treat as unproblematic the patterns and norms of "decision making" in the "private" sphere. As Carole Pateman put it:

> Both sides in the current discussion of the role of participation in the modern theory of democracy have grasped half of the theory of participatory democracy; the defenders of the earlier theorists have

emphasized that their goal was the production of an educated, active citizenry and the theorists of contemporary democracy have pointed to the importance of the structure of authority in nongovernmental spheres for political socialization. But neither side has realized that the two aspects are connected or realized the significance of the empirical evidence for their arguments. (1970, 105)

Pateman's argument with certain contemporary theorists of democracy was that the theory of participatory democracy—as expressed in the work of John Stuart Mill, Rousseau, and G. D. H. Cole—implied much more than a set of protective institutional devices with which to secure the interests of individual members of society. Rather, participation was meant to establish and maintain a "participatory society" by developing certain "psychological qualities and attitudes of individuals" interacting within a specific institutional framework. Where contemporary democratic theorists like Robert Dahl and Harry Eckstein had found sociological evidence in the expressed nondemocratic attitudes and behavior of the "mass man" to support arguments about the pragmatics and ethics of reducing the definition of democracy to a method of selecting between competing elites, Pateman insisted that an explanation of the emergence of such apparently widespread political apathy was imperative. She argued that evidence about the links between personal perceptions of political efficacy and competence and the development of a cumulative (throughout the life-cycle for individuals and over time for groups) pattern of participation opportunities suggested that the possibility of an empirical realization of a participatory society depended upon *providing and institutionalizing these participation opportunities for more and more groups.*

Pateman's evidence was drawn largely from studies of the effects of democratizing decision making in the workplace. But she suggested that "analysis of the concept of participation presented here can be applied to other spheres." (1970, 108) Contemporary feminists, Pateman among them, have concentrated on the way that participatory patterns in "other spheres" such as domestic life, sexuality, cultural production, affective labor—in short, the broad range of sexually divided social roles—have been especially decisive in limiting or expanding women's ability to participate in public decision making. (Sapiro; Pateman 1988; Githens and Prestage 1977; Jaquette; Barry, Welch and Clark)

The tradition of social contract theories of authority and the critique of patriarchalism which those theories offered have been deployed by feminists seeking to make authority accessible to women. Contract theory seemed to promise the theoretical possibility of developing an inclusive authority by providing a logic for the claim that every individual had the equal right to represent herself through electoral action. No one could claim the right to subordinate another without her consent.

Because of the centrality of social contract theory to the question of authority and to the feminist search for a more egalitarian authority system, we should explore its major tenets. The question of whether the notion of authority supported in these theories can be made compatible with the feminist project to include women will be central to this investigation. In fact, I argue, all theories that aim to disengage authority from the male monopoly by challenging the terms of access to political positions of authority, without simultaneously challenging the terms of authority itself, compromise their own political goals. Women gain entry, but at their own expense.

AUTHORITY AS SOVEREIGNTY

From about the fifteenth century, political authority had been conceptualized in modern Western discourse primarily in terms of sovereignty, and sovereignty, or supreme power, whether religious or secular, was understood as the unitary and universal ability to command obedience. In this view political authority was the ultimate source of legitimate political rule. Under pain of various penalties, authority obligated persons subject to it (citizens) to perform specific duties. This modern view had supplanted one competing medieval idea of sovereignty which, as the etymology of the word suggests, connoted superiority, in the sense of a "higher" station, but not necessarily singular rule. As Bertrand de Jouvenal described it, this particular medieval view connected different stations of the social order in an organic web of hierarchically defined patterns of superordination and subordination. In this view each person "had a superior, whether he [sic] was called his seignior, a suzerain, or a sovereign." (171)

Yet this view of sovereignty was not the only one in the medieval period. Within the church the struggle over the rightful claim to sovereign rule reflected in the investiture controversy suggests that later modern interpretations of sovereignty as ultimate rule had their medieval precedents. In addition various usurpations of kingly power and depositions of unsatisfactory sovereigns depended on appeals to a concept of authority as the ultimate source of legitimate rule. For example, the expansiveness of the scope of English royal power was debated in the medieval period around such questions as to whom the good king ought be responsible. "For medieval men, the kingdom possessed authority of its own that in several ways complemented God's, thus suggesting that the king was, in some measure, also responsible to his people." (Dunham and Wood 1976, 738) If anything, this perspective reflected the view that the kingdom itself, represented through the estates, was the site of authority, of sovereignty. (Wood 1975, 277–83)

Sovereignty and duty were intimately connected in medieval constructions. Sovereignty implied a notion of obligation, albeit restricted, to superiors. Such obligation was not self-imposed; that is, it was not the result of individual consent, but followed naturally from distinctions of rank and duty that the social order embodied. (Pateman 1979, 12–13)

The modern Western conceptualization of authority as sovereignty rested on the concentration and monopolization of sovereignty itself in one point or source. Consequently, the "entire substance of Authority" was concentrated in the higher command. (de Jouvenal, 163) The first victory in the process of monopolization had not been in the royal sphere but "was in the Church and the beneficiary was pontifical power." Yet this victory "drove the royal authority in the same direction." (de Jouvenal, 174) Although Luther's theories later shattered the idea that unity was found in a single external source, in fact he had merely replaced an externally imposed unity with a "system of separate unities." (Laski 1968, 21) Thus his arguments reinforced the concept of authority as a form of command-obedience relationship. In fact, as Laski has argued, what changed with the Protestant Reformation was not so much the idea that authority was sovereign rule—the ultimate, unlimited power to command—as "the place in which the controlling factor of unity [was] found." (1968, 23)

During the seventeenth and eighteenth centuries, a gradual shift from monarchical to republican sovereignty took place in Europe: "The representatives of the state must be sovereign, and if the Stuarts abuse[d] their prerogative, the result [was], not its [sovereignty's] limitation but its transference to Parliament." (Laski 1968, 24) Yet the effect of shifting the location of sovereignty from king to Parliament in no way disturbed the concept of authority as a command-obedience confrontation between the ruler and his subjects. Indeed, the move against Charles I by Parliament was justified as an action against the king's body natural, or person, in the name and by the authority of the king's body politic. The Declaration of Lords and Commons on 27 May 1642 read, in part, that "the High Court of Parliament is not only a Court of Judicature, . . . but is likewise a Council . . . to preserve the publick Peace and Safety of the Kingdom, and to declare the King's pleasure in those things that are requisite thereunto, and what they do herein hath the stamp of Royal Authority, although his Majesty . . . do in his own Person oppose or interrupt the same. . . ." (McIlwain cited in Kantorowicz 1957, 21)

By the seventeenth century, the concept of authority had come to imply an absolute will to rule. Theorists argued that what distinguished authority from other forms of willful behavior was its claim to be a power from which there could be no appeal. Divine right theorists dressed this kingly will in sacred robes. It is important to note that although divine right theories were most prevalent in the sixteenth century, the practice of "borrowing from ecclesiology and using ecclesiastical language for secular purposes had its own tradition of long standing." (Kantorowicz 1957, 19) What distinguished divine right theories was that they carried the import of this "Royal Christology" well beyond the scope of linguistic simile into the justification of political authority and obligation itself.

The imperative mood of kingly dictates came to rest on the same foundation as the necessity to submit to the will of God. Divine right theories supported the right of kings to rule through their claims of patrilineal descent from Adam, the original earthly sovereign. These theories contended that dominion had been granted by God to Adam and had passed, through patrilineal descent, to subsequent generations of kings whose claim to rule was based on their established heritage. Such theories enshrined the principle of paternity as the foundation, or origin, of authority and derived the principle of political obligation from it. Patriarchal authority in the family and political authority in the state were considered to be one and the same by divine right theorists such as Filmer. Paternal and regal authority, domestic and political rule, were completely identified.

As Gordon Schochet has convincingly argued, theories of patriarchy as explanations of the origins of political rule had a long tradition in Western social and political thought. From the classical period to the seventeenth century at least, patriarchalism figured as a means to explain the political evolution of states out of families. Aristotle had argued that the polis emerged as a natural growth of the male-dominated household into the village and then from the village into the polis. Cicero had called the family the "nursery of the state."

(cited in Schochet 1975, 22) Aquinas, following Aristotle, had upheld the view that the state and its order represented the natural progression from the principle that "there can be no social life for many persons living together unless one of their number were set in authority to care for the common good." (Aquinas, *Summa Theologica,* I, i, 32 in D'Entreves 1968, 105) In the sixteenth century, Bodin had described political order as a "community of patriarchs or familial heads." (Schochet 1975, 32; Bodin 1962, 1, 47) Yet these early patriarchalists should be distinguished from seventeenth-century patriarchalists because their patriarchalism was limited to an explanation of the origin of governance. Seventeenth-century patriarchalists, on the other hand, used the genesis of patriarchal sovereignty in the family as a direct justification for political obligation.

Patriarchal political thought shifted during this period from explanations of the origin of government in the father-dominated family to justifications "of obedience to the state on the grounds that political authority had originally belonged to fathers." (Schochet 1975, 12) Because of the corrosive effects of contractual theories such as Hobbes's—theories that conceptualized authority as conventional, not natural—justifying obligation to authority through claims that the natural rule of fathers had been extended to monarchs became central to Filmer's and other patriarchalists' defense of nonconsensual authority. "The contractual theory of political obligation . . . contradicted the traditional view that human relationships were the natural outgrowths of the familial association and its paternal authority. The patriarchal doctrine, in response, was transformed from a vaguely articulated social theory into an intentional political ideology." (Schochet 1975, 55)

UNSETTLING PATRIARCHY, REDEFINING SOVEREIGNTY?

Early in the seventeenth century, the father's rule in the family was still held to be natural. Obedience was owed to the father because of his generative role. Patriarchalists during this period had begun to argue, against voluntarist theories of political obligation, that English monarchs could claim their right to rule on the same basis:

> The father was credited with natural authority over his sons: the generation of their lives gave him the right to direct or even negate them. The king, as father of his people, was then credited with

an equivalent power. . . . It is ultimately the biological aspect of paternity which yields to the father his authority. (Coole 1988, 72)

The idea of authority as absolute sovereignty, coupled with the natural, biologically determined right of fathers to rule, established political authority as a naturally hierarchical and naturally paternal relationship. A major rupture with this account of authority's generation had been foreshadowed in critiques of patriarchalism as early as the sixteenth century. In place of the dominant view that society was structured on the basis of natural, patriarchal hierarchies of power and privilege, consent theorists such as Hooker conceptualized society as an essentially contingent set of social arrangements. The work of Hobbes further contributed to debunking the view that patriarchalism was a natural relationship, and to disconnecting authority from paternity as biologically defined. Yet if the new principles of constitutional monarchy and republican sovereignty appeared to loosen patriarchalism's grip, there remained the separate questions about whether women were included among those who founded authority and whether authority itself could now be understood as a gender neutral practice.

Since Hobbes's theory implicitly unsettled patriarchalism as the foundation for authority in the modern state, feminist criticism has been engaged with it, self-consciously or otherwise. The contemporary feminist consensus has been that Hobbes failed to apply consistently his radically egalitarian logic to the analysis of sexual relationships, particularly to the terms of what Carol Pateman has called the "sexual contract." (1988, 43–55) Adhering to a specifically masculinized conception of selfhood, Hobbes's paradigm rested, Di Stefano has recently contended, on a denial of the "maternal contribution to bio-social reproduction." (1991, 103) If the foundation of authority in the modern state rested on a social contract, signalling "the end of a social order structured by kinship and the rule of the father," (Pateman, 1988, 30) patriarchalism continued to thrive in the form of a "sexual contract." Pateman contended that Hobbes never consistently attacked this sexual contract. By means of it, "men claim the right of sexual access to women's bodies and claim the right of command over the use of women's bodies." (1988, 30)

Pateman argued that to fail to recognize the inegalitarian terms of this "original contract" is to reinforce the patriarchal structure of modern civil society despite the subversion of paternal rule as the model for political rule. The sexual contract precludes women's being full and equal members of civil society because it establishes the terms for their "consensual" subjugation to men. But Pateman goes further than criticizing the terms of the sexual contract or the conditions of its "acceptance" by women. For her, contract as a model for equitable social relations, with its corollary idea of the individual as the owner of the property in her person and as possessor of the right to contract, is incompatible with a feminist vision of emancipation which does not make emancipation depend upon the annihilation or suppression of sexual difference. (1988, 30) Women's autonomy "as women" depends upon the supercession of contract, she argues, not its extension to more and more dimensions of civil society.

In this chapter I am interested in deploying Hobbes's arguments strategically to consider something more deeply problematic than Pateman's analysis suggests about the conceptualization of authority as sovereignty, of which Hobbes's theory is a representative version. Rather than ask where women are located in the Hobbesian paradigm, I will interrogate the gendered terrain of authority as Hobbes constructs it.[2] Thus I am less interested in the convention of contract as a device for obligating one to political obedience than with the masculinized *mode* of authority one is obliged to obey. My contention will be that the "sovereignty trap" necessitated Hobbes's retreat to patriarchy despite his otherwise egalitarian arguments. Having weakened the basis for supporting patriarchy on the grounds of biological or natural arguments, the ironic result of his construction of consensually founded patriarchy was the identification of authority more completely with masculinity itself. (Landes 1988)

Pateman seems to be making a similar argument about the increasing masculinization of authority, but for entirely different reasons. Pateman contended that the evolution of patriarchy—from what she called its "traditional" form, which assimilated "all power relations to paternal rule" and which made the paterfamilias the "model or metaphor for power and authority relations of all kinds," through the next stage of "classic patriarchalism," which justified political obligation as an extension of the natural obligation that sons (and presumably daughters) owed fathers, to "modern patriarchy," an institution which roots obligation in the contractual "exchange of obedience for protection,"—transformed patriarchy from the right of fathers to rule to the right of men to rule. To Pateman the structure of patriarchy was largely conjugal, a "part of masculine sex-right, the power that men exercise as men, not as fathers." (1988, 23–25, 22) In this respect Pateman's analysis most closely approximates Catherine MacKinnon's privileging of sexuality—male control of female sexuality—as definitive of women's subordination.

(MacKinnon, "Feminism, Marxism, Method, and the State") Although I agree with the implications of Pateman's analysis—that the masculinization of authority detaches sovereignty from the practices of fathers—I disagree with her ahistorical reading of this evolution as well as with her tendency to represent women as the hapless victims of male sexual exploitation. (cf. Jónasdóttir 1991)

To the extent that contemporary feminist analysis succumbs to the same temptation to establish sovereignty as the mode of authority, it limits the radical import of its critique. Because authority, as sovereignty, became and remained associated more completely with masculinity, contemporary feminist efforts to include women as a diverse group within the practice of authority have confronted their limits in the conceptualization of authority itself. The discourse of feminism seems captivated by this logic: the demand that feminists make often has been cast in terms of access to the instruments of social and political control. If the incorporation of women within the practice of authority increases the number of possible rulers but otherwise leaves undisturbed the mode of authority itself as the exercise of sovereignty—as masculinized protection—then how is feminism different from forms of liberal individualism that so many feminists have argued are inadequate to feminism's radical appeal to constitute a more fully democratic public life, that is, to construct a democracy adequate to the recognition of diversity understood as the "irreducibility of difference"? (Young in Nicholson 1990, 304) Or is the feminist demand for women's inclusion really nothing more than an effort to vindicate women as sovereigns, despite the fact that their exercise of sovereignty would be no different in design and effect from men's? In order to explore these questions, I will consider the way that authority as sovereignty renders anti-patriarchal arguments, both classical liberal ones and more contemporary feminist ones, incoherent.

Hobbes began from the supposition that the state of nature was a state of perfect equality. In the state of nature, he argued, all individuals existed in radical isolation from one another, abstracted from all social relationships. They engaged in individual pursuits motivated by a combination of acquisitiveness and personal insecurity that pitted individuals naturally against one another. Equality in the state of nature consisted in the fact that humans shared the same psychology and the same reasoning which led to "a general inclination of all mankind, a perpetual and restless desire of power after power, that ceaseth only in death." Equality also meant that all individuals were in the same state of insecurity: greed drove everyone to want everything, but the lack of anyone's having adequate "power and the means to live well" made everyone, in the end, vulnerable. Hobbes wrote: *"Nature hath made men so equal, in the faculties of the body and mind; as that though there be found one man sometimes manifestly stronger in body, or of quicker mind than another; yet when all is reckoned together, the difference between man, and man, is not so considerable, as that one man can thereupon claim to himself any benefit to which another may not pretend as well as he."* (1962, 98, emphasis added) Our equality in nature consisted in the fact that no one could *claim*—that is, exclusively, rightfully possess—something as her's (exclusive property) that someone else did not also desire and *could also rightfully claim.*

In the state of nature the principle of equality was so complete, Hobbes argued, that it extended even to relations between the sexes. "And whereas some have attributed the dominion to the man only, as being of the more excellent sex; they misreckon it. For there is not always the difference of strength, or prudence between the man and the woman, as that the right can be determined without war." (1962, 152) In prudence, which Hobbes defined as experience, and in strength, men and women, in Hobbes's view, were relatively equal. They stood, however, in the same relationship, in the state of nature, to the process of obtaining the objects of their desire: they both had the *same natural right to claim* something as "mine." This equal right to claim made insecurity and war the necessary result of the natural equality of all individuals. An individual's natural proclivity and natural right to all those things, without limit, that she desired—"every man [*sic*] has a right to everything"—created the condition of the "war of every one against every one" because "there is no power [in the state of nature] to over-awe them all." (1962, 103, 99) The result was that some would destroy or subdue others until another power great enough to threaten the conquerors had arisen.

Hobbes saw humans as both doomed and saved by their capacity for reason and for discourse, and their resultant tendency toward antagonistic, divisive comparisons with one another. Unlike other animals "without reason or speech," who could live together sociably "without any coercive power," humans needed a sovereign, a "common power, to keep them in awe and to direct their actions to the common benefit." (1962, 131, 132) Here, Hobbes transformed the fundamental principle that Aristotle had identified with our natural sociality—our capacity for speech and discourse—into the very source of our discontent and divisiveness. "The tongue of man is a trumpet of war and sedition." (*De Cive*, V, 5, 168–69). That we cannot agree on the meaning of words, that we appropriate language for the benefit of our own self-interestedness, that we are driven to divisive comparisons with one another, created the human condition: the need for awe-full sovereignty expressed as the need for an authority that can reduce all our wills "unto one will." (1962, 132) Yet our reason and our capacity for speech also enabled us to comprehend and to express the necessity to quit the state of nature and to agree to be conquered, to be subordinated by the Leviathan—that artificial person who speaks, writes, and acts on our behalf. For Hobbes, the sovereign makes the multitude of persons one by containing their differences: "A multitude of men, are made *one* person, when they are by one man, or one person, represented; so that it be done with the consent of every one of that multitude in particular. For it is the *unity* of the representer, not the *unity* of the represented, that maketh the person one." (1962, 127)

Hobbes's rejection of the principle that humans were "naturally" social was a radical departure from the prevailing wisdom. "We do not therefore by nature seek society for its own sake, but that we may receive some honour or profit from it; these we desire primarily, that secondarily." (*De Cive*, 1, 2, 111) Hobbes's argument that we were not born fit for society was a subtle one. He did not deny that we were born into a state of dependency on others. On the contrary, he noted that "to man by nature, or as man, that is as soon as he is born, solitude is an enemy; for infants have need of others to help them to live, and those of riper years to help them to live well." (*De Cive*, I, 2, 220) Yet arguing from this natural state of dependency to a theory of human nature as "naturally" social was unconvincing to Hobbes. We may need others to help us live well, and we may desire to come together, he argued, but these uneducated needs and desires did not constitute the kind of "bonds" made through "faith and compacts" which Hobbes felt founded the social order. In fact, the kind of dependency of "children and fools" precludes their ability to enter into social life:

> But civil societies are not mere meetings, but *bonds,* to the making whereof faith and compacts are necessary; the virtue whereof to children and fools, and the profit whereof to those who have not tasted the miseries which accompany its defects, is altogether unknown; whence it happens, that those, because they know not what society is, cannot enter into it; these, because ignorant of the benefits it brings, care not for it. . . . All men because they are born in

infancy, are born unapt for society. (*De Cive*, 1, 2, 110, emphasis added)

Hobbes's rejection of the proposition that we are naturally social depended on a particular construction of the term "social." Hobbes distinguished the "social" sharply from the state of dependency on others into which we all, as infants, have been born, in which "man, by nature, or as man, that is, as soon as he is born" finds himself. In making this argument he stressed the importance of education for fitting us for society. Yet education was important not only for infants but for "natural man" as well. As Peter Winch has argued, Hobbes, like Rousseau, contended that "a society in which absolute sovereign authority is exercised will not be maintained in the natural course of events: human effort and artifice are necessary. In particular, men must be *taught* to understand those conditions of human life which necessitate its acceptance." (Winch 1972, 233)

What is the significance of the implied analogy between infancy and the human condition in the state of nature? How far can this analogy be carried, since Hobbes's descriptions of the "state of men without civil society" seem to be anything but a state of natural dependency on others? Appreciating this analogy suggests an unarticulated tension in Hobbes's theory between describing humans in the state of nature as radically isolated from one another, dependent on nothing more than their own individual wills for survival, and the recognition, born of fear, that the self's willfulness ultimately depends upon others, even if only on the weakness or self-restraint of others, for its initial successes. Hobbes's "natural man," with her grandiose ego and unbridled sense of others as instruments to achieving greater glory for the self—we enter into society "not so much for love of our fellows, as for love of ourselves" (*De Cive*, 1, 2, 112–13)—seems remarkably infantile. Not out of good will, but out of fear that another will not always be weaker, but may sometimes be stronger than myself, am I moved to seek society. What does this fear represent and what are the consequences of making it the motivation for entering civil society?

Hobbes argued that it was necessary to pass from the state of nature into civil society in order to secure peace. The major motivation behind the establishment of "all great and lasting societies" was "mutual fear." Yet for Hobbes this fear was forward-looking and proactive: it encompassed "foresight of future evil" and people's efforts to "provide so they may not fear." (*De Cive*, I, 3, 113, footnote)

Fear transformed recognition of insecurity into recognition of the need to establish lasting bonds of peace. If "natural man" was like an infant, then she may have the desire for society, but not yet be fit to enter into social bonds. "Man is made fit for society not by nature, but by education. . . . For it is one thing to desire, another to be in capacity fit for what we desire." (*De Cive*, I, 2, 112) For Hobbes, the natural desire for society was a drive or motion toward something that only educated desire could achieve. Taken together these arguments pointed to, and simultaneously elided, the importance of early nurturance to the development of the capacity for social life.

Yet the predominant interpretation of Hobbes's analysis of social life by contemporary feminists has included the claim that Hobbes's theory of selfhood is based on a "masculine outlook and sense of identity" reflected especially in the denial of relatedness and repudiation of natural contingency expressed in Hobbes's view of human nature. This masculinized representation of self has been described by Christine di Stefano in the following terms:

> The need for singular identity and certainty with respect to one's identity and that of other "objects" in the environment, a concomitant of which is panic in the face of threats to such certainty, is another perpetual tendency which may be associated with masculinity. The denial of relatedness would be a feature of masculine identity as well. (1983, 636; cf. 1991, 89)

Di Stefano's criticism of the masculinity of Hobbes's theory of the individual is to be distinguished sharply from the recent arguments of Carole Pateman about the "fraternal" structure of modern patriarchy. To Pateman, the modern social contract is anteceded by a "sexual contract" which ensures that the "law of male sex-right remains operative." (1988, 103) Even after the father's right has been usurped by the fraternal bond "constituted by the forgotten dimension of the original contract," male sexual access to women is guaranteed by the terms of the sexual contract—Pateman's term for the marriage contract of modern liberalism, in which the wife exchanges (sexual) obedience for (economic) protection. Pateman contended that women had to be excluded from participation in the social contract if, in Hobbes's theory, "the contract is to be sealed." "The assumption must be made that, by the time the social contract is made, all women in the natural condition have been conquered by men and are now their subjects (servants)." (1988, 49) But as I will argue below, why Hobbes had to exclude women from the social contract seems to have less to do with some sexual imperative than with the definition of authority as sovereignty.

Pateman's acceptance of the (MacKinnon-esque) definition of "masculinity as sexual mastery" and her projection of a predatory male sexuality across the pages of history have led her to deeply ontological and politically paralyzing generalizations: "A free social order cannot be a contractual order" (1988, 232) and "The individual is a 'patriarchal' category." (1988, 184). Although her aim of working towards the "creation of a free society and the creation of sexual difference as diverse expressions of freedom" is laudable and challenges the liberal feminist assumption of the correctness of gender-neutral laws, her representation of women as the hapless victims of male sexual appetites ironically reinforces the very binary construction—male-individual/female-other—that her critique might point beyond. It also uncritically accepts the idea that sexuality is the essence of femininity. If "contract is the medium through which patriarchal right is created and upheld," (1988, 187) it is also a medium that subverts that right as patriarchal. As Pateman herself has observed: "If marriage is truly contractual, sexual difference must become irrelevant to the marriage contract; 'husband' and 'wife' must no longer be sexually determined. Indeed, from the standpoint of contract, 'men' and 'women' disappear." (1988, 167)

The psychoanalytically informed work of Flax, Chodorow, Dinnerstein and Keller, on which Di Stefano has relied in making her arguments, has rested on the claim that (in Western culture) constructions of masculinity depend upon a flight from the mother, and consequently, a negation of what is retrospectively culturally associated as "female": the centrality of relatedness to others. For men, having a self comes to mean having a rigidly defined sense of identity that necessarily perceives others not as companions but as threats to the impermeable borders of one's own being. For women the consequences of separation from the mother are different. Because mothers are women, the psychic development of "normal" (read heterosexual) femininity, within the context of what has been called the female monopoly on early child rearing, has meant that "girls emerge from this [pre-oedipal] period with a basis for 'empathy' built into the primary definition of self in a way that boys do not. Girls emerge with a stronger basis for experiencing another's needs or feelings as one's own." (Chodorow 1978, 167; cf. Flax; Dinnerstein 1976; Keller 1985)

There seems to be little doubt that Hobbes's understanding of human nature perceived others as threats to an individual's life instead of naturally convivial companions. As Peter Winch has observed, "like everything else in the world, other men [sic] are, for this Hobbist individual, obstacles or instruments in relation to his desires or aversions." (1972, 241) What humans lacked in the state of nature, Hobbes wrote, was a "common power, to keep them in awe and to direct their actions to the common benefit." All human relationships were contingent, "artificial" in Hobbes's words. Society was thoroughgoingly a product of the unreliability of one's individual will to protect one's individual life securely enough from other individuals who were threatening. Although our passions, particularly fear of death, may drive individuals to seek the social means to "commodious living" and to attempt to establish peace by "lay[ing] down this right to all things; and be contented with so much liberty against other men, as he would allow other men against himself," (1962, 104) Hobbes implied that the social was constituted by individuals' common relationship of subordination to the sovereign, instead of being constituted by the relatedness of individuals to each other. For Hobbes the social did not express people's relationship to one another but rather denoted the sharing of a politically guaranteed individual right to enjoy a peaceful private life under the conditions of political domination.

Yet restricting our understanding of Hobbes's analysis to this reading misses a crucial feature of Hobbes's distinction between the state of nature and civil society and the unintended significance of his analogy between the state of nature and human infancy. The ways that Hobbes described human nature in the state of nature parallels what later psychoanalysts would have called pre-oedipal narcissism. It would be anachronistic to argue that Hobbes's descriptions actively employed this discourse. Yet reading Hobbes's theories in light of these later theories provides an opportunity for what Harold Bloom has called a "strong misreading" of these classical texts. This rereading supplements earlier feminist interpretations of the masculinization of selfhood in Hobbes and permits us to consider, in ways that other critics have not, what is so deeply problematic about uncritically accepting Hobbes's theory of sovereignty as a theory of authority. Confronting the limitations of authority conceptualized as sovereignty could serve feminist efforts to make women and women's interests part of the practice of authority.

In the state of nature, as in infancy, we, males and females, do perceive others, primarily the "mother" who protects us, as a threat to our grandiose autonomy. One develops the sense that one's self is fragile and enormously dependent on an "other" for survival and protection. To the extent that we resolve conflicts during this stage successfully—conflicts that reflect the gradual emergence and separation of an "I" from entanglement with another—we perceive ourselves to be "independent" persons. Yet our independence is never fully free from the memory of our earlier dependence and vulnerability, in particular our earlier dependence on the female body/mother/ nurturer. To Hobbes this process of individuation was politically essential. Only an independent person could make promises to another and could agree to "be contented with so much liberty against other men, as he would allow other men against himself." Only an independent person could covenant.

Feminist psychoanalysts do not disagree with this general description of pre-oedipal narcissism and the necessity to transcend it during the later stages of "normal" ego-development. They have argued instead that the resolution of conflicts between separation and merger have different consequences for males and females because it is women who have been the primary caretakers. These consequences have a bearing on our understanding of the sexual significance of liberal theory's making the autonomous individual the hallmark of civil society. The male ego is capable of individuating in ways that more closely fit the model of normalcy. This is because of the different psychic significance for males of being "mothered" by females, a difference that appears to make them more capable of developing rigid ego boundaries. This ego has been made the model of the autonomous self.

It matters significantly that the "other" whom we have feared in our ontological and political infancy is a woman. It is separation from a woman, our distinguishing our bodies from hers, that triggers the process of individuation and codes the development of autonomy in masculine terms. We retreat to the stability of the order of father-Leviathans because it is a "sanctuary from maternal authority." (Dinnerstein 1976, 176) The fact that our "earliest and profoundest prototype of absolute power" occurs in infancy through the experience of the virtually exclusively female monopolization of early child rearing makes male dominion, for both sexes, become "an inexorable emotional necessity." (Dinnerstein 1976, 161, 177)

Yet because the internalization of the process of separation takes place within the context of an already defined symbolic order of sexual difference—a symbolic order which, in Western cultures, assigns priority to the phallus and constructs gender-differentiated social locations for men and women—the consequences of ego development being triggered by a turning away from the woman/mother are distinct for boys and girls: females learn to become women through and in terms of a greater continuity of relationship, whereas males learn to become men through and in terms of a denial of relationship. As long as females continue to learn to become women within the context of a symbolic order of sexual difference which privileges the phallus, which makes individuation depend upon a turning away from the mother toward the father, while it simultaneously reinforces, through the female monopolization of child rearing, the identification of "mothering" with a woman's body, then women will not be able to complete the process of individuation in the same way as men. "The basic feminine sense of self is connected to the world, the basic masculine sense of self is separate." (Chodorow 1978, 169)

If separate selves are the only kinds of selves who can make contracts, then women, who have more relational selves, appear to have been excluded by Hobbes from the group of potential contractors. The masculine self has been privileged as the only self properly educated to enter civil society fully. At this point it is important to recall the significance of Hobbes's analogy between infancy and the nature of human psychology in the state of nature. If, as Hobbes argued, society was not natural to humans but reflected a set of promises made by each one who had been "educated" to the necessity to be *bonded* to all, then Hobbes's understanding of the selfhood sufficient to enter such contracts does not necessarily exclude women as relational selves. Infants and "natural man" were excluded from contracting, but mothers, as the ones *on whom* infants and natural man were dependent, were not.[3] It is not a question of the relationality of self—the desire to maintain connections—which excludes infants, but their utter dependency. If the woman/mother's agency, her "educated desire," included consideration of the effect of her actions on others as well as on her immediate self as part of her consideration of promises; if her sense of self and obligation to others included an ontology of relationship (keeping promises), her agency with and through others did not place her in the same position of dependency as her infant was on her. (Whether something else did will be considered below.)

Feminists have cited the powerful image of the mushroom in *De Cive* as further evidence of Hobbes's masculinized representations of selfhood. (Di Stefano 1983, 1991; Benhabib in Kittay and Meyers 1987) "Let us return again to the state of nature, and consider men as if but even now sprung out of the earth, and suddenly, like mushrooms, come to full maturity, without all kind of engagement to each other." (*De Cive,* XIII, 1, 205) What appears to have been cleverly elided in this single simile is the consequential effect of the fact that men and women are "of women born." At stake here is the very different conceptualization of human behavior that would follow from a focus on humans becoming human within an intersubjectively constituted context of care and nurturance. To have argued that our more than initial dependency on others, primarily women, constructed the conditions of our life's preservation and comfort would have negated the ability to postulate atomistic individuals, "sprung from the earth," as the nature of human reality. The consequences of Hobbes's apparent forgetfulness of mothering, sexuality, life history, and human interdependency extended beyond questions about the adequacies of Hobbes's ontology into the sphere of political rights and obligations:

> In providing us with full sprung and atomistically conceived men and tracing out their hypothetical social exchanges, Hobbes keeps his schedule of human rights to a bare minimum: the right to life, maximum self-defined pleasure so long as it does not interfere with the pleasure or rights of others, and maximum freedom from pain. He makes social and civil obligation a purely pragmatic affair, external to the pre-constituted identity of the subject; such obligation is derived from natural right and, hence, is secondary to it. (Di Stefano 1991, 88)

Yet the interpretation of the mushroom passage is more complex than has been acknowledged. I would argue that it reflected not the unconscious desire to be rid of women and mothering, but an allusive critique of certain theories of procreation and generation which were dominant in the seventeenth century. Feminists have not yet explored how Hobbes's unsettling of traditional biologically based arguments that authority be decided patrilinearly reflected his radical departure from the dominant views about generation and embryology of his time: Hobbes had assigned priority to mothers as procreators.

The theory of procreation in Hobbes's era rested on a neo-Aristotelian interpretation of the biological asymmetry of reproduction—an asymmetry that made biological maternity apparent but which reduced biological paternity to a "cultural construct for which ocular proof was unattainable." (Montrose 1983, 72) Recognizing this asymmetry, theories of reproduction in the seventeenth century postulated that "paternity is procreative, the formal and/or efficient cause of generation; maternity is nurturant, the material cause of generation." (Montrose 1983, 73) Thomas Laqueur has recently explored the history of paternity from the Greeks through Freud and considered the ways that the "conquest of intellectuality over sensuality" (Freud's phrase) represented the triumph of patriarchy. (Laqueur 1990; in Hirsch and Keller 1990, 205–21) Seen in this light, Hobbes's reversal to sensual indicators for determining the mother's prior claim over the father as "lord" of the child, at least initially, is all the more remarkable.

Following Aristotle's claim that menstruation left behind the substance from which the embryo was made, much medical discourse in the seventeenth century sided with the view that the child was made by the man's seed from the menstrual blood." (Crawford 1981, 51) The work of William Harvey discredited this theory. Harvey generally subscribed to a theory of epigenesis, which held that the embryo of certain species developed in sequential stages, instead of another theory of embryology, known as "preformation," which had postulated that the final form existed in miniature from the moment of conception. As to metamorphosis, the simultaneous appearance of all parts of an organism some time after conception, "like mushrooms sprung from the ground," Harvey limited this explanation of the "sudden appearance of the full-sized organism" to insects and lower animals. (Bowler 1971, 222) Insofar as Harvey himself had accepted certain versions of performation, his own arguments gave greater weight to the influence of the egg in this process. He had even gone so far as to suggest that "a partially formed embryo may develop without the concurrence of the male." (Bowler 1971, 229) This theory of "ovism" assigned priority to the egg in the origination of species.

Hobbes was a close friend of Harvey's, and his granting of priority of rule over the child to the mother may have reflected, at least in part, Harvey's influence. Hobbes wrote: "in the state of nature it cannot be known who is the *father,* but by testimony of the *mother,* the child therefore is his whose the mother will have it, and therefore her's." (*De Cive,* IX, 3, 213) Seen in this light, Hobbes's mushroom passage could be read with particular emphasis on the "even now": *even now* that theories of metamorphosis have been shown to be limited to lower species, let us explore the ways that men enter into contracts in the state of nature as if men were sprung from the earth without all kind of engagement with one another.

The fact is Hobbes had acknowledged our dependence on one another and had argued that, precisely because of our *natural* dependence, we were not born fit for society. We had to grow and be

educated to such fitness. In light of his strong, and radically unconventional, insistence on this point, it is more plausible to argue
that Hobbes had embraced a theory of human nature and human
development that not only did not "disappear" mothers but made
them "lords" of their children. His position on this point might have
reflected a predilection for Harvey's theories of ovism, but it is most
consistent with the ontology of his political theory. It is not biology,
or "nature," that creates our obligation to one another. Nor is it our
"natural" dependency. We become obligated to those who effectively
and continuously protect us. In this regard Di Stefano's conclusion
that "Hobbes invokes the figure of the mother when she suits his
purpose of developing an alternative account of legitimate power to
that of the patriarchalists [and] conveniently forgets her after that"
is itself based on an "overly literal loyalty" and overly literal reading
of the "mushroom" passage. (Di Stefano 1983, 85)

It is instructive to interpret this passage not only within the contextual, but also the textual frame in which it was written. Immediately before the infamous, purportedly misogynist allusion to mushrooms, Hobbes has noted that

> in the two foregoing chapters we have treated of an *institutive* or
> *framed* government, as being that which receives its original from
> the consent of the many, who by contract and faith mutually given
> have obliged each other. Now follows what may be said concerning
> a *natural* government; which may also be called *acquired,* because
> it is that which is gotten by power and natural force. (*De Cive,* VIII,
> 1, 205)

Under conditions of conquest, it is much easier to imagine that men
are "sprung out of the earth . . . without all kind of engagement to
each other." This is how the conquered are seen *from the perspective
of the conqueror.* But as I argue below, Hobbes's grasp of the dynamics
of conquest is more dialectical than has previously been acknowledged.

Ironically, Hobbes's critique reinforced the centrality of women's
reproductive biology to the process of procreation. In this light it
seems to make little sense to contend that Hobbes advocated viewing
the persons of civil society as if they were not "of woman born." At
the same time, Hobbes's assignment of "sovereignty" to the mother
in the determination of the "legitimacy" of progeny and his defense
of women as the immediate and original "lords" of their children
radically dethroned traditional biological arguments invoked to sup-

port contentions that the lines of authority should be determined patrilineally. Patriarchal arguments rested on the claim that, since fathers generated children, children were obligated to obey fathers. But in Hobbes's case, the logic of generation supported the rule of mothers, not fathers: "Wherefore original dominion over children belongs to the mother; and among men no less than other creatures, the birth follows the belly." (*De Cive,* IX, 3, 213)

Yet Hobbes did not simply substitute his own, unconventional biological argument for prevalent ones which had been used for determining the origin of authority and for explaining its justification. On the contrary he offered an ethical argument. Hobbes noted that in nature, where there were no civil, matrimonial laws, "either the parents between themselves dispose of the dominion over the child by contract; or do not dispose thereof at all. . . . If there be no contract, the dominion is in the mother." (1962, 152) Hobbes's rationale for concluding that, in nature, women were given the advantage to claim dominion over children depended upon, as we have seen, his contention that unless mothers declared the father's identity, it could not be known for certain who he was, whereas mothers had certain knowledge of their motherhood. So "the right of dominion dependeth on her will." (1962, 152) In the state of nature "every woman that bears children, becomes both a *mother* and a *lord.* . . ." (*De Cive,* IX, 3, 213)[4] Yet Hobbes made the mother's dominion over children depend further on the provision that she continue to nourish it. "But if she expose it, and another find and nourish it, the dominion is in him [sic] that nourisheth it. For it *ought to obey him by whom it is preserved.*" (1962, 153; *De Cive,* IX, 4, 213) Thus Hobbes justified mothers having dominion over children in the state of nature on the grounds of their reproductive biology, but he did not make biology alone a sufficient reason. Given his repudiation of generation alone as a principle for determining rightful rule, he could not have argued otherwise.

> Those that have hitherto endeavored to prove the dominion of a parent over his children, have brought no other argument than that of *generation;* as if it were of itself evident, that what is begotten is mine . . . but two persons, male and female, must concur in the act of generation; it is impossible that dominion should at all be acquired by generation alone. (*De Cive,* IX, 1, 212)

Unless their biological claim was matched by actions to preserve the life of the child, mothers could not justify their continued rule over children. Nor could rulers of states.

For Hobbes all legitimate dominion was based on the ability of rulers to preserve the lives of those who were subject to their rule. Preservation of life was the end, or purpose, "for which one man becomes subject to another." Although, for Hobbes, "covenants, without the sword, are but words," he never claimed that force alone could legitimate authority. The Leviathan, like the mother, must preserve the lives of those subject to their dominion.

THE SEXUAL CONTRACT AND THE CONTRADICTIONS OF CONSENT THEORY

Hobbes's theory has proved deeply troubling to contemporary feminists because of his justification of the legitimacy of governments originally founded in conquest. Hobbes considered two ways that commonwealths were established: by acquisition or by institution. In the latter case, "the citizens by their own wills appoint a lord over themselves." (*De Cive,* V, 12, 172) Hobbes imagined that conquest could create unity. But this unity only became authoritative when those who were subdued accepted the victory of those who had overpowered them. If conquest created situations in which some ruled, or spoke for, others, Hobbes argued that it was as impossible to justify such rule of force *in terms of force* as it was impossible to claim that it was unjust. "Where there is no common power, there is no law: where there is no law, no injustice. . . . Justice, and injustice are none of the faculties neither of the body, nor mind. . . . They are qualities, that relate to men in society, not in solitude." (1962, 101) Justice emerged, for Hobbes, only at the point where everyone had *agreed* to divest themselves of their absolute, natural right to all things and "be contented with so much liberty against other men, as he would allow against himself." (1962, 104) Justice consisted in the freely assumed obligation or duty to be bound to whatever an individual had consented. Even though fear of death and the threat of force might have been the conditions under which one covenanted in the first place, *force became authority through the act of consent.* Conquered peoples were rightfully obligated to obey victors, not because of the victory itself, but only because they had agreed to submit: "It is not therefore the victory, that giveth the right of dominion over the vanquished, but his own covenant. Nor is he obliged because he is conquered; that is to say, beaten, and taken, or put to flight; *but because he cometh in, and submitteth to the victory.*" (1962, 154, emphasis added)

Contemporary feminists have argued that Hobbes's idea of consenting to conquest shared with Locke's acceptance of an unequal marriage contract the same inadequate and ahistorical approach to consent that marked the general irrelevance of liberal paradigms to women's political situation. To writers such as Pateman, women's subordination had been constructed through the terms of the liberal contract itself. Arguments from consent abstracted choice from the historical context in which it was located and ignored the differential social, psychological, legal, and economic conditions which affected women's and men's ability to give consent. The argument that all individuals equally consented to be ruled, either in the private sphere or in the public arena, ignored the extent to which the ability to refuse to consent depended upon both physical, idiosyncratic differences among individuals as well as on socioeconomic factors that would have made it less likely for certain groups to be able to resist at all. Instead of a contextualized theory of choice, liberalism had posited an abstract, unsituated actor who had the same capacity as any other actor to submit to or to resist conquest. Choice was an effect of will; it was not connected by Hobbes either to heart, sexuality, or to embodiment.

Feminists have contended that it was irrational to claim that anyone actually "consents" to be dominated or to be subjugated by someone recognizably superior in strength or social position or economic power. Arguing from consent, when consent has been abstractly defined as the freely-given acceptance of an unequal state of affairs, also sidesteps the absurdity involved in any claim that *links voluntarism with* the acceptance of a *state of unfreedom*. As Pateman has written regarding the terms of consent in marriage and the implied consent of those who apparently "submit" to unwanted sexual advances:

> The identification of enforced submission with consent in rape is a stark example of the wider failure in liberal democratic theory and practice to distinguish free commitment and agreement by equals from domination, subordination, and inequality. Writers on consent link "consent," "freedom," and "equality," but the realities of power and domination in our sexual and political lives are ignored. Contemporary consent theory presents our institutions as if they were actually as consent demands, as if they were actually constituted through the free agreement of equal persons. (1980, 162; cf. Brennan and Pateman 1979, 199)

Pateman suggested that the characteristics of the institutions that "consent demands" are those egalitarian features that permit anyone and everyone to develop a sense of personal autonomy and a "partici-patory psychology," that orientation of mind which reflects an active awareness of one's own efficacy. Feminist research has documented the myriad ways that male-dominated institutions negate autonomy for women. By analyzing the totality of the political-economic order, broadly redefined, that operates behind and before the "moment of choice," feminists have demonstrated how the ways that "the world is organized for us *prior to our participation* as knowers" are critical to understanding women's (and men's) lived experience of choice. (Dorothy Smith in Harding 1987, 94) The proposition that we begin to construct theories "from direct experience" or "from where we are located bodily" reflects, like arguments about the sociology of knowledge, the contention that the always already constituted world mediates the practice of consent. Choice, defined as action taken or not taken, should be comprehended contextually, where the relevant context is understood from within, from the subject's perspective. Context includes the "range of experiences and expectations within which women live." "The weave of relationships and structures which constitute women's worlds" creates the contexts of choice around and through which women must navigate. (Personal Narra-tives Group 1989, 19)

Yet feminist critiques do not acknowledge the degree to which Hobbes's abstracted conceptualization of consent stems from a view of human nature that distinguishes itself from other, more determin-istic, conceptualizations of human behavior, including later feminist ones. If feminist theorists have been quick to locate the structural determinants of consent, they may have been too hasty in character-izing women's positions in modern society as necessarily those of the hapless victims of male oppression. Recent feminist analyses of women's active negotiation of the ways that they have been excluded from traditional arenas of power and influence in a variety of political settings have suggested that women possess a greater degree of resourcefulness, and have more consciously manipulated systems of power to women's own advantage, than was originally postulated by feminists. Context, in the words of one set of critics, "is not a script. Rather it is a dynamic process through which the individual simulta-neously shapes and is shaped by her environment." (Personal Narra-tives Group 1989, 19)

For instance, Soheir Morsy's study of women in traditional rural communities of Egypt offered the view that women's manipulation of the "sick role"—a role traditionally defined as one of dependency on others—provided women ways to escape certain other dimensions of the traditional female role at times that they determined for themselves. Morsy suggested that it was important to understand actions from the perspective of meanings assigned by the actors themselves, rather than only from the position of the "objective," outside observer, in order to comprehend more fully the complex power dynamics that such actions reflected and yet resisted. (1988, 69–90) Morsy claimed that women in rural Egypt were not without some resources to defend themselves against more onerous forms of patriarchy. Similarly, Barbara Calloway's interpretation of Muslim Nigerian women's manipulation of their forced segregation from the male world as a way to transform this male-constructed space into a space for themselves, within which they could voice their concerns apart from men's and could act on them in a political context also implied that the objective determinants of constraint may not appear so unequivocally restrictive from the perspectives of the "constrained" subjects themselves. (1988, 45–68) Both Morsy and Calloway note that their research is not meant to celebrate women's seclusion and subordination as the source of power equivalent to what males exercise, but rather to suggest that relationships of power are more complex and fluid than the dichotomy "superordinate-subordinate" implies.[5]

Writing critically about how Western feminists' paradigm of the universality of male dominance implied the unalterable consequence that women were everywhere and always oppressed by men, Chandra Mohanty argued that women's experiences have been falsely homogenized by the definition of women "as a singular group on the basis of a shared oppression." Falsely universal descriptions of the "average third world woman," or of women in general, have been based on the "crucial assumption that all of us of the same gender, across classes and cultures, are somehow socially constituted as a homogeneous group identified prior to the point of analysis." Mohanty contended that the prevalence in the model of women as victims of an unchanging and unassailable patriarchy " 'colonizes' the fundamental complexities and conflicts which characterize the lives of different classes, religions, cultures, races, and castes." (1984, 335)

In contrast to this kind of reductive research, Mohanty cited approvingly the work of Maria Mies on the lace makers of Narsapur, India. Mies's work suggested, Mohanty continued, that although the lace makers were subjected to patriarchal and exploitative control of their work and its products, these women could not be described as "mere victims of the production process, because they resist[ed], challenge[d] and subvert[ed] the process at various junctures." (1984,

345). Aihwa Ohg argued similarly that there were intersections between Western feminist discourses' constructions of "non-Western" women as unliberated victim and colonial discourses' representation of "the Third World" in fixed, static, "uncivilized" terms. She writes: "By portraying women in non-Western societies as identical and interchangeable, and more exploited than women in the dominant capitalist societies, liberal and socialist feminists alike encode a belief in their own superiority." (1988, 85)

Reading Hobbes's analysis of consent in light of this contemporary research makes judgments such as Pateman's that liberal consent theory rests on a specious claim of autonomy for women more problematic than is ordinarily noted. Hobbes's assertion that the one who appears to be a victim of force in some way, by consenting to or, more precisely, submitting to being subordinate, nonetheless preserves an important aspect of being human, of being an agent against all odds. It deserves reconsideration by feminists. The very act of submission, however determined by the perception of few alternatives in the moment, nonetheless preserves the "victims" humanity because it postulates a recognition of a dialectical moment of willfulness in submission that, ironically, prevents submission from being a complete vanquishing. It seems important to emphasize that judgments are still being made even when the capacity to judge appears overwhelmed by the inordinate power of the oppressor. Not the least significant here is the fact that this idea of consent reflects, as its mirror opposite, the desire and the will to resist.

The critical feature of Hobbes's theory of consent was his connection of consent with trust. Hobbes included three ways that the "right of dominion may be gotten over the persons of men": by mutual contract, by conquest in war, and by generation. (*De Cive,* VIII, 1, 206) The element which each of these three methods of rightful dominion shared in common appeared, on the surface, to be the fact that they were all relationships of dependency and hierarchy. Yet what they shared was the fact that, for Hobbes, what made relations of dominion legitimate, what made rule rightful, was neither force nor subordination, but trust. "The servant that is put in bonds, or by any other means deprived of his corporal liberty, is freed from that other obligation of contract. *For there can be no contract where there is no trust,* nor can that faith be broken which is not given." (*De Cive,* VIII, 9, 209, emphasis added; cf. 207, 127) Trust was the foundation of contract because trust reflected the interdependence and mutual recognition implicit in the relationship of master and slave.

Like Hegel's analysis of self-consciousness, Hobbes's logic of consent rested on the understanding that the lord required the subordinate's *recognition* of the lord in order to be lord. As Hegel had put it, "self-consciousness exists only in being *acknowledged*." (1979, 111, emphasis added) Hegel shows that the relationship between two individuals, each of whom treats the other as not-self, as other, is a relationship of mutual dependency. Each needed the other to become "for itself." Instead of any action on the part of the lord being able to be claimed as the lord's own, what became evident was that the lord needed the bondsman's acting willfully, of her own accord, in order for the lord's desires to be realized. (1979, 112) "They *recognize* themselves as mutually *recognizing* one another." Yet this meant that any complete annihilation of the will of the other, the subordinate, would leave the conqueror only with uncertainty that the struggle was worthwhile. (Bataille, 1977; Benjamin, 1983) Worse still, "conquest" alone cannot provide a *secure* basis for rule.

The recognition that the vanquished, by "escaping", even in the most seemingly ineffectual, "psychological" way—through distancing herself from the moment—has been willful, sullies the conqueror's claim that force alone has been sufficient to secure subordination. Such a conqueror would be plagued by suspicion that the victim was complicitous, by being willful, in structuring the terms of her own defeat. Ironically, the *willfulness* of the victim is precisely what the conqueror needs in order to be *recognized* as conqueror. Yet the realization of this negates the conqueror's claim to singular power in the very moment of apparent triumph. Submission denies to the conqueror what he needs to be master. Submission robs conquest of its own surety. Jessica Benjamin has written: "The exhaustion of satisfaction that occurs when all resistance is vanquished, all tension is lost, means that the relationship [of domination] has come full circle, returned to the emptiness from which it was an effort to escape. Total loss of tension, de-differentiation, means death of the self." (1983, 115)

Subtly, the Hobbesian construction of consent suggests what Hegel's analysis of the lord-bondsman dialectic in *The Phenomenology* treated in more depth: the conqueror's own use of force masks a weakness, a dependency of the victor on the victim, which conquest had intended to deny. Feminists should contemplate these implications of Hobbes's theory of consent before rejecting it cavalierly on the ground that consent is a dangerous mask covering the reality of women's victimization.

In her reading of Hegel, Carole Pateman has recently argued that "Hegel's social order demands a sexually differentiated consciousness." Because the relationship between men and women, structured through the sexual contract, "which constitutes men's patriarchal right over women," is constructed as a relationship of natural subordination, "women are outside the fight to death between master and slave at the dawn of self-consciousness." Pateman continues: "The recognition that a husband obtains from a wife is precisely what is required in modern patriarchy; recognition as a patriarchal master, *which only a woman can provide*." (1988, 179) She contends that the struggle toward self-consciousness, the "mutual acknowledgement and confirmation of self, however, is possible *only if the two selves have an equal status*. The master cannot see his independence reflected back in the self of the slave; all he finds is servility." (1988, 178)

Yet this is a fundamental misinterpretation of Hegel's analysis of the struggle to self-consciousness. The equality of status to which Hegel's theory refers does not imply a "sameness" of social position. The master and the slave do not stand in the same relation to desire or to the object of desire. In fact it is the bondsman, or slave, who is propelled to self-consciousness through the very activity—her work of servitude—which appeared at first to deny her subjectivity, or freedom. The master's interposing of the slave between himself and the object of his desire creates the conditions for the slave's freedom as self-consciousness:

> Desire has reserved to itself the pure negating of the object and therefore its unalloyed feeling of self. But that is the reason why this satisfaction is itself only a fleeting one, for it lacks the side of objectivity and permanence. Work, on the other hand, is desire held in check, fleetingness staved off; in other words, work forms and shapes the thing. . . . It is in this way, therefore, that consciousness, *qua worker,* comes to see in the independent being [of the object] its *own* independence. (1979, 118)

If the man's desire to be recognized as patriarchal master requires recognition by a woman, a "recognition which only a woman can provide," then it is not accurate to say, as Pateman does, that it is "in the brotherhood," or in the fraternity of civil society that "each man can obtain self-confirmation and acknowledgement of his equality. . . ." (1988, 178) The constitution of this brotherhood, and men's recognition as "masters," is mediated by women's existence as objects of sexual desire. Women's sexual "work," like the slave's productivity in Hegel's analysis, gives form and shape to the "thing" which men desire. Women's sexuality, initially experienced as an alienated existence, as being desirable, or as being the object of desire, constitutes what is desired. Through being desired woman confronts her own subjectivity. Following Hegel, woman—in fashioning herself as desirable thing—becomes aware that she herself exists essentially and actually in her own right.

In describing the sexual contract, Pateman has succumbed to the logic of its fictional account of mastery. She has forgotten that the moment of "surrender of one's will is only from one aspect negative; in principle, however, or in itself, it is at the same time positive, viz. the positing of the will as the will of an 'other', and specifically of will, not as a particular, but as a universal will." (Hegel 1979, 138) As the story of the sexual contract implies, the exchange of (sexual) obedience for protection requires obtaining jurisdiction over particular sorts of bodies; that is, female bodies. If having sexual access to women constitutes masculinity within a heterosexual paradigm of sexual difference by creating an arena—private life—against which the (male) public world of freedom is defined, then this very requirement of (sexual) obedience in exchange for protection constitutes simultaneously the moment of vulnerability of the "male protection racket." (Stiehm, 1982) The requirement that women consent to the unequal terms of the heterosexual sexual contract expresses this essential contradiction. Requiring women's consent points, ironically, to the vulnerability, not the certainty, of the sexual contract.

Some feminists have argued that consent theory constitutes a form of victim blaming. For instance, Catherine MacKinnon has contended that grounding arguments for abortion rights on a gender-neutral foundation separates rights from the context of equality that alone can constitute justice. Claims that a woman should have the same private right to control her body as a man have obscured "the unequal basis on which woman's personhood is being constructed." (1987, 123) MacKinnon has insisted that the assertion of a right to privacy as the basis for abortion rights, instead of the defense of abortion as necessary to ensure the equal protection of women before the law, has reinforced the structures that have contributed to the oppression of women by men: inequality in the so-called private sphere has meant that women have been denied the ability to be autonomous beings in control of their own personal identities. The right to privacy is constructed only by abstracting from this unequal context of privacy. To MacKinnon women have been victims of male coercion in the private sphere especially because women have been defined by men in terms of their sexual availability for men. "Sex doesn't look a whole lot like freedom when it appears normatively less costly for women to risk an undesired, often painful, traumatic, dangerous, sometimes illegal, and potentially life-threatening procedure than to protect themselves in advance." Under conditions of gender inequality, the context of privacy within which women get pregnant has been "forced sex." (1987, 95, 96) Within this context women have been provided with little, if any, basis to resist the attacks of male predators. MacKinnon implied that women who rationalized their submission, or who claimed to autonomy, to choice, were merely deceived or self-deceiving.

> This right of privacy is a right of men "to be let alone" to oppress women one at a time. . . . This is an instance of liberalism called feminism, liberalism applied to women as if we *are* persons, gender neutral. It reinforces the division between the public and the private that is *not* gender neutral. . . . It keeps some men out of the bedrooms of other men. (1987, 102)

Yet are feminist theories of women's structured inequality better served by emphasizing women's conquest and its corollary—women's victimization—or by exploring the paradox of choosing to submit? In 1979, commenting on the use of the "oppressed group" model for the study of women's history, Gerda Lerner noted that, although oppressive restraints were undoubtedly aspects of women's historical experience,

> the limitation of this approach is that it makes it appear that women were either largely passive or that, at the most, they reacted to male pressures or to the restraints of patriarchal society. Such inquiry fails to elicit the positive and essential way in which women have functioned in history. . . . Treating women as victims once again places them in a male-defined conceptual framework: oppressed, victimized by standards and values established by men. The true history of women is the history of their ongoing functioning in that male-defined world *on their own terms.* (1979, 178)

An equally fruitful approach to women's political experience would be to explore the thesis that many women have manipulated male-defined consent *on their own terms.*

DISAPPEARING WOMEN AND THE PATRIARCHY OF SOVEREIGNTY

Although Hobbes contended that the principle of natural equality precluded anyone's claiming the *right* to rule another because of superiority of strength of body or of mind, or because of conquest, feminists have pointed to Hobbes's inconsistency about the implications of his attack on force, or custom, as justifications for authority. In his theory, they have argued, married women disappeared into a family that Hobbes had presumed was patriarchal, constructed as he had argued it was by civil laws favoring the father's rule. Although Hobbes had noted that parental power *should* belong equally to both parents, and although he had rejected the idea that dominion belonged to the man "as being of the more excellent sex," nevertheless, he had argued that fathers *would* rule, since, for the most part, he claimed, "commonwealths have been erected by the fathers, and not the mothers, of families." (1962, 152; *De Cive,* IX, 16, 219) In founding states, fathers had made civil laws favoring themselves.

Feminists have concluded that Hobbes's eventual exclusion of women resulted from a fatal theoretical slippage away from a consistent critique of all relationships based on force to an assumption that traditional male domination in the family, and by implication in the state, was acceptable and rational. Because Hobbes had assumed the appropriateness of women's legal subordination to male rule in the family, he succumbed to the lure of residual patriarchal ideas. Thus, Diana Coole noted that Hobbes "could subvert women's equal authority in the family only by conceding a natural superiority to men." (1988, 83)

Yet what such accounts miss is the extent to which Hobbes's commitment to a conceptualization of authority as sovereignty, that is, to authority as the *unitary* right to rule, both in the family and in the state, led him necessarily to retreat to patriarchal justifications of women's subordination in the family and to their subjection to male-dominated institutions in the state. In other words, what Pateman called modern "fraternal patriarchalism," which she claimed enabled men to "claim right of sexual access to women's bodies and claim right of command over the use of women's bodies," (1988, 17) presented itself as a convenient yet indispensable device with which to complete arguments about authority as a practice founded in the act of consenting to obey a *singular will* outside of, and even at odds with, one's own.

Although Diana Coole has implied that Hobbes *intended* to subvert his own arguments about women's equivalent authority in the family, the fact was that his falling into the "sovereignty trap" logically required him to undermine women's share in authority. Hobbes's attack on patriarchy as an unacceptable justification for authority in the state necessarily remained incomplete *because* he accepted sovereignty, or univocal rule, as the only appropriate model for authority. The relationship between this conceptualization of authority as sovereignty, the search for political stability, and the exclusion of women, materially and symbolically, from the practice of political authority, needs to be explored systematically.

Ursula Vogel has commented that the " 'sovereignty-requirement' on which virtually all Natural Law theorists agree[d] rest[ed] on the premise that in the family—as in the state—there must be an unquestionable authority for issuing final decisions." (1988, 147) Hobbes was no exception. Yet, she argued, there were, given the contractual basis of marriage, several options for solving the problem of who the one who would rule (be in authority) might be. In principle, rule could be, as Hobbes himself allowed, contractually assigned to the mother, to the father, or to both. Although it is certainly true that these options may have existed within the scope of Hobbes's thought, the recurrence to patriarchal assumptions about male rule within the family and the state presented itself as a solution to the problem of deciding on the "appropriate" gender identity of rulers. Sovereignty as controlling paradigm for authority required that someone should have the determining voice. "No man can obey two masters." Sovereignty, as I will argue further in the next chapter, also was linked, in Hobbes, to the need for the representation of the indivisibility of the represented through the sovereign's body politic. On the symbolic level then, the concept of sovereignty as unity negated the possibility of including divisible bodies—women's bodies—in the scheme.

Pateman has argued that the exclusion of women from entering the original contract followed from contract theorists' definition of the individual.

> The body of the "individual" is very different from women's bodies. His body is tightly enclosed within boundaries, but women's bodies are permeable, their contours change shape and they are subject to cyclical processes. . . . Physical birth symbolizes everything that makes women incapable of entering the original contract and transforming themselves into the civil individuals who uphold its terms. (1988, 96)

Because their capacity to give birth makes women "naturally subversive of men's political order," they must be excluded from the making of the original contract. They are excluded, Pateman has argued, by the terms of the marriage contract which make them subject to the rule of men and which legitimate men's right of sexual access to women's bodies. Yet this interpretation seems weak in the case of single women, who remain independent of the unequal terms of the marriage contract. Moreover, it misses the extent to which, in both Hobbes and Locke, it was the model of authority as sovereignty that led them to subscribe to a modern patriarchal determination of the sexual division of labor. Especially in Hobbes, the need for political order led to a theory that stressed the singularity of the will of the sovereign. Even in the case of Hobbes's recognition of the possibility of authority being vested in an "assembly," the focus is not on thereby ensuring the representation of a plurality of interests, but the manufacture of univocality, the reduction of diversity to singularity, the incorporation of difference in unity.

Women's bodies subvert order symbolically in Hobbes's theory because Hobbesian order depends upon unity. In Hobbes the sovereign's body is undivided and his voice is univocal. The political commonwealth derived from a basic covenant among men (and Hobbes generally means *men*), unfettered by attachments, who entered into a compact to be ruled. It consisted in their agreement:

> to confer all their power and strength upon one man, or upon one assembly of men, that may reduce all their wills, by plurality of voices, unto one will: which is as much to say to appoint one man, or assembly of men, to bear their person; and every one to own, and *acknowledge himself to be author* of whatsoever he that so beareth their person, shall act, or cause to be acted, in those things which concern the common peace and safety; and therein submit their wills, every one to his will, and their judgments to his judgment. (1962, 132, emphasis added)

In Hobbes's conceptualization authority is, quite literally, written into the office of the sovereign, the one who represents, or "bears the person of," the divided multitude that created him, or authored him into existence in the first place. Yet Hobbes's notion of authorship is a curious one, because it ceases, as an ongoing practice, in the very moment that its first product, the covenant, is crafted. From that moment it is the actor, the Leviathan created by authors of the covenant, who speaks, writes and acts on their behalf, and in their name, or by virtue of the authority, or "right of doing any action," that they have conferred upon him. With this original authorizing of the "artificial person" to speak or act on our behalf we agree to accept his words, speeches, and acts as our own by definition.

Participation in authority here amounts to the equal obligation of all contracting parties to abide by the dictates of the sovereign.

Participation in this kind of authority amounted to the annihilation of difference because difference was understood to be divisive and destructive. In fact, Hobbes's point was that the sovereign was to make the multitude into one by overcoming their differences: "A multitude of men, are made *one* person, when they are represented by one man, or one person, represented; so that it be done with the consent of that multitude in particular. For it is the *unity* of the represener, not the unity of the represented, that maketh the person *one*." (1962, 127)

This aspect of Hobbes's theory of authority—the annihilation, or at least the transcendence, of difference in the moment of authorizing— has been generally ignored by feminist scholars. Instead they have concentrated on the fact that his theory viewed the foundation of authority in all areas as essentially contingent, but that he inconsistently applied this principle to women's situation: "Each abstract entity, taken singularly, is an 'individual' with specified 'natural' characteristics. But this means that the conception of 'natural' freedom and equality is incompatible with patriarchal authority, whether that authority is exercized in the state or in the family." (Brennan and Pateman 1979, 184) Indeed, as Brennan and Pateman have observed, Hobbes had no argument with the patriarchalists' assertion that authority relationships were structured homologously throughout society. The difference in his theory was that he insisted that these structures were based on convention and not on mere nature.

Yet Hobbes's denaturalization and depersonalization of authority, which separated his theory from a patriarchal tradition that had connected authority to "persons and their special (divinely ordained) attributes," (Di Stefano 1983, 639) existed on the same plane as the patriarchalists' argument that authority was sovereignty. This has had significant consequences for feminist efforts to include women and female interests with authority defined as the singular right to speak for another. From the feminist perspective of changing the shape of rule, in the final analysis it matters little whether women would have been chosen as the ultimate authorities in families or in states if the principle of authority remained sovereignty. Unless the principle of women's ruling invoked a different norm for deciding questions of how to represent divided interests, unless, in other words, women's speaking authoritatively meant transcending the principle of authority as sovereignty, the selection of women over men as rulers, in families or in states, would not have made, and does not make, a difference in the conceptualization of authority as a final, unimpeachable command. In other words, opting for women to represent families or to be the representatives in polities, could not, within the logic of authority as sovereignty, change the way authority was practiced as a command-obedience relationship.

What feminists like Pateman have objected to in Hobbes has been his fundamental unwillingness to take criticisms of patriarchal ideas about the *foundation* of sovereignty to their logical conclusions. Yet my argument is that even if Hobbes had addressed more consistently this sex—and race and class—bias, the masculinism of his theory of authority was rooted in the universalizing form that authority as sovereignty took in his system, and not simply in the fact that women, as individuals, were not fully included as contract makers. The fact is that Hobbes's conceptualization of the sovereign individual ultimately abstracted from the social contexts of embodiment, lineage, and location that make people the *specific* persons they are. Such a conceptualization of sovereignty negated the political significance of all historically constructed differences—of class and race as well as of sex. That was its purpose. Individuals became what they were because of their *separation* from everything—physically, culturally, and historically—which connected them to others like them. Consequently, even if women had been recognized as "authors" of the covenant, the representational system that their authored covenant might have created necessarily excluded women's sexuality and the female gender, and every other particularized aspect of being human, from it by definition. Difference, in the sense of a distinguishable practice of being a self in connection with others, a self who was at once separate *and* connected, was occluded by a political formalism that recognized neither a substantive nor a formal basis for resisting the monotonal and monolithic speeches of the person, the Leviathan, whom all have authorized to speak and act for them.

In order to become such undivided unities who spoke for all, no matter for whom specifically, it could be argued that women would have to transcend their embodied experiential, divided, and dividing selves. Hobbes's theory of authority deauthorized "maternal authority," an "authority indelibly personal and organically based" which "cannot be characterized in the simple linear terms of commandments and prescriptions with merely behavioral consequences." (Di Stefano 1983, 639) Yet at the same time, as I will argue in the next chapter, Hobbes coopted "maternal interests" and the symbolism of the "maternal body" to justify the rule of the sovereign. The need for unity was so strong in Hobbes that, once the commonwealth had been created, women's mothering was appropriated by the sovereign. Nature, Hobbes wrote, provided the nutrition that supports the commonwealth, coming from the "two breasts of our common mother, land and sea. . . ." Yet the body of the commonwealth was described in terms that subverted Hobbes's earlier understanding of human reproduction. Procreation occurred; the children of the commonwealth were its "colonies." But it was "men sent out from a commonwealth . . . to inhabit a foreign country" whose actions reproduced these children. The colonies may understand that the metropolis was their mother, but if they were "discharged of their subjection," then this mother-commonwealth "require[d] no more of them than fathers require[d] of the children, who they emancipate and make free from their domestic government, which is honour, and friendship. . . ." (1962, 185, 190)

Hobbes's addiction to authority as sovereignty effectively undermined maternal authority, because such rule was personalized rule by divided rulers. Hobbes's sovereign protected his subjects by disassociating preservative care from the marks of femininity, those marks signaling the dismembering and divisive effects of factionalism. Feminists who criticize Hobbes's exclusion of women from the practice of sovereignty should ponder the effects of allowing any sovereign, male or female, to capture the discourse of authority, speak in a univocal voice, and reduce all of our different wills to one. As we will see, even those who have been critical of feminist theory for failing to recognize its own claims to sovereignty have not always been able to avoid the temptation toward univocality. Even as they criticize those whose voices have been dominant, there remains a tendency to reproduce the same dynamics of exclusion in the struggle for sovereignty within feminism.

Notes

1. I am not arguing that this is in fact what all women do; rather, I am contending that this has been a dominant way that women's values and duties have been represented. As we will see in the following chapters, "protection" is not without its violent dimensions, and so an invocation of it does not in itself solve the problem of how to distinguish between authority and coercion. See Arendt, *On Revolution* (1963) and John Schaar's analysis of Melville's *Benito Cerino* in *Legitimacy and the Modern State* (1981).

2. A note about interpretative strategies is useful here. There is considerable debate among Hobbes scholars, as among students of textual analysis in general, about the correct way to interpret texts. The deontological school, championed by Howard Warrender's *The Political Philosophy of Hobbes* in 1957, was an approach that stressed reading Hobbes's concept of political obligation as central to the Hobbesian project as a whole. Subsequent studies, such as Quentin Skinner's, stressed the importance of contextualizing Hobbes's arguments, and thus emphasized the influence of historical factors—explicitly the "engagement controversy" spawned by the execution of Charles I in 1649. In my rereading of Hobbes, I deploy a combination of approaches: I center on constructions of sovereignty in Hobbes's work, *Leviathan,* a work I consider motivated at once by the immediate political problems which Hobbes saw as troubling his times, *and* informed by a particular effort to shape the times accordingly; at the same time, I read below the surface of the text to certain meanings in tension with one another. In this sense my reading is contextual and deconstructive.

3. Diana Coole (1988) has discussed at length Hobbes's apparent extension of contracting to describe the relationship between infants and parents. It remains problematic to claim that Hobbes, who had explicitly excluded infants from those who could contract, seriously believed that "consent" legitimated the parent's authority over the child. It is true that he wrote that the parent's dominion was "not so derived from the generation, as if therefore the parent had dominion over his child because he begat him; but from the child's consent, either by express, or by sufficient arguments declared." (1962, 152) Since no relationship of rule can be legitimated by force, or appeals to natural authority, logically Hobbes had to extend this principle to his consideration of relations between parents and children. However, the emphasis in his critique of "natural" parental authority—that is, his critique of the claim that parental rule was justified through the principle of generation—tended to stress the duty to which parents' consenting to care for their children bound them. As far as the obligation of children is concerned, as Gilbert Meilaender has observed, "the obligation of the child to obey its parent is rooted in the fact that within the institution of the family the child gets nourishment and preservation of its life." (1973, 403) Consent creates the *right* of the parent's dominion; protection creates the obligation to obey.

4. Recent developments in the field of reproductive technology, such as frozen embryo storage, in vitro fertilization, and "surrogacy" arrangements appear to confound the identity of mothers as well as fathers. Is the mother who is lord the one whose egg constitutes half the genetic makeup of the fetus, or is it the one who carries the fetus in her body, or the one who cares for the child? Hobbes's emphasis on the "bearing" of children would seem to side with a privileging of birth over genetics, but the issue has been compli-

cated by the intervention of modern technology into the process of conception and birth. See Keller's discussion, "Feminism, Science, and Postmodernism."

5. Both Morsy's and Calloway's analyses read women's situations, or the contexts of choice, in ways that are different from a feminist narrative, like MacKinnon's, that picture women as the captives of the context within which they find themselves. Morsy and Calloway urge us to see a more complex picture of the contexts of choice as women experience and negotiate them. Yet Morsy's and Calloway's accounts share an aspect of the view of the women-as-victims narrative. They, too, rest their accounts on "women's experiences," although they read these experiences in multiple ways simultaneously. In the "victim" narrative of women's experiences, women's worlds are seen as wholly constructed by male domination—as in the pervasiveness of the ontology of the "sexual contract"—yet women somehow manage to grasp the "truth" of their complete domination and also to "speak it," thereby "breaking the silence." As Wendy Brown has put it, in this narrative 'feelings' and 'experiences' acquire a status that is politically if not ontologically essentialist—beyond hermeneutics." (1991, 73) Both Morsy and Calloway are more or less self-consciously involved in hermeneutical enterprises, defending what they regard as *interpretations* of experience. In this sense they avoid some of the pitfalls of arguing from experience that I explore in detail in chapter 5.

2

What Sort of Body Is the Body Politic?

When she's good we call her a painter; when she's bad we call her a lady painter. (Atwood 1978)

She must learn *to paint her world with colors chosen more often than not by men for men to suit their realities.* She-her *has always conveyed the idea of a personal and gender-specific voice. In order to be taken more seriously, she is therefore bound to dye this voice universal, a tint that can only be obtained through words like* man, mankind, he-him. . . . *Such a convenient way to generalize and transcend the sex line. (Trinh 1988)*

Woman's space is not a field in which her bodily intentionality can be freely realized but an enclosure in which she feels herself positioned and by which she is confined. (Bartky 1988)

What a magnificent body! . . . Shouldn't I like to see it on the dissecting table. (Turgenev 1941)

Introducing the bent handle of a spoon, I saw everything as no man had ever seen before. . . . The Speculum made it perfectly clear from the beginning. . . . I felt like an explorer in medicine who first views a new and important territory. (Sims 1976)

[I]n all times, kings and persons of sovereign authority, because of their independency, are in continual jealousies, and in the state and posture of gladiators; having their weapons pointing, and their

74

*eyes fixed on one another; that is, their forts, garri-
sons, and guns upon the frontiers of their king-
doms; and continual spies upon their neighbors;
which is a posture of war. (Hobbes, 1962)*

INTRODUCTION

Within the dominant discourse of political theory, the representational matrix within which authority is recognized is gendered in a
specific way. Insofar as what authority *is* remains connected to ideas
of sovereign control, then the marks of authority will remain connected to those signifying sovereignty. This representational matrix
sustains the connection of authority with masculinity. The marks or
signs of authority imply a specific corporeality. We look to the bodies
of individuals who claim authority; to the positions they occupy; and
to the ways they appear, gesture, speak, and act for signs that they
do so authoritatively.

Feminist film theorists have contributed in important ways to
the analysis of representation. They have demonstrated that the
dynamics of the dominant position in film structures this position
most frequently as one occupied by a male figure who is "free to
command the stage . . . of spatial illusion in which he articulates the
look and creates the action." (Mulvey 1988) Their work provides
important insights into the representational system that signifies
authority as masculine. Such theorists also have questioned whether
altering the "sex" of the person in the dominant position in film—
the position of the one who commands the stage and creates the
action—changes or reinforces the fundamental structure of the dominating position as a "masculine" one. E. Ann Kaplan asks:

> Can we envisage a female dominant position that would differ
> qualitatively from the male form of dominance? Or is there merely
> the possibility of both sex genders occupying the positions we now
> know as "masculine" and "feminine"? . . . In all these films [of the
> 70s and 80s with the so-called liberated woman on screen], when
> the man steps out of the traditional role as the one who controls the
> whole action, and when he is set up as sex object, the woman then
> takes on the "masculine" role as bearer of the gaze and initiator

of the action. She nearly always loses her traditionally feminine characteristics in so doing—not those of attractiveness, but rather of *kindness, humaneness, motherliness.* She is now often cold, driving, ambitious, manipulating, just like the men whose position she has usurped. (1983, 28–29)

Since I am concerned with analyzing the dominant *representational matrix* constructing the form of authority as masculine, the relevance of film theory's analysis of the *representation* of the female form is significant. Film theory draws heavily on poststructuralist accounts of language, accounts that argue language is anything but the transparent vehicle for the communication of meaning. Calling attention to the ways that film texts structure meaning through the deployment of an elaborate system of codes, and position subjects in relation to these texts through a complex set of rhetorical devices, film theory stresses the spectacular and specular aspects of modern ideologies of power. In particular, feminist film theory, provides us with a methodology for reading texts by reflecting on the significance of the representation of women's bodies in filmic-public space in ways that both contribute to the development of the narrative in a particular direction and disrupt it simultaneously. I draw on their insights in order to consider what difference the representation of sexual difference makes, what difference imagining the female body's presence in public space makes, to the elaboration of the dominant narrative about political authority.

Within a symbolic order that privileges the phallus—in other words, a symbolic order that reads the significance of sexual difference within a socially established interpretive practice that assigns power and priority to the phallus by constructing the female form as incomplete, as lacking—recognizing women as authorities appears to require the erasure of those marks which would situate her within the "traditional" sphere of femininity: marks such as "kindness, humaneness and motherliness."

Here I explore the marking of authority and the corresponding erasure of "the feminine." My approach is genealogical in the sense that it is "a kind of attempt to emancipate historical knowledges from . . . subjection, to render them . . . capable of opposition and of struggle against the coercion of a theoretical, unitary, formal and scientific discourse." (Foucault, *Power/Knowledge,* 85) Recent feminist criticism has deployed the concept of gender differences against patriarchal constructions of them to argue that the history of women's experiences and women's voices about those experiences suggests the development of alternative ways of seeing and knowing. As I argue later, the uncritical use of the category of unmediated "experience" as the foundation of feminist epistemology is problematic. Nevertheless, what I am concerned with here is the emancipatory effect of ironically recovering the marks of the "female" body and "women's" epistemologies and reconnecting these to the practice of authority. If practices of nurturing and preservation which Hobbes had accepted as authority's purpose and its justification were reattached to the signs of the female body, what would happen to the meaning of authority itself and to the shape of the body politic?

The texts that serve as epigrams for the opening of this chapter move backwards in time, traversing discursive, gendered boundaries as well as historical epochs. Together, they invoke the problematic relationship between women and language, between the female body and public space, and between the woman's body and the body politic. If authority is about being entitled to speak, and if the words spoken represent the author, even if he is absent, then the question of whether woman, as absence (of the phallus) incarnate, can speak representatively, authoritatively, emerges as a haunting query.

Within the context of a masculine, phallogocentric discourse, woman has nothing to say. As Linda Zerilli has put it, "woman" cannot be represented within "a system of representation which refuses to recognize female sexual difference and which converts it, instead, into a *rien a voir*—the absence of the phallus." (1991, 261) To grant to woman an untranslatable "différence" would be to dismantle the phallic signifying economy and those "representational epistemologies that privilege evidence derived from the (male) gaze." (Hawkesworth 1988, 450) Such representational epistemologies construct the female body as a body to-be-looked-at, as spectacle, and simultaneously, anxiously, as a (threatening) body, a body whose mysterious *rien a voir* must be constrained and conquered. Dispelling the anxiety at the core of these epistemologies requires that the sovereign (male) body, the conquering body, stand in the jealous posture of a gladiator, guarding the conquered territory, "weapons pointing . . . eyes fixed," assuming a "posture of war." Within these terms, can the spectacular body represent the body politic? Can she assume the posture of a gladiator? Can woman enter the symbolic order as a speaking subject of authority without becoming caught within the " 'specular logic' of patriarchal discourse"? (Zerilli 1991, 263) Can an authority speak multivocally?

Gendered bodies. Bodies politic. Disciplined and controlled bodies. Today we are in the throes of debates about the nature and meaning of bodies female and male. Fascination with technologically sophisticated, ever-more precise instruments with which to satisfy our urge to "fathom the secrets of nature, and the collateral hope that, in fathoming the secrets of nature, we will fathom the ultimate secrets (and hence gain control over) of our own mortality" (Keller in Jacobus, Keller, Shuttleworth 1990, 177) represent only one type of impulse to explore the body. Its mirror image is the projection of the characteristics of the human onto the inventions of technology, as in the "smart bomb," thereby erasing the question of the smartness or stupidity of the people who made them or the people who deployed them. Yet as the Gulf War demonstrated, and continues to demonstrate, the presence of (arguably) female bodies in certain spaces, perhaps most especially, the space of destruction and death, provokes cultural and psychological responses that range from aversion to pride. The conflict between female bodies and public space becomes particularly acute.

Feminist theorists have had a long history of engagement with philosophies defining the female body and its proper place. A whole range of discourses, including the discourses of science, aesthetics, political theory, anthropology, and even geography, have deployed metaphors and codes signalling the female body, ascribing and appropriating that body "as a sign of other struggles than women's own." (Jacobus, Keller, Shuttleworth 1990, 10) Recognizing the ways that negative images of women have been used to map binary oppositions such as those between mind and body, subject and object, culture and nature, inside and outside, sacred and profane, public and private has led feminist scholars to contest particular representations of the female body and to demonstrate the ways that different discourses "not only construct but depend on the very institution of gender," an institution which was claimed to be discovered or merely observed; not constituted, but found. (Jacobus, Keller, Shuttleworth 1990, 7; cf. Showalter, 1990; Jordanova 1976; Young, *Throwing Like a Girl;* Gilman 1985) One of the most highly charged issues emerging within contemporary feminist theory's exploration of "the body" is the question of the relationship between bodies as matter and bodies as representation.

Judith Butler has argued recently that even feminist efforts to maintain distinctions between bodies and the cultural systems of meaning that saturate them—between, in other words, sex and gender—perpetuate the fiction that there is such a thing as "the female body" apart from specific discursive practices that name any body as female in the first place. Both sex and gender, in her view, are best conceptualized as "performances." Specific power relations, she argues following Foucault, produce the "trope of the maternal body." Seeing even the maternal body as an un-natural body would mean that the "maternal body would no longer be understood as the hidden ground of all signification, the tacit cause of all culture. It would be understood [instead] as an effect or consequence of a system of sexuality in which the female body is required to assume maternity as the essence of its self and the law of its desire." (*Gender Trouble*, 92) Yet if the maternal body is an effect of a "system of sexuality," of what is the "system of sexuality" an effect? In what system is the law of heterosexual desire rooted? Butler's analysis fails to take up this question; instead, the system of sexuality becomes an effect of itself.

My concern here is in part a reflection on whether the recent de(con)structive explosion of the "maternal body" represents a feminist alternative to modern science's desire to unlock the secrets of life and thereby control them. I read ironically these efforts to reduce the female body to a (mere) effect of discourse, and the (anxious) denial that this body has any material reality apart from specific, endlessly malleable, cultural readings of it. They share, along with modern science's effort to control and reproduce life technologically, the same refusal to accept the limitations and implications, for all of us, of our emergence not from the head of Zeus, but from the body of a woman. What is refused is not only the "fact" of our mortality, but also the "fact" of our natality: that we came out of the body of some woman in particular, that we have a past, that we are not self-made. (Vergès, "Memories of Origin") The result of this refusal, I argue in chapter 4, following Arendt, is the construction of the fantasy of autogenesis and the foundation of authority in domination. As a way toward refusing this refusal I propose to take a strange detour. I ask: what sort of body is the body politic and find in the work of Thomas Hobbes some interesting replies.

SOVEREIGNTY THROUGH INCORPORATION

Leviathan, Hobbes wrote, was that "artificial man" created by the covenant—an agreement among men to "confer all their power and strength on one man, or upon one assembly of men, that may reduce all their wills, by plurality of voices, to one will." (1962, 132) The covenant breathed life into the soul of Leviathan and fabricated his corporeal existence out of the diverse parts, the individuals, who agreed to make themselves one. What kind of body did Leviathan have? With what sort of voice did he represent the commonwealth? With what stature and posture did he "keep them all in awe"? What discursive field surrounded his pronouncements? Hobbes tells us that the body of Leviathan was created not through birth, but through incorporation—the conjoining of various parts to construct an artificial body of "greater strength and stature than the natural." Leviathan's "soul" was sovereignty, a force "giving life and motion to the whole body." (1962, 19)

Yet if Leviathan as body politic represented the fabricated unity of otherwise warring subject-parts, without whom every one would remain the enemy of every one, the body politic itself was represented by the sovereign "actor," the one who speaks and acts by authority for all. This actor speaks in a univocal, monolithic voice and inhabits an undivided body:

> And in him consisteth the essence of the commonwealth; which, to define it, is *one person, of whose acts a great multitude, by mutual covenants with one another, have made themselves every one the author, to the end he may use the strength and means of them all as he shall think expedient, for their peace and common defense.* . . . And he that carryeth this person is called SOVEREIGN. (1962, 132)

The body politic represented the unity of subjects, a unity achieved through their symbolic incorporation. Each member of the body politic gave up, or renounced, the right to all things in exchange for protection through the commonwealth. Yet this unity had to be enacted, performed. The person of the sovereign represented the body politic by *performing* their unity, *speaking and acting as if they were one* by *being* one himself, undivided and indivisibly one. On the stage of public life, bearing the outward appearance of a man, acting in the name of everyone, but no one in particular, the sovereign performed the real unity of all. Could women be such sovereign persons, or is the performance of sovereignty dependent upon masculine representations of embodiment, in other words, on a gendered performance[1] of sovereignty?

Here I interrogate the marks of authority, the codes of being in authority. My concern is not with whether women can become political rulers. That is historically incontrovertible. Rather, I propose to examine how different practices of ruling, different cultural codes for signifying authority and for establishing claims to rule, appropriate—yet also mask—characteristics that have been associated with the "feminine," simultaneously colonizing the "feminine" while displacing women symbolically from the founding moment of public life.

My contention is that what we construe as being in authority, and acting authoritatively, has depended upon representations of authoritativeness that privilege masculinity—male bodies and masculinized knowledge and practices. The menstruating body, the body-with-a-womb, the birthing, fecund body, the lactating body, the menopausal body, the more docile and more specular or to-be-looked-at body—it is difficult to imagine such bodies being in authority. (Bartky 1988; Young *Justice and the Politics of Difference,* 141–59) Authority, understood as the issuance of sovereign commands, represents a masculinized practice just as authoring, understood as a discursive practice "dominated by the sovereignty of the author," has represented masculinity.

By reading sovereignty as a specifically gendered performance, I want to provoke a reconsideration of where accepting the boundaries of traditional concepts and practices of authority leaves us. When feminists have argued that women have neither learned how to be in authority nor how to establish themselves as authorities, they have accepted the conceptualization of authority itself as unproblematic. In contrast, I claim that the marks of authority recognized in the dominant discourse of political theory mask forms of embodiment and expression, modes of knowing, roles, contexts, and practices of judgment that have been constructed culturally as "feminine." In order to be recognized as authorities, women rulers must either de-feminize themselves, by taking up the masculine position, or they must de-sexualize themselves, representing themselves as "exceptional women," as women who will not be women. Correspondingly, male rulers must strongly assert their distance from and control over the "feminine."

In bourgeois democratic discourse, with its ideology of the expansive, limitless, unbounded self, political control itself becomes increasingly sexualized as the sort of rule needed to avoid what Rousseau called the "disorder of women." (1968, 109; cf. Pateman, "The Disorder of Woman; Bloom 1987; Elshtain 1990, 107–18; Jones 1989) Yet the representation of disorder as female and order as male is ironic. In *The Horrors of the Half-Known Life* (1976), G. J. Barker-Benfield explored how, the more the unbounded self was represented as the democratic self, especially in nineteenth-century America, the more authority itself was viewed with suspicion. Insofar as the unbounded, democratic self became the ideal self, political discourse retrospectively characterized any "central government as essentially antagonistic to the individual, an encroaching, castrating threat." (Barker-Benfield 1976, 24) This unbounded and disorderly self, of course, was the self-made, self-sufficient *man*. The threat to masculine, democratic selfhood was represented as the threat of limitations on freedom and autonomy, the threat of castrating, female authority. Women were simultaneously cast as the threats to male autonomy insofar as they represented the confinement of domesticity, and when they stepped outside the boundary of private life, as the embodiment of disorder itself. By describing women as disorderly and in need of being controlled by strong men, "men were projecting onto women what they feared from themselves. So in a real sense women did represent order, in virtue of not being free, of not being men." (Barker-Benfield 1976, 48)

> Democratic men adopted the 'general principle that it is good and lawful to judge all things for oneself,' denying the authority of past beliefs; hence 'the power which the opinions of a father exercises over those of his sons diminishes as well as his legal power.' . . . The father could no longer command his sons *ex officio patris*. He could, however, guarantee himself authority over his wife and daughters. (Barker-Banfield 1976, 27)

Once authority was conceptualized as men's "control over" women, instead of fathers' control over children, male and female, the dissociation between the "female" and authority became exacerbated in modern Western democratic culture. Yet the connection between masculinity and sovereign rulership has a deeper and longer history. The masculinization of control has its roots in a tradition of political discourse that represents sovereignty as a stable, self-regenerating, disciplined body politic.

Hobbes understood authority as sovereignty and represented it metaphorically as the "soul" of the body politic, giving "life and motion to the whole body." Yet in Hobbes's text, this life-giving force was disconnected from the practice of mothers even though, as we shall see, sovereignty depended upon the discourse of nurturant protection for its justification. The body politic was brought to life, in Hobbes's text, through the reproductive activity of men's wills. Significantly, if we examine the dominant texts on authority in modern political theory from Hobbes through Schaar and Raz, we discover a similar tension and sexual ambiguity within the gendered order that authority is understood to impose. John Schaar has written, for instance, that "an authority is one who starts lines of action which others complete. Hence, he is, metaphorically, the father of their actions." (1981, 26) The modern age is a "fallen world." It is a world without authority; it is "fatherless." (1981, 75, 77) Authority is clearly a gendered practice. Schaar continues, "the words *nature* and *nation* come from the same root, the word for birth. Etymologically, a nation is a birth, hence a group of persons made kindred by common origin. Nations are also continuously reborn, through the death of old customs and institutions and the generation of new ones." (1981, 47) Yet the exercise of authority is so powerfully gendered in masculine terms that its identification by Schaar with the founding of communities constitutes a symbolic birth unique among all births; it is a birth without mothers. "Nations and communities are 'born.' *And birth requires a father or author,* the one who, whether mythologically or actually, brought the original laws and customs, thereby making a people a people." (1981, 47, emphasis added)

The birth of a nation, the founding of authority, here represents political natality as a masculine act of origination. This conceptualization of authority disconnects authority from women and the symbolically female even while its rhetoric deploys metaphors of origination. Women's birthing represents the disorderliness of the state of nature; only a second "birth," a birth that produces an "artificial man," a birth that results from men's wills, can rid nature of this dis-ease. Yet, ironically, in Hobbes's *Leviathan* this second birth is a return to the womb/tomb: the body politic becomes re-membered through the process of incorporation. All are swallowed up within the body of that "great Leviathan" and made one.

Women's bodies, especially the "maternal body," as divided and dividing bodies, subvert order symbolically in Hobbes's theory because Hobbesian order depends upon unity. In Hobbes's text the sovereign's body must be undivided and his voice univocal. In fact the split between the "feminine," the female body as body politic, and political rule also has had a long history in Western discourse.

PATRIARCHY, PATRILINEARITY, AND WOMEN'S GENERATIVITY

In early theories, the patriarchalism of the state was the result of claims that the state's origins could be traced back to the father-dominated family. The patrilinearity of descent lines invoked to establish hereditary justifications of legitimate rule also worked significantly to distance women from political authority. In the case of medieval France where, by the thirteenth century, "blood right became the predominant element in royal legitimacy," the legitimacy of succession through patrilineal lines was cast into doubt by the consequences of women's sexuality. (Wood 1976) Patrilineal succession depended upon the fidelity of queens. An adulterous queen threatened the legitimacy of a monarchy that was defined as legitimate virtually exclusively on the basis of heredity. An adulterous queen's children, regardless of their sex, had to be excluded from succession because of the possibility that their father might not have been the monarch. Ironically, patrilinear descent rested on the uneasy foundation of women's ultimate control of these lines through their exclusive knowledge of whether the heir apparent was unconditionally the offspring of the king himself. Read on a symbolic level, the exclusion of women from rights of succession, as occurred in France, may have signaled an effort to restrain the power that women's reproductive role gave them to manipulate patrilinearity.

Thomas Laqueur recently has argued that earlier debates about the biology of human reproduction assumed cultural and political significance.

> Much of the [medieval] debate about the nature of the seed and of the bodies that produce it was in fact not about bodies at all but about power, legitimacy, and the politics of fatherhood. . . . The "fact" of women bearing children has never been in dispute and has nonetheless counted for relatively little historically in establishing their claims to recognition or authority over children or property. ("The Facts of Fatherhood" 211; cf. *Making Sex*)

It would be more accurate to say that the "fact" of women bearing children *has been made to count for very little historically*. This "fact" can be made to count for quite a lot, depending on different political circumstances, a "fact" Laqueur should have recognized.

The intensity of the debate about reproduction, and the significance in France of excluding women from succession point to a fear engendered by the instability of claims to paternity which contributed to the need to harness women's power to bear children through an elaborate bio-philosophical discourse that made this power "count for relatively little historically in establishing [women's] claims to recognition or authority." (Laqueur, "The Facts of Fatherhood," 211) One senses the same fear behind Laqueur's participation in the contemporary version of this debate about the significance of differences between female and male bodies, and bodily "products," to the sexual politics of motherhood and fatherhood, as well as the relevance of this politics to the shaping of the body politic.

Laqueur attempts to demonstrate that, ontologically, there is little difference between "biological" fatherhood and "biological" motherhood. This is so, he contends, because a sperm can be invested with as much psycho-cultural weight as an ovum.

> The "fact" of motherhood is precisely the psychic labor that goes into making [emotional and imaginative] connections, into appropriating the fetus and then child into a mother's moral and emotional economy. The "fact" of fatherhood is of a like order. If a labor theory of value gives parents rights to a child, that labor is of the heart, not the hand. ("The Facts of Fatherhood," 212)

But the "hand" is not the "womb." (Nor is it accidental that Laqueur uses "hand," the part of the male body used to produce the sperm for donor insemination—a process in which Laqueur confesses he almost participated—to stand for the [male] body.) Laqueur's theory assigns an ever more "shrinking significance" to female birthgiving than some of the theories of human reproduction he examines. (Ruddick in Hirsch and Keller, 226) His anti-essentialist, supramaterialist theory of fatherhood makes it more difficult to invest the vagina, the womb, or the breast with authority in the one arena, generativity, in which women as birth-givers could be seen as authorities, or as augmenters. Laqueur's effort to bring fathers into an equal (read same) relationship to child care, however laudable, rests on strategies closer to medieval representations of reproduction than he seems to realize. Scientific discourse in the medieval period worked to wrest control of birth from women while, at the same time, representing the act founding the body politic as a birth, but a birth without women. Shrinking the significance of female birthgiving by equating the ovum and the sperm was, and is, a significant strategy in the establishment of the primordial Law of the Father.

Interestingly enough Hobbes's position in these debates, as taken up in the course of *Leviathan,* is more complex than might be imagined. Hobbes unsettled traditional biological arguments that authority could be decided patrilineally. He departed radically from the dominant views about generation and embryology in his time by assigning priority to mothers as procreators. He wrote: "in the state of nature it cannot be known who is the father, but by the testimony of the mother, the child is therefore his whose the mother will have it, and therefore hers." (*De Cive,* IX, 3, 213)

Because Hobbes assigned "sovereignty" to the mother in the determination of the "legitimacy" of progeny and defended women as at least the original "lords" of their children, his arguments differed markedly from traditional biological arguments used to claim that the lines of authority were naturally patrilinear. If patriarchal arguments obligated children to obey the fathers who generated them, in Hobbes's case the logic of generation supported mothers' rule.

Yet Hobbes did not rest his argument justifying authority on biological claims alone. On the contrary he supplemented his theory of the origin of authority in contract with the contention that the obligation to obey authority was a function of the protection that authority secured. The mother's dominion over children depended on her continued protection of them. "But if she expose it, and another find and nourish it, the dominion is in him [sic] that nourisheth it. For it *ought to obey him by whom it is preserved.*" (1962, 153, emphasis added; cf. *De Cive,* IX, 4, 213) Thus Hobbes justified mothers' claiming dominion over children in the state of nature as a function of their reproductive biology without making biology alone a sufficient rationale for their dominion. Unless a mother's biological claim was matched by her diligent preservation of the life of the child, she could not justify her continued rule over children. Hobbes used the same logic to explain the legitimacy of rulers of states.

THE EXCHANGE OF OBEDIENCE FOR PROTECTION: *LEVIATHAN* AS PHALLIC MOTHER

Hobbes rested the sovereign's claim to legitimate rule on his ability to preserve the lives of those subject to his rule—the exchange of obedience for protection. In this sense Hobbes conflated the purpose of political society—protection—with the conditions of legitimate authority, an awareness of which most of Hobbes's contemporaries, both critics and acolytes, appeared to have shared and deployed in their own arguments. As Quentin Skinner has observed, "the deduction that the capacity to be given protection constitutes sufficient grounds for political obligation can also be found in many of the 'engagement' tracts expressed in exactly Hobbes's terminology of 'mutual relationship' between protection and obedience. . . ." (129) Skinner continued: "all [Hobbes's] critics assumed that as Hobbes had made obligation depend on protection, so he had intended to teach that when a citizen is not adequately protected, then his obligations cease." In this analysis, Skinner is directly dissenting from Warrender's reformulation of Hobbes as an "essentially natural law philosopher." (1957, 322) Not paying attention to the grounding of obligation in protection turns Hobbes, Skinner contended, "into the most incredible figure of all. He has to be represented as presenting a traditional type of natural law theory in a manner so convoluted that it was everywhere taken for the work of a complete utilitarian. . . ." (1972, 140; cf. Barry 1972, 37–65; Schochet in Dietz 1990; and Herzog 1989) Preservation of life was the end, or purpose, "for which one man becomes subject to another." Yet it also became the basis for the legitimacy of rule, in Hobbes's view. Hobbes specifically rejected the view that force alone could legitimate authority. The sovereign, like the mother, must preserve the lives of those subject to "his" dominion.

Recently, feminist theorists such as Sara Ruddick have contended that among the distinctive features of "maternal thought" are its interests in the preservation, growth and [social] acceptability of the vulnerable child. (1980) Ironically, since Hobbes saw natural man in precisely those terms—like a vulnerable child—he justified authority in relation to those same interests. Yet certainly the image that we conjure of Hobbesian authority in Hobbesian terms, the voice and figure of the Leviathan, has been strongly linked to masculine rule! The Leviathan seems so much more like a man than a woman. His disciplinary role, his sword-wielding hand, his very awesomeness, evoke images of masculinity much more than of femininity; he reminds us of fathers not mothers. Nonetheless, reading Hobbes against the grain, I argue that there is a paradoxical wedding, in Hobbes's delineation of sovereign authority, of the external features of paternal, disciplinary rule—the body of the father—with maternal, preservative interests—the caretaking of the mother. Hobbes paired maternal interests with the paternal, disciplinary power to originate and enforce laws.

Sovereign rulers had a duty to secure the safety of their people. Their purpose was to protect against internal and external threats to the people's security in order that their subjects would grow and prosper in peace: "But because dominions were constituted for peace's sake, and peace was sought after for safety's sake; he, who being placed in authority, shall use his powers otherwise than to the safety of the people, will act against the reasons of peace, that is to say, the laws of nature." (De Cive, XIII, 4, 258) Sovereigns were entrusted with absolute power in order to procure the "safety of the people. . . .

But by safety here is not meant a bare preservation, but also all other contentments of life, which every man by lawful industry, without danger, or hurt to the commonwealth, shall acquire to himself." (1962, 247) Safety, Hobbes had argued in *De Cive,* consisted in "not the sole preservation of life in what condition soever, but happiness," or "liv[ing] delightfully." Sovereigns should study how "to furnish their subjects abundantly, not only with the good things belonging to life, but also with those which advance to delectation. . . . with such whereby they may grow strong and lusty." (*De Cive,* XIII, 4, 259–60) To see that their subjects "live delightfully" and "grow strong and lusty" were the interests that sovereigns had in securing a well-ordered peace.

Hobbes joined the sovereign's interests in preservation and growth of the commonwealth to an educative interest. This educative interest, like Ruddick's definition of the interest in social acceptability as one of the interests governing maternal practices, has as its focus the training of subjects in the norms of the dominant culture, "in the ways and desires of obedience." (Ruddick 1980, 355) Repeatedly Hobbes argued in *Leviathan* that the sovereign's "procuration of *the safety of the people*" was to be accomplished "by a general providence, contained in public instruction, both of doctrine, and example; and in the making and executing of good laws. . . . (1962, 247) David Johnston has argued that Hobbes's aim in *Leviathan* was to initiate a process of "cultural transformation" in order to "lay the foundations required for any truly rational polity to come into being." (1987, xx) Public indoctrination in the principles and rights of the sovereign— especially about the inviolability and intractability of sovereign rule—had to be, Hobbes wrote, "diligently, and truly taught; because they cannot be maintained by any civil law, or terror of legal punishment." (1962, 248) People had to be carefully schooled in the need for unquestioning obedience to authority as the most secure foundation for prosperity. "Take away in any kind of state, the obedience, and consequently the concord of the people, and they shall not only not flourish, but in short time be dissolved." (1962, 250) More than that, Hobbes imagined the establishment of days of public instruction in the new civic religion he had articulated in order to ensure the perpetuation of sovereignty from one generation to the next. At these assemblies the people would "after prayers and praises given to God, the sovereign of sovereigns, hear those their duties told them, and the positive laws, such as generally concern them all, read and expounded, and be put in mind of the authority that maketh them laws." (1962, 251)

Yet if these were sovereignty's "maternal interests," they were best represented, in Hobbes's theory, by the sovereign's "masculine" body politic—an artificial undivided and indivisible body, yet a body, curiously enough, that was formed through the incorporation of the many in the one, a body that represented "a real unity of them all." (1962, 19) Individuals who form the commonwealth were swallowed up by it. This self-contained body politic—generated out of men's will, motivated by their desire to avoid death—represented their unity. The sovereign preserved and protected the lives of his subjects and educated them to obedience by *representing* the unity of the commonwealth through both the unity of his own undivided body politic and the certainty of his speech. His body politic was not born of woman, but fashioned artificially by human covenant. Art imitates nature, Hobbes argued; and "by art is created that great LEVIA-THAN called a COMMONWEALTH, or STATE, in Latin CIVITAS, which is but an artificial man; though of greater stature and strength than the natural, for whose protection and defense it was intended. . . ." (1962, 19)

Yet the need for the Leviathan's body politic to be undivided, and the requirement that the one in whom sovereign power was invested by the covenant be able to represent, to signify, unity in his own person—to "bear one person"—suggest the impossibility for this body politic to be represented by a dividing, birthing body. The phallic symbolism of sovereign unity becomes apparent when we consider what gender-coded textual devices Hobbes used to signal the threat of political dissolution, of faction and sedition. These textual clues will return us later to consider the consequences of conceptualizing authority as sovereignty.

Hobbes defined seditious opinion as a "poison" that worked to divide the city against itself. What is the substance and origin of this poison? In several critical places in *De Cive* and *Leviathan,* Hobbes's discussion of sovereignty's loss under conditions of civil war is marked by telling allusions to *Medea:*

> For *folly* and *eloquence* concur in the subversion of government, in the same manner (as the fable hath it) as heretofore the daughters of Pelias, king of Thesally, conspired with Medea against their father. They going to restore the decrepit old man to his youth again, by the counsel of Medea they cut him into pieces, and set him in the fire to boil; in vain expecting when he would live again. So the common people, through their folly, like the daughters of Pelias, desiring to renew the ancient government, being drawn

away by the *eloquence* of ambitious men, as it were by the witchcraft
of Medea; divided into faction they consume it rather by those
flames, than they reform it. (*De Cive*, XII, 13, 255; cf 1962, 250)

Factionalism was represented here as the dismemberment of the
father's body, as seditious patricide by daughters whose actions were
fired by the "eloquence of ambitious men." Instead of renewing the
ancient government, the flames of these men's factious speech, like
the "witchcraft of Medea," consume the body of the father, "the
decrepit old man"/"the ancient government." He cannot be brought
back to life again.

These images resonate with powerful sexual overtones: threats
to the body politic are represented as the virtually cannibalistic,
castrating actions of murderous women. The allusion to Medea
evokes other discursive connections between political dissolution
and male dismemberment. In *Medea* dismemberment occurred twice:
Medea killed her own brother and scattered the pieces of his body
before the pursuing ships of her father, King Aeetes; and Pelias,
Jason's uncle, was killed and dismembered by his own daughters,
who had been tricked into thinking their father would be rejuvenated
by this act. Finally jealous Medea, discarded by Jason for a new wife,
kills her own sons after having murdered Jason's new wife and
Creon. These murderous women are truly castrating: they divide the
male body and sever all other blood connections to men—to sons,
fathers, brothers.

Yet the relationship, and its dissolution, which triggered the murderous actions was Medea's marriage to Jason. It is not that women
were intrinsically murderous, they *became* murderous when they
attached themselves to fickle and ambitious men; or they were
tricked into murder by the venomous speech of witches who were
attached to such men. The commonwealth could be protected from
such murderous witches only if its protecting sovereign was obeyed.
If the "old man" could not be re-membered, the New Man, the artificial man/Leviathan, could be formed by men's willing him into existence and then renouncing their ability to dissent as long as he
continued to protect them. The phallic sword of the Leviathan would
protect against the dismemberment of castrating "women," who were
really ambitious men, by protecting everyone against the insecurity
of having to rely on any one private individual for protection:

And from hence it comes to pass, that where an invader hath no
more to fear, than another man's single power; if one plant, sow,

build, or possess a convenient seat, others may probably be expected to come prepared with forces united, to dispossess, and deprive him, not only of the fruit of his labour, but also of his life, or liberty. And the invader again is in the like danger of another. (1962, 99)

Under these conditions, where no one has any more to fear than "another man's single power," there is no security. Yet Hobbes's Leviathan possesses the power to "over-awe them all"; he possesses what might be called a super-phallus. The unity of the commonwealth is ensured by his phallic power to overawe them all, thereby creating the conditions under which all subjects, men and women, will be protected and nurtured as long as he can jealously guard against the threats of dismemberment from within and without. Ever watchful of danger from the threats of externally instigated invasion of the body politic by foreign forces or of internally generated dangers by the factious speech of traitors, the sovereign stands, eyes fixed, sword poised.

Yet if all subjects are overawed by this Father, who nonetheless "mothers them," who encourages their industry and their happiness, the relationship of subjects to the sovereign is defined by the fact that they all, men and women alike, now *lack* the phallus. The fear of dismemberment, of castration, is alleviated, ironically, by the self-castration of "particular men" whose anxiety and loss is assuaged by the unmitigated rule of the Leviathan who "maketh the person *one.*" He alone possesses the Phallus and has been authorized to speak and act for them. Civil laws binding the body politic together are the "artificial chains" that those who created the artificial man "fastened at one end, to the lips of that man, or assembly, to whom they have given the sovereign power; and at the other end to their own ears." (1962, 160) Speechless and voiceless, "feminized" subjects—these are the citizens of Hobbes's civil society.

In light of my argument that "citizens," in Hobbes's view, become speechless and voiceless, Pateman's claim that "civil fraternity" is based on an association among brothers, an association that, in modern times, "refers not to a blood relation, to the sons of one father, but to men bound by a common recognized bond" is called into question. In Hobbes's case all men become "sisters" in relationship to the castrating Leviathan, because they lack the common power to protect themselves adequately—they lack the phallus/sword that the Leviathan alone possesses. (1988, 78, 80) Indeed, Hobbes specifically allows for cowardice on the battlefield—what he calls "feminine courage"—because, he argues, no one can call unjust any effort to protect one's own life, an inalienable right from Hobbes's view. "And there is allowance to be made for natural timourousness; not only to women, of whom no such dangerous duty is expected, but also to men of feminine courage. . . . To avoid battle, is not injustice, but cowardice." (1962, 165)

But what if the sovereign ruler had been a woman?

THE RULE OF VIRAGOS: AN EXCEPTIONAL CASE?

In the case of medieval England, where royal legitimacy had been less exclusively dependent on heredity, the consequences of a queen's known adultery were not as unsettling as in France. Yet in England, too, the legitimacy of women rulers eventually was challenged. This challenge was especially forceful the more insistently patriarchy was invoked as the principle for legitimating authority and for establishing political subjects' obligation to obey.

In early Tudor England, there had been little theoretical discussion of the justification of political obligation. Yet both the Reformation and the existence of two successive women rulers on the throne of England from 1553 to 1603—Mary and Elizabeth, the daughters of Henry VIII—coupled with the succession controversy triggered by Elizabeth's childlessness had stimulated heated discussions about obligation and laid the foundation for more systematically articulated patriarchalist theories of political authority later in the Stuart period.

There had been a long tradition of debate about the status of women well before the accession of Mary Tudor to the throne. Humanists during the Renaissance had concerned themselves principally with the question of women's intelligence and their proper education. Abundant works on both sides of the argument considered women's capacities.

> Apologists for the whole sex defended the intellect, physical prowess, virtue, and other qualities of women and cited in support of their contentions such illustrious women of the past as Semiramis, Camilla, Judith, Deborah, Hester, and Zenobia—to name only a few of the many whose stories were repeated throughout the century. (Phillips, "The Background," 6)

Detractors, on the other, had argued that women were the embodiment of misrule and disorderliness.[2] By their very nature as inferiors, they were meant to be subordinated by men. ("Woman on Top" in

Davis 1975) From around the 1540s, works in England began to concentrate on the specific question of women's right and ability to exercise civil authority. (Phillips, "The Background," 6) Salic law in France had precluded the possibility of a woman ruler. In England that possibility remained alive. When Mary Tudor came to the throne in 1553, the possibility became reality.

Immediately after Mary's accession, Parliament had passed an act confirming the legality of a woman ruler. "That the Regal Power of this Realm is in the Queen's Majesty, to be as fully and absolutely as ever it was in any of her most Noble Progenitors, Kings of this Realm." (*Lord's Journals*, I, 453, in Phillips, "The Background," 8) Nonetheless, the legitimacy of women rulers continued to be debated vociferously. Perhaps no one was more virulent in his condemnation of women rulers than John Knox, who published his *First Blast of the Trumpet Against the Monstrous Regiment of Women* in 1558 (ironically, the year Elizabeth was crowned): "To promote a Woman to beare rule, superioritie, dominion, or empire above any Realme, Nation, or Citie, is repugnant to Nature; contumelie to God, a thing most contrarious to his reveled will and approved ordinance; and finallie, it is the subversion of good Order, of all equitie and justice." A woman ruler, Knox complained, was a "monstre in nature . . . a woman clad in the habit of man . . . a woman against nature reigning above man." (Laing 1844, iv, 373, 416) Mary Tudor's Catholicism was the factor that most immediately had prompted Knox to write the *First Blast*. Yet the debate about female rule which ensued under Protestant Elizabeth's reign extended beyond this religious issue to include the general question of women's right to exercise sovereignty.

Various sides in the debate employed religious arguments to strengthen their case. Knox argued that God had expressly forbidden women to rule. "For the same God, that in plain words forbiddeth idolatrie, doth also forbidde the authoritie of women over man; as the words of St. Paule . . . do plainly teach us." (1844, 414) John Aylmer, one of Elizabeth's earliest defenders, retorted by writing as God himself:

> Murmur ye at myne anointed, because she is a woman? who made man and woman, you, or I? yf I made hire to lyue: may I not make hir to reigne? If I apoynt hir to the office? can I not adourne hir, and make hir hable to discharge it? Why then (you of litle faithe) eyther feare you my good wil: or mistrust you my power? . . . What letteth, that she may not as well represent my maiestie, as any of you all? If I be

> best represented by the shining ornamentes of the mynde, and not the outwarde sturdines of the body: why may not she haue at my hande that any of you have? wisdom to gouerne, justice to punish, clemencie to pardon, discrescion to iudge . . . can I not make a woman ruler to be a good ruler ouer you, and a mete minister to me? (in Phillips, "The Background," 16)

John Calvin took a more moderate position on the issue. Interpreting the rule of women as "visitations of God's anger," he argued that although such rule "was contrary to the legitimate course of nature," when virtuous viragos headed states it expressed some divine purpose. Under such conditions female government must be accepted as legitimate. The poet Spenser appears to have shared this latter perspective. Male authority was authority's proper form, but there were divinely ordained exceptions. Virtuous women were naturally born to "base humilitie, unless the heavens lift them up to lawfull soveraintie." (1924, V, v, 25)

What was common to both Calvin's and Spenser's distinction between virtuous viragos and vicious viragos was the catalogue of moral and intellectual capacities that they claimed virtuous viragos possessed. These capacities were reflected in the particular order that their rule instituted. In Spenser's epic, *The Fairie Queene,* Radigund, a vicious virago, and Britomart, a virtuous virago, were alike in their marital valor: they were equally courageous on the battlefield. Yet military prowess was insufficient grounds for legitimating women's exercise of sovereign authority. "Admirable as such prowess may be, any authority based exclusively upon it [wa]s a violation of natural law and order and [wa]s bound to produce an abnormal state of political and social affairs." (in Phillips, "The Woman Ruler," 220) For Spenser, this abnormality consisted in the subversion of the natural sexual division of labor. Radigund's rule, the rule of the vicious virago, was corrupt because she disarmed men, clothed them in "women's weeds," and forced them to do women's work. Britomart's rule, the rule of the virtuous virago, was just because she ruled temporarily and in order to reinstate the divinely established proper sexual order; she repealed the liberty of women "which they had long usurpt; and then restoring to mens subjection, did true Justice deal." (1924, V, vii, 42) The authority of the virtuous virago was legitimated *because* she reinstituted the patriarchal order. Virtuous viragos were needed to conquer vicious viragos. Ironically, legitimate female authority was accepted as a means to reinforce women's natural subjugation to men.

On the symbolic level, the image of women ruling created an anxiety about the legitimacy of their authority reflected in a number of events and in different cultural representations of rightful rule, such as those in Elizabethan drama and poetry. Throughout Mary's and Elizabeth's reign, repeated rumors circulated of the survival of Edward VI, son of Henry VIII. Significantly, these occurred most frequently "in Mary's reign after it was evident that she would not have a child" and in Elizabeth's "in the last two decades of her reign." (Levine 1986, 61)

> Queenship provoked questioning of the legitimacy of the ruler, a questioning that coincided with the further turmoil brought on by the Reformation. Just at a time when ceremonies that had brought comfort for centuries were being stripped away, so too the familiar figure of the king, God's anointed, was being replaced by that of a woman. The issue of legitimacy was brought even more sharply into focus because neither Mary nor Elizabeth had sons to succeed them. (Levine 1986, 41)

Although it is true that there were other periods of English history in which the legitimacy of the sovereign was doubted and when there were rumors of the survival of previous monarchs and pretenders to the throne, it is important to emphasize that in this case it was the sex of the ruler herself that had created anxiety about legitimacy. The political status and sexual identity of the female monarch were seen by some to be in direct conflict. The very figure of authority— her corporeal existence—appeared to some to represent not order, but the institutionalization of misrule itself. A "Woman on Top," not as part of a parodic mockery of dominant institutions which was meant to reinforce them, but *as* the dominant institution itself, was indeed perceived as dangerous. It meant the world *was* upside down. (Clark 1980, 98–127; Davis 1975) As such it created conditions which led to the representation and articulation, with renewed vigor and greater systematization, of patriarchy as proper rule. Even Aylmer's defense of Elizabeth had "admitted . . . that men are normally better qualified for [rulership] than women." (Phillips, "The Background," 16) Elizabeth herself, as well as the dramatists and court scholars of the period, played at reversing the reversal; she and they worked to reinscribe patriarchy within the context of its official inversion.

Writing about the significance of the reinscription of patriarchy reflected in Shakespeare's *A Midsummer Night's Dream,* Louis Adrian Montrose noted that "with one vital exception, all forms of public and domestic authority in Elizabethan England were vested in men: in fathers, husbands, masters, teachers, magistrates, lords. It was inevitable that the rule of a woman would generate peculiar tensions within such a 'patriarchal' society." (1983, 64–65) The fact that neither regent had heirs only heightened the tensions. Ironically, Elizabeth's efforts to maintain her legitimacy depended upon her distancing her political authority—her body politic—from her sexual identity, her body natural, while at the same time calling attention to her femininity.

The general device readily available to her, and one with which she appeared quite familiar, was the juristic notion of the "King's Two Bodies":

> For the King has in him two Bodies, viz. a Body natural, and a Body politic. His Body natural . . . is a Body mortal, subject to all Infirmities that come by Nature or Accident, to the Imbecility of Infancy or Old Age, and to the like Defects that happen to the natural Bodies of other People. But his Body politic is a Body that cannot be seen or handled, consisting of Policy and Government, and constituted for the Direction of the People, and the Management of the publick-weal and this Body is utterly void of Infancy, and Old Age, and other natural Defects and Imbecilities which the Body natural is subject to, and for this Cause what the King does in his Body politic cannot be invalidated or frustrated by any Disability in his natural Body. (Plowden in Kantorowicz 1957, 7)

Elizabeth was a proficient manipulator of this doctrine. (Axton 1977, 39) Yet the problem confronting Elizabeth rested on whether this doctrine would be flexible enough to accommodate the perplexing situation of the peculiar disability of the monarch who inhabited a woman's body. Was the doctrine of the two bodies adequate to this situation? In 1588, on the occasion of her address to her troops anticipating the Spanish invasion, Elizabeth noted that she knew that she had "the body but of a weak and feeble woman; but I have the heart and stomach of a king, and of a king of England too." ("To the Troops at Tilbury, 1588," in Rice 1966, 96; cf. Montrose 1983, 77) Elizabeth's choice of body parts—heart and stomach—to represent her sovereignty suggests she perceived that the woman ruler must not only call attention to the ways that the body politic of the monarch overrides the body personal—because the political body is immortal—but must also assume a fundamental schism of her body personal into two parts: the human and the female. The heart and stomach divide themselves further, as metaphors, into referrants to the protection and courage which the monarch's body politic represents, and to the two parts of the body arguably most closely connected to the female: the heart, site of emotions, and the stomach, or belly, associated with birth. To legitimate her rule, Elizabeth had developed an elaborate and ingenious strategy by which she transformed her sex from political liability into political advantage for a half century.

Antonia Fraser has noted that "because her sex is foremost what makes the Warrior Queen remarkable, her sexuality must always be called into question." (1989, 12) Elizabeth's sexuality was called into question in terms of the marriage and succession problem. In 1566, at the age of thirty-three, Elizabeth addressed members of the houses of Parliament on this question. She indicated that she would marry, "although of my own disposition I was not inclined to." Declaring that she would "never break the word of a prince spoke in a public place," she reiterated her intention to "marry as soon as I can conveniently, if God take not him away with whom I mean to marry or myself, or else some other great let happen. I can say no more except the party were present and I hope to have children, Otherwise I would never marry." Cleverly allowing herself the loophole of "inconvenience," Elizabeth neared the end of her speech with the observation that "although I be a woman I have as good a courage answerable to my place as ever my father had." She called attention to her femininity to deny its relevance to the legitimacy of her rule. ("On Marriage and Succession, 1566," in Rice 1966, 78, 81)

Elizabeth's ability to maintain her position of authority depended on a paradoxical ploy: reinforcing patriarchy while simultaneously distancing herself from it. She became the exception to the rule. Fostering the development of an elaborate cult of the Virgin Queen and thereby distancing herself from patriarchal domesticity, she simultaneously reinforced a code of female subservience in the domestic sphere. In Elizabeth's England "it became more difficult to obtain a divorce . . . than in previous centuries." (Bassnett 1988, 41) Elizabeth's resistance to marriage and her self-conscious manipulation of her role as Virgin Queen reinforced her rule by constructing her as a female monarch outside the boundaries of patriarchy. Her own life history supported this further: Henry VIII had had Mary declared illegitimate after the birth of Edward. The later declaration by Thomas Cranmer, Henry's adviser on matrimonial affairs, that Henry's marriage to Anne Boleyn was null and void bastardized Elizabeth as well. It was reinforced by Parliament's passage in 1536 of the second Act of

Succession. (Plowden 1984, 13–23; Bassnett 1988, 19) Elizabeth's own father had situated her outside patriarchy, adding symbolic significance to Elizabeth's exploitation of the Marian cult.

At the same time she brilliantly deployed a wifely and maternal discourse to express the particular nature of her rule:

> I am already bound unto an Husband, which is the Kingdome of England, and that may suffice you: and this . . . makes mee wonder, that you forget yourselues, the pledge of this alliance which I haue made with my Kingdome. (And therewithall, stretching out her hand, shee shewed them the Ring with which shee was giuen in marriage, and inaugurated to her Kingdome, in expresse and solemne termes.) And reproach mee no more . . . that I have no children: for every one of you, and as many are English, are my Children, and Kinfolkes. (Camden in Axton 1977, 38–39)

The peculiar nature of her claim to rule was that, as a woman ruler, married to and mother of her people, she contended that she had a wifely and motherly *duty to be in authority*.

Marrying her nation and nurturing her people instead of any children merely of her own body enabled Elizabeth to distinguish herself as a singular woman; a woman who would not be woman. Her female body natural was subsumed by her female body politic. Elizabeth had turned her traditionally female role into the very justification of her apparent reversal of patriarchy. Hers was a discourse that aimed to reverse the reversal that a "Woman on Top" appeared to represent. The highlighting of her "*difference* from other women may have helped to reinforce [male hegemony]. . . . The royal exception could prove the patriarchal rule in society at large." (Montrose 1983, 80)

Yet there remained anxiety about the stability of authority resting with a queen who would not marry. Both Elizabeth's dangerous and incestuous metaphors of being, at once, mother and wife to the nation, as well as her adoption of the symbol of the phoenix—self-regenerating the nation from the ashes of her body instead of from her living womb—were mirrored in the frequent entreaties, by Parliament and councilors, that the Queen marry, and marry properly. The image of Jocasta, and the disastrous results of Jocasta's marriage, haunted. Dramatic presentations at the Inns of Court, and Shakespeare's own plays, can be interpreted as efforts to "restore the inverted Amazonian system of gender and nurture to a patriarchal norm." (Montrose, 1983, 81) Both Shakespeare's plays and the renewed, albeit altered, accounts of patriarchalism in the seventeenth century could be seen as reflections of and responses to the gendered hierarchy that Elizabeth invoked but from which she separated herself. These cultural products and theories together constructed a homologous view of authority in the family and authority in the state with specific consequences for the shape of authority and the signs that marked its presence. Because it was argued that "political power was merely an extension of natural and absolute paternal authority, the obligation of the subject to obey his sovereign was identical to the unquestioning obedience a child owed its father." (Schochet 1975, 64)

Even when, in the same century, social contract theorists such as Hobbes and Locke broke the connection between political authority and paternal authority, the fundamental incompatibility between authority, understood as a hierarchical relationship between ruler and ruled, and representations of the feminine remained and continued to signal misrule or disorder. This disjunction has persisted today at the level of the beliefs that structure the recognition of those in authority. Beliefs about the shape that rule must have in order to be acknowledged as rule remain saturated with gendered codes.

THE DISCERNING MARKS OF AUTHORITY

In most of the literature of modern political theory, being *in authority* has been understood to be a property of rules and offices created by rules. "Individuals possess it [*in authority*] by virtue of holding an office in an organization, such as a state, a corporation, a university, or a trade union, that is (partially) governed by more or less formalized or codified rules." (Flathman 1980, 17) Yet the existence of rules alone does not ensure the existence of authority, since "there can be no authority unless participants in a practice governed by rules *believe* that the putative rules are in fact the rules." (Flathman 1980, 21, emphasis added) Thus, "the criteria by which authority is established in the association in question . . . are given by . . . *values and beliefs* shared among the members of the association." (Flathman 1980, 30, emphasis added) Authority, in this formulation, depends both upon the *recognition of rules* and their *acceptance as the rules-that-ought-to-be-rules.*

Situating authority on the terrain of beliefs that structure the recognition of rules as rules forces us to confront the question of how beliefs about the acceptable *shape* of rules intrinsically mediate our perception of what counts as rules in the first place, and who can be recognized as legitimate articulators of rules in the second place. An "imaginative geography" effects a conceptual cartography of "rules" and limits their shape to those that mirror dominant modes of rule formulation: a Mercator projection of the rules that not only places the West at the center of the map but also depends upon a particularly gendered geography of rules.

Pierre Clastres has asked whether, "when there is neither coercion nor violence, it is impossible to speak of power." (1987, 11) His studies of Amerindian societies led Clastres to conclude that "power exists . . . totally separate from violence and apart from any hierarchy." The failure to conceptualize power apart from violence reflected the limit encountered by the imaginative geography of political anthropology: "the limitation of the West itself." (1987, 22, 25) Clastres called for a "Copernican revolution" which would de-center the West's attraction for defining itself as the force of gravity in the universe. (1987, 25–26) I am interested in asking whether, if there is neither sovereignty nor univocal, monolithic commands, and if the body politic is represented by a "divided" female body, it becomes impossible to speak of authority. What are the marks that enable us to recognize someone's being "in authority" (Flathman 1980) and thereby to grant legitimacy to her efforts to influence and give meaning to what Arendt called our "actions in concert"?[3]

Claims to legitimacy, understood as different "names" for rules, have been structured through gendered codes insofar as the beliefs shaping the recognition of these claims reflect androcentric values. As a result of the filtering of claims through a discursive economy that privileges masculine practices, certain values and beliefs have been hidden or disqualified from the legitimating sphere of values and beliefs that could be called authoritative. The task at hand for a feminist theory of authority is to effect a Copernican revolution in the conceptualization of authority that enables us to break with Western sovereign masculinity's fascination with itself.

Notes

1. Performance is not my metaphor, but Hobbes's. In the famous chapter 16 of *Leviathan*, Hobbes wrote that

a *person,* is the same that an *actor* is, both on the stage and in common conversations; and to *personate* is to *act,* or *represent* himself, or another. . . . Of persons artificial, some have their words *owned* by those whom they represent. And then the person is the *actor;* and he that owneth his words and actions, is the AUTHOR; in which case the actor acteth by authority. (1962, 125)

2. For a sample of works of this period that generally defended women, see the texts cited in Phillips, "The Background," 5–32. For an earlier defense, see Christine de Pisan, (1982). See also the discussion of the roots of this debate in Joan Kelly (1982).

3. The entire passage within which Arendt's phrase "action in concert" appears is worth quoting at length because of the connection it draws between legitimacy and a bringing together of people for political action:

Power needs no justification, being inherent in the very existence of political communities; what it does need is legitimacy. The common treatment of these two words as synonyms is no less misleading and confusing than the current equation of obedience and support. Power springs up whenever people get together and act in concert, but it derives its legitimacy from the initial getting together rather than from any action that may follow. (1970, 52)

3

Gender and the Marks of Authority, or, Why Are There No Good Women Rulers?

Most of the men whom the reader will encounter in these pages were innovators. They did not just rule; they founded a new nation-state or recast its institutions. They did not just arrange or spread the teachings of others; they created new systems of thought. Whatever the particular feat of innovation, it was closely bound up with the most intimate hopes, memories, and fears of the statesman or thinker. The major themes of this volume, then, are leadership as a process of innovation and leadership as a recurrent interplay between private personality and public performance. (Rustow 1970, 1)

The satiric BBC show "Spitting Image" once offered a blistering portrayal of Margaret Thatcher's leadership. The year was 1985. Occasioned by Thatcher's approval of American use of British airbases for attack missions against Qadaafi of Libya, "Spitting Image" showed Margaret Thatcher appearing before Parliament to explain her decision and to insist on parliamentary support of her foreign policy. As the acrimoniousness of Labour Party members' speeches against Thatcher's Iron Ladyism reached a fever pitch, Thatcher was shown ripping open her blouse to reveal underneath her suit not the breasts that would mark her as female, but a hyperdeveloped and excessively hairy chest. The message was unambiguous: the Iron Lady was really a man in drag.

In the modern West, leadership is strongly culturally coded with signs of masculinity. Consequently, women whose leadership styles transgress the gendered boundaries of behavior risk being delegitimated as rulers. At the same time, the masculine coding of leadership means that a woman ruler appears to be an oxymoron. The proverbial double bind confronts women rulers with a dilemma only few manage to resolve: call attention to the feminine and risk losing authority, or adopt masculine norms and risk social disapprobation.

The problem seems exacerbated in the case of women whose rule is intended to subvert the dominant social order, especially if their leadership directly challenges the dominant codes of masculinity or contests the gendered boundaries of public space. Commenting on the still intense scrutiny of public women's appearance and physical being, Sheila Rowbotham noted that Thatcher had managed to open "a space for Conservative women to extend the range of their public presentation and take on a certain diverse angularity. . . ." (*New Society,* 20 March 1987, 28) She contended that for Labour women, or any groups of women whose move into the public sphere was predicated on "opposing the status quo in a period of reaction," the situation confronting them was less flexible:

> By forcing the women with public roles who seek change to personify ideals which do not make sense in everyday life, by divesting them of both passion and angularity, we diminish them. . . . The anxieties which accompany the persecution of radical women who deviate are considerable, for the codes of rebellion and submission are frantically reassembling and dissolving. The preoccupation with appearance is the surface clue. It is an indicator of a profound panic around identity, power and desirability. These are the nerves that paralyze, trapping the discordant discontent of increasing numbers of women who those in power would prefer to ignore. (ibid.)

In this chapter I explore the ways that the codes of being "in authority" have been structured. Along with Rowbotham I would argue that these codes mask a certain anxiety about "identity, power and desirability" provoked by the sign of a woman ruling.

The standard analysis of authority in modern Western discourse begins by defining authority as a set of rules governing public life issued by those who are entitled to speak. In these terms an authority is someone who is *official* (occupies a public, professionalized role recognized as having the capacity to issue rules), *knowledgeable* (has knowledge that meets certain epistemic criteria for issuing rules), *decisive* (possesses singularity of will and judges dispassionately so that the rules will be enforced), and *compelling* (constructs political obedience to the rules ordering public life through institutionalized hierarchy). In other words, those who are "in authority" are perceived as being so because they exhibit characteristics of office, knowledge, judgment, and will associate objectively and formally with the practice of ruling. In this chapter I will consider the characteristics of office and knowledge and, in chapter 4, examine those of judgment and will.

In the literature on rulership and leadership, the gender neutrality of these four characteristics has been accepted axiomatically. That "American public leadership is a man's role today," Wendell Bell, Richard Hill, and Charles Wright have argued, is not a product of the way we conceptualize public leadership. "No matter what concept of leadership is adopted or what methods for locating leaders are employed," they continue, "most studies document the fact of male dominance in public affairs in the United States." (1961, 34). Overcoming obstacles to female leadership is not judged to be an effect of changing our conceptualization or practice of leadership, but of changing women themselves so that they will no longer be personally apathetic, lack interest in politics, or be mired in those situations which distract from their ability to become public leaders. (1961, 35, 54)

Lest the reader leap to the simple conclusion that this victim-blaming tendency is an effect of chauvinistic scholarship, it is important to note that the burgeoning feminist literature on political women supports similar conclusions. Although feminists tend to place more stress on the structural obstacles to women's being better represented in positions of public authority than on sociopsychological explanations, the general assumption of feminist literature remains that the conceptualization of public authority is unproblematic, gender neutral. The issue for feminist researchers has been to demonstrate the existence and continued operation of sexism in the form of differential public career opportunities for women and men. Studies of the career paths of "women in leadership positions, particularly at the very highest levels of public decision-making," uncover "the challenges and opportunities the future leader faced in her climb to the top." (Thompson 1991, 1) Women have fewer chances to "climb to the top" either because informal mechanisms, such as the privilege of incumbency, the male club network, or the disciplinary effects of sexual harassment or more formal mechanisms, such as the structure of particular electoral systems, operate to keep women out. (Darcy et al., 1987)

On the basis of studies of political women, feminists have concluded that political leadership is male because women have been systematically denied access to it. My concern in this chapter is not to dispute the incontrovertible fact that women occupy disproportionately fewer appointive or elected public offices than men. Nor would I contest the fact that there are specific political systems—notably those structured as multiparty parliamentary systems—that are more advantageous than others to women's success as candidates for public office. That women are highly motivated to seek public office and that there remain significant systemic barriers to translating this motivation into greater representation in official positions of authority has now been generally accepted as the wisdom of the newest studies of women in public office. (Darcy et al., 1987, Rule 1981) My interest in this chapter is with the broader philosophical question of what our understanding of the meaning of being "in authority" becomes, or what conceptualization and practices of rulership and legitimacy we sustain, when we limit our analysis of being "in authority" to accepted constructions of the four characteristics listed above. My claim is that descriptions of those who act as public authorities—public spokespeople—and of the norms and rules that they articulate, generally have excluded characteristics culturally coded as "feminine." In Western political thought, office, knowledge, judgment, and command have been connected more immediately to masculine than to feminine modes of being and action.

Since there have been few women rulers in any political system in any epoch, the exclusion of signs that are gendered female from the practice of being in authority seems unremarkable. The exclusion of "the feminine" appears simply to be an effect of the practice of authority rather than being recognized as political authority's foundational moment. But if we argue that the very definition of authority as a set of practices designed to institutionalize social hierarchies and to ensure that political subjects obey leaders' commands contributes to the separation of "women-qua-women" from the process of authorizing, we might provoke the Copernican shift in our conceptualization of authority that could disrupt Western sovereign masculinity's representation of itself as the center of the universe.

Seeing how authority has been reduced to the institutionalization of a system of domination that requires the construction of the citizen as obedient subject can help reconnect this practice to those specifically gendered codes that were hidden by the gender-neutral discourse with which authority has been described. This is because patterns of domination and submission often have been defined as such in gendered terms. As Joan W. Scott has remarked, "gender is a primary way of signifying relationships of power." (in Weed 1989, 94) Recognizing that those codes used to signal relationships of authority are gendered codes denaturalizes them, as well as challenges the assumption that masculinized bodies best represent the body politic.

If we argue further that the (apparent) dichotomy between compassion and authority, between feeling and cognition, between empathy and judgment contributes to the association of the authoritative with a masculine voice, then the specific constellation of offices associated with public leadership; the limited kinds of knowledge qualified as legitimate knowledge; the narrowing of practices of political judgment to practices of a commanding, dispassionate gaze; and the monolithic nature of the willfulness of authorities become more noticeably gendered, too.

To sustain this argument it will be necessary to consider what "women-qua-women" signifies and to admit the danger that, by delineating the "feminine" we imply a distinction from the "masculine," and thus risk reinforcing the very stereotypes about representations of "woman" that feminists have intended to subvert. Yet if investigating the gendered codes for recognizing an authority requires a strategic invocation of signs of sexual difference—those historical constellations of embodiment, voice, role, and wisdom that have been taken to represent one gender or another—the strategy can be defended as a discursive device intended to subvert, to probe beneath the surface of what have masqueraded as the objective, genderless marks of authority. Diana Fuss has argued that risk and danger are inherent in all discursive strategies. Risking essentialism, she contended, can "operate as a deconstructionist strategy." A "strategy of any kind is a risk because its effects, its outcome, are always unpredictable and undecidable." The effects of a particularly risky strategy depend upon historical circumstance, cultural context, and subject-position. "What is risky is giving up the security—and the fantasy—of occupying a single subject-position and instead occupying two [or more!] subject positions at once." (1989, 19)

This genealogical project is meant not to uncover some "essential" masculinity hiding out there but to recover the ways that specific practices of legitimation depend upon what has been excluded for establishing their own credibility. Legitimation depends upon saying both "I am this" and "I am not that." Or, more precisely, "I am this because I am not that." A genealogical approach to reading the characteristics of being "in authority" is intended, in other words, to provoke reflection on the fact that the artificially binary separation between masculine-feminine is the effect, among other things, of a particular discourse about and marking of authority, and never only its foundation.

Noticing the way that discourses about authority both produce and reflect certain distinctions between the masculine and the feminine might free difference from the understanding we have of difference as "special identity." In more concrete terms, it might permit sexual difference to be freed from the paralyzing code of "different from," a code which continues to force the comparison, often within hierarchical terms, of one (core) identity, understood to be normative, with another. (Trinh 1988, 95, 96) The strategic reversal implied by counterpoising abstract with concrete, thought with feeling, and authoritative decision making with compassionate judgment in terms of a masculine-feminine binary is intended to focus on what has been excluded or derogated through these contrasts and to demonstrate the implication of one in the other. My effort is not to replace one (masculine) set of marks of authority with another (feminine) set of marks but to contribute further to the displacement of the binary logic to which analytical thinking is often subjected.

If, as I have argued, we continue to assume that authority is the sovereign right to command obedience or to enforce interpretations, then it matters little whether the claim to such rights to command or interpret are established by appeals to age-old traditions, to the possession of a "gift of grace" (charisma), or to an invocation of the rules. The point remains to command by whatever means. By any route, women as women, as signs of what cannot be represented through the univocality or singularity of authority, remain excluded. Feminist theorists have not always avoided the "sovereignty trap" when describing how to recognize authority in feminist theory and practice. Feminists continue to talk about being recognized as leaders without challenging what leadership means, often implicitly defining a leader as one who can elicit obedience or conformity in others. Yet it should be possible to investigate fruitfully the question of the connection between gender and different marks of leadership without necessarily falling into the sovereignty trap.

In particular, appeals to the significance of traditions of women's cultures, and the charismatic appeal of women's "grace under pressure" suggested by the writings of some feminists, especially those who have argued against seeing women as victims, imply the possibility that other marks of leadership might provoke us to think differently about being "in authority." If read against the grain of the construction of them as merely more personalized forms of command, these traditions and practices suggest alternative conceptualizations of who and what leaders are, what they do, where to find them, and what their dialectical relationship to the communities of which they are a part might be. At the same time, the implications of feminist criticism of the "masculinity" of rule-governed practices of authority—the discharge of business "without regard for persons"— need to be addressed directly as we imagine the kinds of bodies politic that would be most friendly to diversity and difference. Would a woman-friendly body politic be one in which we have abandoned rules and the legal discourse of boundaries in favor of the endless multiplicity and radical individuality of experience? Or is some kind of "objective discharge of business," some set of rules and markers of boundaries, essential as a "protection" against power's inevitable tendency toward displacement but not disappearance?

RECOGNIZING AUTHORITIES: THE DISCOURSE OF PUBLIC LEADERSHIP

Ask any introductory political science class to define public authority for you and they will recite the litany of official roles, the public offices of government, described in the modern constitutional state. Rulership and public leadership are assumed to be the practices of those who occupy the official institutions of the state. The list might be broadened to include, in modern industrial societies, "business executives, officials of voluntary institutions, heads of religious organizations, leaders of labor unions, [and] military officers." (Bell, et al., 1961, 6) But an underlying assumption in the construction of the list will be that public leaders, rulers, are those who occupy the representative, spokesperson position in any organization regarded as directly or indirectly connected to the practice of being in public authority. It follows that since women occupy few of these roles, few women are regarded as public authorities.

Even if the strongest version of this formal-institutional definition of public authority is held—that authority is wielded by anyone who occupies one of the recognized offices of authority, regardless of what people believe about the value of actions taken by the person in office—it remains difficult to deny, as Richard Flathman has demonstrated, that the identification of those offices rests in the final analysis on a set of presupposed, although not frequently articulated, "values and beliefs shared among those who participate in the practice [of authority]." (Flathman 1980, 20) Flathman continues by observing that the dependence of authority on values and beliefs extends beyond

> the necessity of knowing what authority is and the necessity of certain criteria for identifying instances of it. It posits *acceptance of some set of propositions according to which it is right or proper that there be authority at all and that such authority be established, lodged, distributed, exercised, and so on in this or that manner....* A *mark* of authority is necessary in order that the B's be able to pick out the A's [authorities] and the X's [their commands] from the welter of phenomena with which they (the B's) are presented. (1980, 20, emphasis added)

In other words, where authority is lodged in any system is an effect of certain beliefs and values about where it ought to be lodged. These values and beliefs vary culturally and historically. Together they constitute the criteria marking authority by locating it in particular offices and roles and not others.

A variety of systems for mapping the different constellations of belief undergirding authority have been articulated in Western political theory. One of the most influential modern typologies for distinguishing among the "marks" of authority is Max Weber's formulation. Weber cataloged three types of legitimate rule—rational, traditional, and charismatic. Each of these three kinds of claims to legitimacy was, he argued, paralleled by a "type of obedience, the kind of administrative staff developed to guarantee it, and the mode of exercising authority." (1947, 325; 1978 (1), III, i, 213) Thus, forms of rulership, or what Weber called "imperative control" (*Herrschaft*), were differentiated from one another in terms of the appropriate forms of response to the form of rule, the different methods of structuring and administering rule, and the signs by which authority was recognized in the first place. Do any of these forms of rulership depend upon representations that privilege masculinity, or are they all gender neutral? Our response to this question depends upon where authority is lodged in these different systems and the gendered consequences of lodging authority in different places.

Weber argued that the hallmark of modernity was the gradual shift from personal to impersonal, rational rule. Instrumental rationality, the model of modern authority, was the pursuit of established ends by the most efficient means. The fundamental characteristics of rational legal authority were the "continuous conduct of rule-bound official business," where each office extended to a specified sphere of competence (jurisdiction) and where the "organization of offices follows the principle of hierarchy; that is, each lower office is under the control and supervision of a higher one." Qualifications for office-holding within the administrative staff of rational legal authority are determined to exist if "a person . . . has demonstrated an adequate technical training" for the role. Finally, "administrative acts, decisions, and rules are formulated and recorded in writing." (1978, (I), III, ii, 3, 218–19) In this conceptualization, authority was lodged in hierarchically arranged offices, each with limited jurisdiction, and its operations were catalogued in written records, thereby presumably enhancing the rationality, continuity, and efficiency of its actions.

Weber made the emphasis on office over person one of the distinguishing characteristics of bureaucratic authority. It was this feature which permitted rational legal systems to administer authority over human beings with the highest degree of efficiency. "Bureaucratization," he wrote, "offers above all the optimum possibility for carrying through the principle of specializing administrative functions according to purely objective considerations. . . . 'Objective' discharge of business primarily means a discharge of business according to *calculable rules* and 'without regard for persons.' " (1978 (II) XI, 6, 975) This disregard of the personal operated with respect not only to the discharge of the business of authority; it extended equally to the relationship between an officeholder and the office held. Weber argued that "in the rational type case, there is also a complete absence of appropriation of his official position by the incumbent." (1978 (I), III, ii, 3, 219) In this sense the person belongs to the office, or, more precisely, is erased by the office, rather than the other way around.

Locating authority in the office itself, rather than in the specific person who occupies it, subjugates all personal dimensions of authority, all specifically human characteristics of ruling, to the "objective," public engines of hierarchical control. On the one hand, this separation of the personal, or charismatic, dimensions of authority from the practice of authority in rational legal systems appears to establish authority in the most gender-neutral terms. The more that ruling is depersonalized, the more its characteristics transcend the boundaries of sex. Anyone, regardless of sex, can occupy an authoritative office. On the other hand, the question of the gender of rational legal systems of authority depends upon the extent to which ruling constituted as "objective discharge of business . . . 'without regard for persons' " itself could be considered a gendered practice. Is ruling practiced as instrumental rationality a masculinized practice? (Ferguson 1984)

Wendy Brown has argued that "Weber's analysis of modern political and economic institutions reveal instrumental rationality to have been harnessed to specific projects of manhood. . . . These projects include a quest for freedom defined as liberation from constraint and power defined as domination." (1988, 152) Weber's ultimate inability to avoid connecting instrumental rationality to mechanisms of social control and domination has had serious consequences for the modern conceptualization of politics linked to this form of administration. Brown pays particular attention to the effects of this system of administration on the reproduction of gender:

> The complete realization of rationalized economic and political life, with its qualities of disciplined obedience and conformity, creates men who are calculable and predictable, models of behavioralist analysis, fully conditioned into automatons. This last turn suggests that it is not the feminine alone that is imperiled under conditions of rationalization. . . . The will to freedom, control, domination, and power . . . has engendered such total systems of domination in the form of capitalism and the bureaucratic state that *manhood itself, at the moment at which it is fully realized, is wholly crushed.* (1988, 162, emphasis added)

In other words, "the most rational form of exercising authority over human beings" rests upon the routinization of experience and the annihilation of any inner life, an inner life that Weber identified as "the feminine." (Brown 1988, 128–29) But it rests as well on the devirilization of most men by their transformation into uniformly disciplined cogs in a "ceaselessly moving mechanism." Regardless of sex, bureaucratic leaders are masculinized because they are above the merely subjective pull of everyday life, and their followers are feminized because they are subjected to the soulless commands of rationalized, instrumentalized, and institutionalized manliness.

Weber distinguished rational legal authority most starkly from the characteristics of charismatic authority. "Bureaucratic authority is specifically rational in the sense of being bound to intellectually analyzable rules; while charismatic authority is specifically irrational in the sense of being foreign to rules." (1978, (I), III, iv, 10, 244) The charismatic ruler or leader elicits obedience to authority by the appeal to the "gifts of grace" that distinguish the ruler as genuine in the first place. These "gifts" are signs that attribute extraordinary powers or abilities to an individual. Weber wrote that "charisma" applied to "a certain quality of an individual personality by virtue of which he is considered extraordinary and treated as endowed with supernatural, superhuman, or at least specifically exceptional powers or qualities." (1978 (I), III, iv, 241) Charismatic authority is further distinguished on the basis of the fact that "there is no hierarchy ... there is no such thing as a bailiwick or definite sphere of competence"; nor is there any "system of formal rules, of abstract principles, and hence no process of rational judicial decision oriented to them." (1978 (I), III, iv, 10, 243) To the extent that the "gifts of grace" by which charismatic rulers establish their authority are not limited to exclusively masculine representations, this mode of authority may be more capable of accommodating marks of "the feminine" as indicators of authority.

Yet Weber's characterization of the "gifts of grace" linked them at least in "primitive circumstances" to the "peculiar kind of quality of thought as resting on magical powers, whether of prophets, persons with a reputation for therapeutic or legal wisdom, leaders in the hunt, or heroes in war." (1978 (I), III, iv, 10, 241) The power of charisma, Weber wrote, "rests upon the belief in revelation and heroes ... it rests upon 'heroism' of an ascetic, military, judicial, magical, or whichever kind." (1978 (II), XIV, i, 3, 1116) Wendy Brown has noted that Weber's conceptualization of "heroism" is descriptive of a hero who "wears the mantle of classical manhood and wields modern manhood's creation, the massively powerful nation-state." (1988, 167) Weber's list of those characteristics thought to be charismatic seems more indebted to masculine representations of a reputation for greatness than feminine ones. This is not so much because, in the history of Western cultural traditions, women have been outside the arenas of magic, prophecy, piety, folk wisdom, or the hunt and the battle as that the parameters of these arenas, in the West, came to be defined increasingly in opposition to the East and to the feminine, or to the East as feminized "other."

Originally, Mesopotamian and Levantine creation stories explaining the origins of the universe (cosmogonies), as well as the particular ordering of human society that resulted, drew analogies between this creativity and women's procreativity. Feminine powers of reproduction were invoked not only to explain the origins of earthly life, but also to legitimate earthly monarchical rule. Patricia Springborg has written that

> It is no distortion to claim, I believe, that the creativity principle in Ancient Egypt represents a generalization, beyond gender speci-

ficity, of the feminine. . . . It was incumbent upon the pharaoh to match the creativity of woman in his leadership function as shaper of society, builder of the temples and recreator of the gods. But at the same time he must extend to his subjects the protective (ka) arms of the mother-goddess, Good Shepherd of his Sheep, in his moral role as guardian of his people. (1991, 11–12; cf. Allen, 1986)

The legacy of Egypt, Springborg continued, bequeathed early forms of a welfare state operating under the aegis of a beneficent monarch as well as "the conceptualization and symbolism of royal office and monarchy as an immortal institution," the use of "original symbols of female empowerment" in the "regalia of monarchy," and the appropriation of " 'metaphors of birth, sexuality, a release of new energy, a surge of vitalism,' as essential to the legitimation of new charismatic leaders as of old." (1991, 13, 6, 16)

The history of the Western cooptation of feminine powers of generativity in representations of the "birth of the state" as an essentially masculine act of political natality both suppresses and ironically preserves the connections between charismatic rule and female symbology. Weber credits charisma with being the "specifically creative revolutionary force of history," since, "in its most potent forms, [it] disrupts rational rule as well as tradition altogether and overturns all notions of sanctity." (1978 (II), XIV, i, 4, 1117) Yet the marks of potency of charismatic authority require that it be thoroughly detached from the everyday, from all "systematic economic activities," and "free of the ordinary worldly attachments and duties of occupational and family life." (1978 (II), XIV, i, i, 1113) To work its effects, Weber argued, charisma must be in the world, yet not mired in it. Charismatic leaders must prove themselves as "unprecedented and absolutely unique and therefore Divine." This is why, Weber contended, prophetic or artistic charismatic rulers frequently adhered to "the rule of celibacy." (1978 (II), XIV, 1115, 1114)

The generativity of the charismatic leader lies in the limitlessness and the for-the-sake-of-itselfness of its actions. If charisma gives birth to power, its purpose is not to care for or to preserve the issue, but to generate anew, to create again "out of the anxiety and enthusiasm of an extraordinary situation." (1978 (II), XIV, 4, 1117) Charisma, even when it has an economic object, is unconcerned with meeting "ongoing, routine demands." Against continuity, charisma is self-determined and sets its own limits. "Its bearer seizes the task for which he is destined and demands that the others follow him by virtue of his mission." (1978 (II), XIV, 1, 1111, 1112) One is reminded here of Jesus's words to his disciples: "Abandon thy father and thy mother and come follow me." Bearing "specific gifts of body and mind . . . considered 'supernatural,' " the charismatic leader transcends "the sphere of everyday economic routines" and leads his followers to greatness. (1978 (II), XIV, 1, 1112, 1111)

For Weber, bureaucracy and patriarchalism share one important characteristic, even though they are "antagonistic in many respects." Their common characteristic is that they are rooted in continuity. As an alternative to continuity which harnesses creativity to a mission in order to escape from "the channels of workaday routines," Weber's construction of charismatic authority offers minimal purchase on a symbolic order that would include the marks of the feminine as generative of an order requiring not constant disruption and beginning again, but nurturing protection. One can read in the following mournful prose Weber's regret that the necessary loss of charisma signals the reduction of "collective excitement" to the boring routines of everyday existence: "Every charisma is on the road from a turbulently emotional life that knows no economic rationality to a slow death by suffocation under the weight of material interests: every hour of its existence brings it nearer to the end." (1978 (II), XIV, 6, 1120) The collective, orgiastic "high" of charisma stands as an alternative to the mundane, tedious, and, Weber thought, ultimately soulless "duties of occupational and family life." It is a utopian alternative that, as with Plato's *Republic,* Weber nonetheless recognized was doomed to suffocate under the weight of the everyday.

Weber's discourse constructs a diametric opposition between charisma and the mundane. The heroic leader rises above the ordinary masses to lead them to greatness, and then resigns himself to a slow death as material reality routinizes the agonistic struggle and regiments the "anxiety and enthusiasm of an extraordinary situation" that gave birth to the hero in the first place. The charismatic ruler lives above and beyond the masses he inspires. By contrast Bettina Aptheker's recent work on women's resistance strategies suggests an alternative conceptualization of charisma as grace under pressure. Less visibly expressed as the superhuman actions of the supernaturally gifted, less likely to be connected to what Aptheker terms oppositional politics and power struggles, this grace under pressure emerges out of the everyday, the "dailiness of women's lives," yet exerts a strong counterforce to the dominant and deadening routinization of the mundane. (1989, 173) "To see women's resistance," Aptheker writes, "is also to see the accumulated effects of daily, arduous, creative, sometimes ingenious labors, performed over time, sometimes over generations." (1989, 173)

The Weberian elaboration of charisma has left us with a legacy that identifies the phenomenon with the most striking actions of those who are most graphically distant and different from us. The creative force of charisma, according to Weber, derives from its ability to distinguish itself from the ordinary plodding of ordinary people. It can only work its effects outside the terms of the "established order." To do this it must prove itself again and again by "working miracles," "performing heroic deeds," or "bringing well-being to his followers." (1978 (II), XIV, i, 2, 1114) The tendency has been to interpret these required proofs in the most literal sense. As a result we only notice the miracle at the moment of its having been worked; that is, at its flashpoint. Left outside the scope of this definition are the miracles worked within and through the ordinary; miracles that "have a profound effect on the fabric of social life because of [their] steady, cumulative effects." (Aptheker 1989, 173)

The creativity of charisma, in this sense, is not opposed to the everyday, nor is it opposed to traditions per se. Aptheker contends that women's actions of resistance are informed by the "logic of survival." Yet in the course of efforts to survive, women's resistance strategies augment and alter the structure and purpose of even the more traditional rituals and institutions.

> [Family and community] networks have played a crucial role in facilitating women's resistance both on the job and in marriages, families, and personal relationships. While family and work may compete with one another for a woman's time, a kind of family networking system is adapted by many women on the job to provide a key avenue for resistance. . . . This network operates every day and in innumerable ways. At its core is the protection of women's dignity. (1989, 175)

Understood in these terms, charismatic leadership becomes not the isolated heroic action of the saint but the collective, creative, even mundane activity of an otherwise marginalized group to evidence grace under pressure as a way of securing dignity. The extraordinariness of the ordinariness of this kind of leadership is captured by Adrienne Rich:

> The women are salvaging and building what they can, refusing to go quietly, putting up a struggle to the death. Every ordinary woman is extraordinary. The grandmothers, the mothers on the street, the angry housewives, the women in the empty office buildings late at night, the women who never planned this city, never

had a thing to say about its priorities. . . . (cited in Aptheker, 1989, 179)

Here leadership is represented as the process of building dignity from the scraps and shards of life. As extensions of their everyday roles, these charismatic leaders are not extraordinary because they possess some oracular power or supernatural capacity, but precisely because they do not. Rich evokes women's traditional roles as mothers, grandmothers, and service workers to suggest that out of these traditional roles an alternative system is forged, one which emerges from the resistance strategies of ordinary people, people who have never planned cities or influenced the public policy agenda in an official way.

By rejecting the opposition between the charismatic ruler and the everyday, this model of leadership as "grace under pressure" provides a more inclusive model than Weber's, one that is more amenable to different representations of gender as well as of different classes, races, and ethnicities. The importance of this model, for my purposes, lies not in the extent to which it draws on "women's experiences" but in the degree to which its alternative to the graceful/mundane dichotomy permits the articulation of knowledge of the creative processes of leadership and resists the pyrotechnic definitions of heroism that continue to subjugate all other understandings of the heroic. If heroism includes not only the more visibly displayed forms of prowess, but also the myriad of "means by which people find meaning in life and what religious, philosophical, or ethical understandings underscore their courage, commitments, methods of confronting suffering, ideas of justice, and efforts to change themselves and the world," (Buss cited in Aptheker 1989, 211) it represents an alternative to Weber's understanding of charisma. Precisely because it is not detached from the "ordinary worldly attachments and duties of occupational and family life" it is accessible to the many disparate values and practices that propel life "in practical ways every day." I call this characterization of charisma "prudentialized charisma."

"Prudentialized charisma" should be distinguished from the type that motivated Weber's mournful nostalgia for a "turbulently emotional life that knows no economic rationality." Prudentialized charisma makes its way through the mundane without simply conforming to the immediate demands of the everyday. In its very dailiness and persistence it stands, in Bettina Aptheker's words, as the "bedrock that gave meaning to life and served as an underpinning that made all else possible." (1989, 190) Understood in these terms, prudentially charismatic leaders make everything possible precisely because they recreate the conditions of life which, in Hannah Arendt's phrasing, remind us of the action we are capable of by virtue of having been born. Because they remind us of the action that we are capable of, prudentially charismatic leaders who exhibit grace under pressure may be more compatible with democratic traditions of participatory community which engage the actions of citizens and less subject to the whims of demagoguery than Weber's charismatic superheroes.

SPOKESPERSONS AND CENTERPEOPLE

Both Weber's understanding of bureaucratic authority and his construction of charismatic authority continue to influence modern studies of leadership. Together they contribute to the assumption that leadership is marked by its visible officiality, its measurable efficacy, or its existence as the property of specific persons. One recent example of this, marked strongly by Weberian frameworks, is James MacGregor Burns's *Leadership*. Burns is careful to stress the symbiotic relationship between leaders and followers, but his tendency is to identify leadership in traditional terms. In her study of gender and grassroots leadership in a hospital organizing drive, Karen Sacks remarks that the prevalent notion of leadership equates "public speakers and negotiators with leadership" and accepts "the distinction between 'organizing' and 'leading.'" (in Bookman and Morgan, 1989, 79) She argued that adhering to this conceptualization of leadership promoted class, race, and gender biases because it "implicitly equated political leadership with the movement's public spokespersons," consequently obscuring "an equally crucial aspect of leadership, that of *network centers,* who were almost all Black women. . . . Though women and men took leadership, they did so in different ways." The establishment of network centers by what Sacks calls "centerpeople" is a leadership activity, where leadership is understood "to be a collective and dynamic process, a complex set of relationships rather than the mobilization of parallel but individual actors." (in Bookman and Morgan, 79, 77)

Shifting the understanding of the roles of leadership from the official spokesperson definition that dominates the field to conceptualizing leadership roles to include those strategies responsible for the creation of action networks and consciousness shaping is relevant to my argument about gender and the marks of authority for several reasons. First, it builds on the mainstream argument that women are less likely to become the "official" spokespeople for any organizations, despite the fact that their actions are critical to the creation of the organization in the first place and to the sustaining of its work. Aptheker writes, for instance, that

> women have been marginalized in or excluded from the centers of power like trade unions, political parties, social movements, and the armed forces, from which men have waged their resistance. Women's strategies have pivoted from different centers and engaged different priorities. Often the choices women make about how to resist and in what ways are made outside the rules and outside the boundaries of conventional politics. (1989, 180; cf. Evans, 1980; Jones and Vergès 1991)

The reasons for this exclusion of women have to do with what political sociologists have long taught us—different groups have differential relations to the structure of political opportunities because of the operations of systemic classism, racism, and sexism. But to conclude on the basis of this relative exclusion that women's roles are not leadership roles concedes too much to the dominant tradition without considering its biases—particularly the way it privileges the officials over the networks.

Besides this, as feminist scholars and scholars of so-called "minority discourses" have demonstrated, having an official voice is also a function of what kind of voice the system is willing to hear. Those who speak in "different" voices—that is, different from what has been normalized as the "authentic" voice of authority—cannot become the official spokespeople for a group because their grammar and logic are discredited as particularistic, vernacular, or idiomatic. Official voices speak the language of universalized discourse and engage with the rational speech of rational political actors. Other voices ramble.

In the dominant discourse the voice of authority is heard as a commanding voice; the actions of authority are recognized as unambiguously purposive and goal oriented. Articulating judgments in a different voice, the "female" voice of would-be authority may speak in compassionate tones inaudible to listeners attuned to harsher commands. Hence in the dominant discourse, much of compassion is taken as nonauthoritative, marginal pleadings for mercy—the supplicant gestures of the subordinate. Even when the attempt to make authority compatible with agency modifies this view by providing a "space" for the exercise of judgments on the part of those subject to authority as "an absolutely central part in the practice of *in* authority," (Flathman 1980, 124) the ideal of autonomy and participation in rational discourse excludes certain forms of expression, linked metaphorically and symbolically to "female" speech, from those which make authority coherent. For example, sociolinguists recently have argued that female patterns of speech reveal a different expressiveness than do male patterns. Rhythms, nuance, emphasis, gesture, and assertiveness, in tone and syntax, appear to vary with gender. Nevertheless, we define the masculine mode of self-assured, self-assertive, unqualified declarativeness as the model of authoritative speech. "Female" hesitancy and other-oriented language patterns, considered as the marks of uncertainty or confusion, are derogated. (cf. Illych; Trinh 1988; Young, *Throwing Like a Girl*) Sack's research demonstrates how, in the network model, attention is focused less on people dictating to others what is to be done than on mechanisms that construct conditions of dialogue and communication that are perceived to establish the lifelines of the organization. (Collins, *Black Feminist Thought*)

Finally, the activity of leadership as network building draws on familial, communal, and life-cycle events to express its logic. Leadership, in this view, becomes a practice for establishing networks that sustain connections among members of a political group and augment formal ties by means of "rituals that stress family and life-cycle events and make use of a familylike set of symbols that cross racial and class lines." (Sacks in Bookman and Morgan, 1988, 81; Collins *Black Feminist Thought*, Aptheker 1989)

Of course, the history of symbols connected to the recognition of leadership or rulership in Western political thought also frequently drew on family metaphors to establish the marks of authority. As we saw in Hobbes, the sovereign was represented as the protector of his people like the father was the protector of his family. Hobbes wrote that the "marks [of sovereignty] whereby a man may discern in what man, or assembly of men, the sovereign power is placed" consist in the indivisible powers created by the covenant. These marks are the rights "of making rules . . . of judicature and decision and decision of controversy . . . of making war and peace . . . of choosing all counselors . . . of honour and order." (1962, 139) They are marks that stress actions of rule making, conflict resolution as final decision making, and of creating order as the signal marks of being in authority. What is unique about women's use of familial symbols in their descriptions of their leadership practices?

Several factors differentiate traditional theoretical invocations of family metaphors from what is implied by Sacks's analysis of leadership as the activities of network building by center people. Leadership is not the personification of the one who rules like a patriarch, or even a matriarch. Instead it is an activity of groups who construct dynamic social networks of communication and dialogue patterned on the family. Equally important is the linkage between leadership as network building and specific family rituals and symbols that have been connected to women, as well as between such leadership and the skills of mediation, conflict resolution by reconciliation, and the emotional as well as cognitive support and advice often associated with women's domestic roles.

Finally, the analogy between the leader's actions of initiating a group's organization and creating collective goals and strategies, even if not directly making pronouncements about them, and leadership as political birth giving should not go unnoticed. The chapter's opening epigram from Dankwart Rustow's volume on leadership explicitly connects leadership to the activities of founding and creating; a leader is an innovator. Again, Springborg argues that connections between rulership and women's reproductive activities were not lost on the ancient Egyptians.

> Although from the beginning there is no doubt that the first monarchies are patriarchal, the processes of empowerment are female. The awesome power of the first women, Hathor and Isis, Tiamat, Ishtar, and Anath, resides in their reproductive capacities, as powers of creativity of which the social power of kings is merely imitative. . . . The "birth of the state," no mere metaphor, was a symptomatic act in which all reigning dynasties sought their legitimacy. (1991, 4)

Springborg reminds us that the "perennial mouth-womb symbolism of Greek mythology" was more explicit in ancient Egyptian symbols. Egyptian iconography celebrated placentas and uteruses as symbols of the foundational powers of kings. This connection becomes metaphoric in Greek civilization, where the verbal birth of the polis through men's dialogue with one another displaces the birth of the social network from women's bodies. The privileging of word over flesh continued through early Christendom into modern European representations of stately authority. If Foucault is correct, the modern dynamic of disciplinary power functions primarily through the later privileging of vision—the gaze—over voice. (Foucault, *Power/Knowledge;* Jay) Nancy Love has recently pointed to the importance of metaphors and imagery in the epistemological and political projects of theory and has contended that the primacy of vision over voice granted the epistemological primacy over the political. (1991, 85–86) Grounding feminist theory more in voice than in vision might better connect it to a "political epistemology and the democratic politics accompanying it" she writes. (1991, 95)

Modern official leaders remain those who can be seen and who are recognized as representing and speaking for the group. One could argue, however, that their "speaking for" has become more and more detached from substance and more and more a matter of style. The visible marks of leaders are that they "look like" leaders; even their speeches are subject to visual tests for credibility rather than substantive assessments of their persuasiveness. Judging the credibility of a ruler as public spokesperson often depends upon evaluating the forcefulness of gestures used to make a point, as well as of facial expressions, of "body language." (Lakoff, 1991) The more the emphasis is placed on the visible marks of being in authority, on the outward signs of leadership, on "looking like" an authority in a public office, the more leadership becomes disconnected from those cultural codes representing women and women's roles. The reason for this is not that women are incapable of exhibiting such signs; rather, these signs have been defined in terms of a gendered discourse about rulership. This discourse privileges spokespeople over centerpeople and masculinized signals of singular presence over the prudential charisma of grace under pressure or over sustained connectedness, and gives priority to the heard over the hearer, the visible over the invisible, the phallic over the womblike. Not only are the outward signs of leadership connected to differences between masculine and feminine, they also are linked to racial, ethnic, and class codes that normalize official roles of leadership. Often these codes are interlinked.

The values and beliefs about officeholding as a mark of leadership depend upon the gendered boundary of the definition of "office" in the first place. Shifting perspectives about what constitutes the marks of leadership from public spokesperson to network creator and sustainer radically alters our view of the origins and structures of the social order. (Wolf 1972)

THE EPISTEMOLOGICAL FOUNDATION
OF LEADERSHIP

In Western political thought, we inherit from Plato the idea that what creates the foundation of legitimate rule is the ruler's possession of, perhaps even monopolization of, knowledge about the "good society." In modern theories of rulership, the idea that one has "expertise" about matters of the public good is taken as at least one of the qualifying characteristics for recognizing those in authority. The legitimating of authority by knowledge, whether that knowledge is ethical or technical, departs from Hobbes, for whom the recognition of the sovereign precedes any acknowledgment of the sovereign's capacity to know and to judge. The right "to be judge both of the means of peace and defence" and "of what opinions and doctrines are averse" belongs to those in authority as a function of their being instituted as authorities, in other words, as those who act, judge, or speak on behalf of obligated subjects. The right to declare what is to be known, defined by Hobbes as "the whole power of prescribing the rules, whereby every man may know, what goods he may enjoy, and what actions he may do, without being molested by any of his fellow subjects," is "*annexed* to sovereignty" at its institution. (1962, 137, 138, emphasis added)

As far as women's relationship to authority is concerned, there seems to be no intrinsic problem with privileging knowledge as the source of authority, insofar as what counts as knowledge is open. Although Plato argued that women, too, should have access to the training in dialectics that was to form the foundation for proper knowledge for political rulers, the assumptions that he made about what constituted the tenets of that epistemological system could be argued to rest on anthropomorphic, ethnocentric, and masculinist assumptions about what was important to be known by philosopher rulers. This is, perhaps, an anachronistic reading of Plato. Yet Plato was at no pains to disguise his antipathy toward the body, the processes of reproduction, and sexuality, as well as the vicissitudes of desire. (Brown 1988, Okin 1978) Let reason be bled of any connections to the passions, to the unfortunate fact of our embodiment, except insofar as the body could become a finely honed instrument of the soul. The dualism between body and soul, sense and reason in Plato's epistemology continues to influence contemporary Western theories of knowing.

Plato's assumptions about knowledge are anthropomorphic insofar as the human enterprise of knowing is defined as the political subjugation of the realm of the "merely" natural needs of everyday survival and the satisfaction of daily wants to the "higher" realm of ideas and the abstract. Self-sufficiency and the subjugation of nature are privileged over dependence and passion's rule over reason. Arendt has argued that Plato's analogy between ruling and the crafts, or the "activities of making, fabricating, and producing," ultimately betrayed Plato's instrumentalization of reason. (1968, 113) Page du Bois extends this argument by linking Plato's analogy between knowing and making to his privileging of masculinity. She contends that Plato's representation of the work of the philosopher rests on an "appropriation of the reproductive metaphors of Greek culture used to describe the place of women and his use of this metaphorical network to authorize the male philosopher." (1988, 169) In Plato's dialogues women are, she concludes, excluded "from true *eros,* and therefore from philosophy, from access to the truth." (1988, 171) The masculinization of Platonic reason, and the subsequent androcentrism of Western theories of knowledge, is the result, in du Bois's interpretation, of the appropriation of the female powers of reproduction to the male philosopher. "The male philosopher becomes the site of metaphorical reproduction, the subject of philosophical generation; the female, stripped of her metaphorical otherness, becomes a defective male, defined by lack." (1988, 183)

Feminist criticism of the androcentrism of Western epistemology has continued to be rich and prolific. Not untypical is the summary of feminist criticism of traditional Western theories of knowledge offered by Sandra Harding:

> The androcentric ideology of contemporary science posits as necessary, and/or as facts, a set of dualisms—culture vs. nature; rational mind vs. prerational body and irrational emotions and values; objectivity vs. subjectivity; public vs. private—and then links men and masculinity to the former and women and femininity to the latter in each dichotomy. (1986, 136)

Following du Bois's analysis we might add that this dichotomization operates to displace the "female" while, simultaneously and ironically, appropriating the female's powers to the masculine act of knowing.

If what counts as knowledge has been defined androcentrically, then feminist criticism of dominant theories of knowledge can be understood as attempts to broaden the basis of knowledge, of what counts as knowing and the known, by searching for "theoretical

connections between gender and specific ways of knowing."
(Hawkesworth 1988, 535) Increasingly this criticism has been extended to include a critique of dualistic thinking, or what Joan
Cocks has called the "oppositional imagination," as foundational of a
patriarchally defined knowledge about the meaning of sexual differences. (1989, 1; cf., Trinh 1988, 39; Barbara Johnson in Johnson
1987, 12)

If knowledge has been connected to leadership, then the implication of feminist criticism is to challenge the limited kinds of knowledge upon which leadership has been alleged to be founded. Other
modes of knowing would alter the practice of leadership in ways
more representative of women insofar as these other modes of knowing could be said to signal the "feminine." At its deepest level, the
feminist critique of epistemology challenges mainstream Western
thought not by asking how women know or what women's ways
of knowing are but, rather, what practices of knowing have been
disqualified because they have been feminized and how practices of
knowing and the modes of leadership connected to them would be
changed if these suppressed modes of knowledge were reintegrated
into the practice of authority.

Much of the earlier feminist criticism of the bias of specific areas
of discourse focused narrowly on the question of the sex of the researcher or the identity of the knower. This mode of inquiry, the
traces of which are to be felt strongly in the so-called "standpoint
epistemologies," tends to reduce the project of feminist epistemological criticism to the question of the presence or absence of different
types of knowers in the knowledge-production process. By collapsing
the question of the more adequate representation of women to the
question of the identity of the representer, where identity is equated
with surface appearances, this approach conflates concern with representation of alternative interests and values into concern with
whether the representer looks like members of an excluded group.
Although *who* the representer is remains an important consideration
and is one response to the issue of how better to represent women,
ultimately this mode of inquiry reaches a theoretical dead end, leading to the confusion of acting "like" or "as" a woman with being a
woman.

One problem with such a subject-centered approach to the politics
of representation is that it fails to permit the articulation of general
criteria for distinguishing among competing claims about reality
made by similarly situated subjects. How do we separate the desirable forms of political life advocated by those who look like us from

the undesirable forms? How do we define "women's interests"? Is being female a sufficient condition for defining who can represent women? Is being female a necessary condition for defining who can represent women? Clearly we need a set of criteria for determining the relationship between knower and known that moves beyond a biologistic or naturalistic equation between being X and knowing about X. As I will develop further in chapter 5, the need for such a set of criteria extends into the politics of theory building in feminist circles; that is, to the question of who can speak for or about whom.

Patricia Hill Collins has isolated the difficulty of having adequate criteria:

> A definition of Black feminist thought is needed that avoids the materialist position that being Black and/or female generates certain experiences that automatically determine variants of a Black and/or feminist consciousness. . . . But a definition of Black feminist thought must also avoid the idealist position that ideas can be evaluated in isolation from the groups that create them. (*Black Feminist Thought,* 21)

Collins's recognition of the limits of biologistic definitions is laudable, but exactly when a theorist is to be accused of developing interpretations that are isolated "from the groups that create them" remains vaguely defined. Does Nanci Caraway's work, *Segregated Sisterhood,* a text written about black feminist thought by a white feminist, stay closely enough connected to the groups about which she speaks to qualify? Moreover, Collins's argument begs the question of how to define the relevant group that creates the ideas of that group in the first place. Collins argues that the category of "race" is a highly contested category whose meaning is crucially shaped by history, politics, and ideology. This makes who is "in" the relevant group difficult to define. Race is, she contends, more socially constructed than are gender categories, which rest on "clear biological differences distinguishing females from males." (*Black Feminist Thought,* 27) Yet many would argue that the imputation of gender from biological differences between men and women is also highly questionable. Each of the categories of race, sex, and gender are dramatically unstable. Nevertheless Collins's defense of a definition of Black feminism that is nonexclusionary, even though it takes Black women's self-defined experiences as central to its project, promotes the kind of dialogue and political solidarity that I think is central to the building of alternative structures of authority.

To retain coherence, many of those who defend standpoint episte-mologies as more accurate modes of knowledge constitution assume that the perspective of the most marginalized has the greatest degree of truth because this perspective is claimed to be the least tainted by power. (Hawkesworth 1988, 544–46; Brown 1991; Pitkin, 1967) Yet standpoint epistemologies, a variation of the general category of building knowledge from experience, rest on a fundamental miscon-struing of materialist analysis and a reductionistic account of Marx-ian claims about the relationship between consciousness and lived experience. As Marx argued in *The German Ideology* about the work-ing class, marginalization itself—defined as one's social location on the periphery of a given social order—is no *guarantee* of critical political insight. We need to distinguish between occupying a social position of powerlessness and developing critical consciousness of that position.

The shift in emphasis in feminist critiques of epistemology from knower to known has been valuable, for reasons I will explore in more detail in chapter 5, since it enables us to escape the impasse resulting from any claims that genuine knowledge is the unmediated product of immediate apprehension or lived experience. This shift puts greater stress on critical examination of the "theoretical consti-tution of the empirical realm," the elaboration of those rules, norms, and standards for "assigning meanings to observed events, bestowing relevance and significance on phenomena, indicating strategies for problem-solving, and identifying methods by which to test the valid-ity of proposed solutions." (Hawkesworth 1988, 549) My critique here is engaged with the theoretical constitution of the rules, norms, and standards of what is, can be, or should be known by the ruler. Thus I am less concerned with "the effects of the exclusion of women from participation in those traditions [by which knowledge has been constituted]" (Hawkesworth 1988, 551) than in the ways that gender figures in the elaboration of a discourse about what constitutes au-thority in the first place.[1]

Distinctive forms of knowledge are connected to the different mod-els of authority found in the Weberian typology. Traditional author-ity seems least dependent on any form of knowledge because, as Weber described the basis of traditional authority, obedience to tradi-tional leaders "is owed not to enacted rules but to the person who occupies a position of authority by tradition or has been chosen for it by the traditional master." (1978 (I), III, iii, 6, 227) Authority is the result of occupying a position of culturally recognized status. To the extent that the traditional leader has discretionary powers "in that sphere which tradition leaves open to him," Weber argued that

> so far as his action follows principles at all, these are governed by considerations of ethical common sense, of equity or of utilitarian expediency. They are not formal principles, as in the case of legal authority. The exercise of power is oriented towards the consideration of how far the master and staff can go in view of the subjects' traditional compliance without arousing their resistance. (1978 (I), III, iii, 6, 227)

Even in this area of discretionary power, the legitimacy of the ruler is based less on formalized knowledge than on either conventional wisdom, or on the ability of the leader to act with prudence and to demonstrate the conformity between his current actions and "precedents and earlier decisions." (1978 (I), III, iii, 6, 227)

Traditional authority is not altogether disconnected from knowledge in the form of what Weber calls "ethical common sense." In this respect traditional forms of authority are compatible with those modes of conventional wisdom that have been defined by feminist scholars as emerging from women's struggles with the dailiness and routine of life. (Aptheker 1989) Yet both charismatic authority and rational-legal authority are systems more clearly dependent on particular knowledge practices for their legitimacy. In developing both of these models, Weber specifically invoked different forms of knowledge to explain their legitimacy. As discussed above, the magical knowledge that the charismatic leader possesses can be described as spiritual, medical, military, or ideological. Its characteristic authenticity, however, lies in its demonstrable ability to work certain effects; it must be proved again and again. Its otherworldliness, or super-ordinariness, must nonetheless effect change in the world of the ordinary or, more precisely, be believed to have effected change. "The only basis for [charismatic authority] is personal charisma so long as it is proved; that is, as long as it receives recognition and as long as the followers and disciples prove their usefulness charismatically." (1978 (I), III, iv, 10, 244)

Yet charismatic purposiveness is specifically distinguished from bureaucratic authority, or rational purposiveness, in the sense that charismatic authority is not "bound to intellectually analyzable rules." Nor does the accomplishment of tasks or the effecting of change in itself have any *practical* significance to the interests of the followers of charismatic authority. The working of charisma reinforces belief in the leader by effecting an internal transformation among believers. The accomplishment of tasks by the charismatic ruler, although taking place on the terrain of the mundane, is disconnected from any rational-technical, means-ends, or survival concerns. Instead, the "power of charisma rests upon the belief in revelation and heroes, upon the conviction that certain manifestations—whether they be of a religious, ethical, artistic, scientific, political or other kind—are important and valuable." (1978 (II) XIV, i, 3, 1116) That people believe such manifestations have value in and of themselves, and that these proofs of charisma do not need to be attached to higher ends, distinguishes charismatic knowledge from bureaucratic rationality.

In this respect the kinds of knowledge possessed by those whom I have termed "prudentially charismatic" rulers are less likely to be seen as important and valuable in themselves precisely because they are the kinds of knowledge that work their effects incrementally, cumulatively, and not in any immediate or cataclysmically miraculous way. The difficulty of even perceiving that observable effects result from an unglamorous activity repeated again and again, often without the benefit of an audience, has been reflected upon in different ways by anthropologists and sociologists of women's work as well as writers of literature. (Walker 1983; "Everyday Use" in Walker 1973; Oakley 1975) The knowledge of plodding methodism, of the endless repetition of tasks of perseverance and preservation, whose effects are constantly being undone, often has been represented as "feminine." It is the knowledge of "women's work." It is not the knowledge of the hunt but of plowing and planting; not the knowledge of heroically destructive combat but of attentive caretaking; not the knowledge of miraculous cures but of preventative medicine.

It is interesting to note that Weber specifically rejected the idea that "reason" and "intuition" were radically distinct, or that certain kinds of knowledge, such as scientific ideas, are rational and other sorts, such as religious, artistic, or ethical, are merely intuitive. "The mathematical imagination of a Weiserstrass, for instance, is 'intuition' in exactly the same sense as is that of any artist, prophet—or demagogue." (1978 (II), XIV, i, 3, 1116) In this regard his claim that different sorts of knowledge have the same psychological roots would be amenable to the sorts of arguments that feminist theorists have been making about redefining rationality to include forms of cognition disqualified because they do not conform to standard forms of detached, scientific observation. Yet the very efficiency with which scientific or technical rationality can achieve ends, or "deliver the goods," when delivering the goods becomes more and more of an end in itself, dictates the supercession of substantive rationality in any form by what Weber termed "rationalism." "Rationalism," for Weber, consisted in the erasure, or the rendering irrelevant, of the *substance* of a creator's ideas. It represented the triumph of the calculable over the incommensurable, the subordination of the substance of all knowledge to the interests of efficiency, predictability, and stability.

With the establishment of authority in the form of bureaucratic or instrumental rationality, the connection between knowledge and authority becomes most complete. "Bureaucratic administration means fundamentally domination through knowledge." (1978 (I), III, ii, 5, 225) But what sort of knowledge serves as the foundation of bureaucratic authority? Weber argued that the distinctive type of knowledge that made bureaucratic administration specifically rational was technical knowledge augmented by the knowledge that the holders of power come to have "growing out of experience in service. For they acquire through the conduct of office a special kind of knowledge of facts and have available a store of documentary material peculiar to themselves." This specialized knowledge becomes the store of secretive knowledge produced through the "striving for power." (1978 (I), ii, 5, 225) Bureaucratic administration then seals the store of knowledge and transforms it into "official secrets." The rule of experts, who come to define for themselves the character of knowledge qualified as such, is the hallmark of rational-legal authority. It is a closed system of domination.

The technical knowledge marking bureaucratic administration is knowledge driven by the goal of productivity for the sake of itself and the desire for greater and greater control over the world as the means of achieving "the actor's own rationally pursued and calculated ends." (1978 (I), I, 2, 24) Within the scope of instrumental rationality, ends are "rationally" pursued when assessment of the "behavior of objects in the environment and of other human beings" are treated as " 'conditions' or 'means' of the actor's own . . . ends." (1978 (I), I, 2, 24) This calculus includes the rational weighing, or "consideration of alternative means to the end, of the relations of the end to secondary consequences, and finally of the relative importance of different possible ends." (1978 (I), I, 2, 26) The "peculiarity of modern culture," Weber wrote, "and specifically of its technical and economic basis, demands this very 'calculability' of results." (1978 (II), XI, 6, 975)

The instrumentally rational assessment of different possible ends excludes the "determination of action either in affectual or traditional terms." (1978 (I), 1, 2, 26) "Affectual terms" were those which emerged out of the subject's feelings; "traditional terms" were those defined by "ingrained habituation." Weber acknowledged that action also could be understood in "value-rational" terms, that is, in terms of a "conscious belief in the value for its own sake of some ethical, aesthetic, religious, or other form of behavior, independently of the prospects of success." (1978 (I), I, 2, 25) But the unconditionality of commitment to such values—the fact that they would act as ethical or aesthetic limits on the pursuit of certain goals—meant that any action motivated by value-rational terms could be viewed as instrumentally rational only with respect to the selection of the means to achieve desired ends.

More importantly, the unconditionality of commitment to such things as "duty, honor, the pursuit of beauty, a religious call, personal loyalty, or the importance of some 'cause' no matter in what it consists" (1978 (I), I, 2, 25) meant that value-rational action was limited with respect to its ability to motivate the construction of a system of state power whose goal was the unlimited accumulation of power for the sake of itself. Ironically, power is the one value-rational goal, unnamed as such, that escapes the Weberian calculation that all ends determined value-rationally are, from the point of view of instrumental rationality, "irrational." This is because, for Weber, power has been conceptualized strictly in instrumentally rational terms. Power, defined as power over those conditions of life conceived as external constraints on human action, is measurable, calculable, and unlimited. Once this absolute value has been rendered in calculable terms, it leaves the sphere of value-rationality and enters the sphere of instrumental rationality. But how did the unlimited accumulation of power for its own sake become the self-legitimating goal towards which bureaucratic authority was inexorably oriented?

That the unlimited accumulation of power for its own sake becomes the purpose of state power is the result, in Weber's analysis, of the possibility of accomplishing this end promised by the ruthless efficiency of bureaucratic administration. "The decisive reason for the advance of bureaucratic organization has always been its purely *technical* superiority over any other form of organization." (1978 (II), XI, 6, 973) Such technical superiority is marked by the system's ability, in Marcuse's phrase, to "deliver the goods." It becomes impossible to assess the superiority or inferiority of the goods delivered within the terms of instrumental rationality itself because bureaucratic authority has succeeded in "eliminating from official business love, hatred, and all purely personal, irrational, and emotional elements which escape calculation." (Weber 1978 (II), XI, 6, 975) Instrumental rationality, or the justification of action in terms of the extent to which it is "best adapted to the normal interests of the actors as they themselves are aware of them," is distinguished by its "clarity of self-consciousness and freedom from subjective scruples." In this sense Weber declares that instrumental rationality is the "polar antithesis of every sort of unthinking acquiescence in customary ways as well as of devotion to norms consciously accepted as absolute values." (1978 (I), 1, 4, 30) Cast in these terms, where instrumental rationality is represented as "self-consciousness and freedom," where custom becomes "unthinking acquiescence," and where "norms consciously accepted as absolute values" become forms of "devotion," the logos of instrumental rationality becomes definitive of knowledge itself. In other words knowledge can only be characterized as such to the extent that it is distinguished from the realms of either custom or value.

The critique of instrumental rationality offered by the Frankfurt School introduced us to a set of now familiar arguments about the political consequences of the dominance of what Marcuse called "technological rationality" as a way of legitimating public decisions and political authority. Technological rationality, Marcuse wrote, "shapes the entire universe of discourse and action, intellectual and material culture. In the medium of technology, culture, politics, and the economy merge into an omnipresent system which swallows up or repulses all alternatives." (1966, xvi) The instrumentalism of technical rationality puts it at war with ambiguity, uncertainty, or any form of knowledge that cannot easily be transformed into immediately useful information. Particularized knowledge, knowledge less subject to formulaic translation, knowledge related to custom, knowledge of ethical or substantive values, or knowledge whose "usefulness" lies in its noninstrumentality, such as aesthetics, becomes disqualified as knowledge under the rubric of instrumental rationality.

Building on the insights of critical theorists, I want to ask a question that is only implicit in their analyses: What connection is there between knowledge as technical or instrumental rationality and gender? Are the submerged discourses rendered silent by the logic of instrumental rationality discourses connected in any way to representations of the female or feminine? Here I will be calling attention to what Nancy Fraser has called the failure of critical theory to "theorize the patriarchal, norm-mediated character of late capitalist official-economic and administrative systems." (in Benhabib and Cornell 1987, 55) My interest is in the potentially liberating effects of the specific sorts of "particularistic," not-only-utilitarian, modes of knowing implicit in the feminist reinterpretation of the social meanings of sexed and gendered bodies, and in what consequences these modes of knowing have for restructuring the meaning and practice of authority.

Kathy Ferguson has argued that

> bureaucratic capitalism separates us from others without freeing us, resulting in isolation rather than autonomy; it ties us to roles and rules rather than to people, weighting us with connections that deny community. Feminist discourse and practice entail a struggle for individual autonomy that is *with others* and for community that *embraces diversity*—that is, for an integration of the individual and the collective in an ongoing process of authentic individuation and genuine connectedness. (1984, 157)

She contends that this alternative feminist discourse on rationality is the result of "buried historical knowledge about women, about what women have done, spoken and dreamed, sought and found" and of "women's invisible and disqualified knowledge about themselves and their world, knowledge that has been inadequately elaborated because it is dismissed by the powerful as 'naive knowledge, located low down on the hierarchy, beneath the required level of cognition or scientificity.' " (1984, 157–58) In chapter 5 I will investigate further the assumptions behind such claims about women's knowledge of the world, since they are common to feminist standpoint epistemologies. For now I want to explore the question of gender and rationality at the level of representation, not lived experience.

THE "EPISTEMOLOGICAL EFFECTS OF COMMODITY PRODUCTION": CARING LABOR AND THE CRITIQUE OF BUREAUCRATIC AUTHORITY AND ITS "ILLUSORY COMMUNITY"

Instrumental rationality is the calculating practice of goal-oriented individuals who evaluate the merit of actions from the perspective of their own private interests. Its modern variation in political theory is rational choice theory. As Nancy Hartsock has observed, "the subjectively defined nature of rationality is central to the construct of rational economic man." (1983; 85; cf. Held, 1990, 321–44) Instrumental rationality is the "epistemological [underpinning] of the market model" (Hartsock 1983, 92) of social life and bureaucratic authority. But it is more than this. For Hartsock this particular mode of rationality reproduces not only class domination but a specifically gendered system of power. Hartsock's efforts to construct a specifically feminist historical materialism derive from her contention that neither Marx nor Marxian theorists have considered how instrumental rationality has been linked to manliness as much as such theories have connected instrumental rationality to a specifically bourgeois ideology.

Although I agree with Hartsock that Marx failed "to take account of or analyze the genderedness of power," and that "Marx's theory is useful more as a methodological guide to the feminist theorist than as an adequate theorization of domination," (1983, 139) I want to reread Marx's critique with a stress on the "more" rather than the unspoken "merely," a word whose traces are to be found lurking behind the "more" in Hartsock's phrasing as in so much of feminist theory. My effort to reread Marx has less to do with my desire to vindicate Marx than the political urgency of alerting ourselves again to the significance of his materialist analysis. In the contemporary period, when so much of feminist theory, as I argued in the introduction, has been captivated by a slick discourse about discourse, Marx's deconstruction of the discourse of political economy anchors the feminist project politically.

My interpretive strategy will be to consider Marx's critique of capitalism gendered even though he does not directly talk about women's productive activity, or women in general, to any great extent. To contend that Marxian analysis of productive activity would be relevant to theorizing gender only if it specifically engages with theorizing women's activities leads to the inevitable and, I think, erroneous, conclusion that since Marx "failed to analyze the work of women and their specific relations to the process of capitalist production, and failed to recognize the importance of social conflicts other than class conflict," Marxian theory can be of little direct help "on the specific question of the ways power is gendered." (Hartsock 1983, 146, 145)

Seyla Benhabib makes an indictment similar to Hartsock's when she contends that Marx's critique is locked in a paradigm that gives primacy to production and understands production in a narrowly economistic way by basing production on the "model of an active subject transforming, making, and shaping an object given to it." She argues that such a model is not at all "adequate for comprehending activities like childbearing and rearing, care of the sick and the elderly." "Can," she asks, "nurture, care, and the socialization of young children be understood in the light of a subject-object model when they are activities which are so thoroughly *intersubjective?*" (in Benhabib and Cornell 1987, 2) The problem with these interpretations is their reduction of Marxian theory to the "truth" (or "falsifiability") of its literal, as opposed to its metaphoric or ironic, reading of capitalism and capitalist instrumentalization of productive activity. Moreover, both impute too much to the ability of any author to domesticate and contain the significance of the insights of his or her theory.

Contrary to Hartsock and most feminists' assessment of Marx, I want to argue that the ways in which Marx talked about human productive activity are compatible with what feminist theorists have called the work and the thought of caretaking, the reflective actions of a connected self whose behavior becomes alienated and incomprehensible outside of the framework of human community. Consequently Marx's critique can provide the foundation for a feminist materialist critique of instrumental rationality if read against the grain of our, and perhaps Marx's, assumption of the genderlessness of capitalism. Marx's critique alerts us to what specifically human characteristics are sacrificed to the logic of value defined as exchange value. Marx identified alienated labor with a mode of productive activity that reduced the "purpose" of human activity to its instrumental function. What escapes the orbit of the instrumentally rational understanding of human action are those characteristics of labor as sensuous activity, of action as the action of embodied persons with many-sided (*genusfahig*) pleasures, who interact with the world in ways that express their need for and connection to others—the characteristics of caring labor that feminists have defined as "feminizied" caretaking practices.

Benhabib writes that

> it is only within the last ten years, and largely through the work of radical feminists, that the vision of human liberation in feminism has come to the fore. Although there is no agreement in the contemporary Women's Movement as to what this vision entails precisely, there is consensus around a *minimal utopia* of social life characterized by nurturant, caring, expressive and nonrepressive relations

between self and other, self and nature. (in Benhabib and Cornell 1987, 4)

Yet Marx's paradigm of labor defines productive activity in precisely these same terms. For Marx, labor is the many-sided human practice of working in and on the world; it is acting in connection with and empathy for the needs of others. Labor is transmuted into instrumental activity under the logic of capitalist accumulation. Reading Marx against the grain of traditional feminist interpretations is significant for feminist theory at this moment in history for several reasons. First, it suggests a way to avoid reducing gender as a category to "things about women." It also permits us to avoid dehistoricizing feminist theory by connecting feminism to traditions from which it can continue to draw insights and support. Finally, reading Marx's understanding of labor as intersubjective action in the context of the priority of community enables us to situate the feminist defense of caretaking as paradigmatic of nonalienated human labor within the context of a specifically political-economic critique of institutions of domination.

The kind of knowledge produced and legitimated by bureaucratic authority is knowledge of calculable rules whose derivation and application are "dehumanized." Instrumental rationality is knowledge and judgment developed and produced "without regard for persons." Both Marx and Weber linked this practice of rationality to the calculability required of a system of production based on exchange, in other words, to capitalism. Historicization of the critique of instrumental rationality is exemplified in Marx's analysis of the labor theory of value. Marx's analysis is particularly valuable for feminist criticism of instrumental rationality because it permits us to ground that critique materially in specific, historical practices of manhood instead of "naturalistically" claiming that instrumental rationality is an effect of the way men think about the world. Marx's deconstruction of commodity fetishism in *Capital* provides a methodology for linking instrumental rationality symbolically with specific codes of masculinity. Conjoined to the interests of feminist epistemology in excavating submerged alternative discourses connected to knowledge constructed from "women's experiences," both the critique of an episteme of exchange and the demystification of commodity fetishism provide the foundation for a feminist materialist critique of instrumental rationality.

Marx's work can be understood as an elaborate analysis of the discourse of political economy, a deconstruction of the framework of capitalism as reflected in the theories and practices of exchange economies. Political economy purported to analyze "the relation of human to human" but, Marx argued, it confused "the *estranged* form of social intercourse" with "the *essential* and *original* form corresponding to human nature."[2] (1975, II, 225, emphasis in the original) Political economy substituted the community in the form of exchange and trade for the human community. Instead of understanding human relations as necessarily communal—that is, as relations oriented towards others—political economy understood these relations as *necessarily* mediated by exchange. In other words, in the discourse of political economy, the most basic human relations are to be understood primarily as commercial relations. Instead of seeing human activity as necessarily social, political economy treated the social as incidental. The social value of human activity was defined as its instrumental value measured in terms of exchange. In the discourse of political economy, human social activities were not immediately useful, immediately identical with themselves, but were understood to be the product of the movement of private property. Hence, Marx wrote that within the system of private property, "social nature only comes into existence as its opposite, in the form of estrangement." Human "social" relations became nothing more than "reciprocity in alienation."

Marx intended to demystify exchange relations by revealing them to be the alienated form of human social relations, the annihilation of genuine community. He began with a critique of money, the medium of exchange or "universal equivalent." The ability to represent the value of things in terms of money suggests that money, as measure of value, is neutral. Yet, Marx argued, the apparent neutrality of money obscures the real relationships which are the presupposition of exchange—"the inner, implicit, hidden social relationship or *class relationship* between commodities." (1975, II, 211) The existence of money presupposed that human social relations were already circumscribed by property relations. It meant, further, that social relations and social activities were estranged from individual life; social relations were understood to be an effect of the exchange of products, so that exchange appeared to be the purpose of human activity:

> The essence of money is not, in the first place, that property is alienated in it, but that the *mediating activity* or movement, the *human*, social act by which persons' products mutually complement

one another, is estranged from the individual and becomes the attribute of money, a material thing outside persons. (1975, II, 212)

Here Marx implies that productive activity ("mediating activity") is an implicitly social and, therefore, human activity. The discourse of political economy failed to grasp this fact because it treated human social relations as the result of relations between things. It ascribed human qualities to objects and reduced all social relations to the single relation of possession, itself an anti-social relation. Although even relations of possession require social recognition in order to become real ("the power which I attribute to my object over yours requires your *recognition* in order to be a real power") (1975, II, 226, emphasis added), they can hardly be called social relations since, Marx contended, they are nothing more than destructive relations of "mutual plundering." Social relations, thus, appeared in the form of the "mutually *exclusive possession* of our respective products." Social relations within the system of private property appeared as the *"abstract relationship* of private property to private property"; that is, as relations between objects instead of between people. The individual was estranged from her/himself as a human being because she/he no longer understood her/himself as a subject but, rather, viewed her/his own products as the subjects. As a consequence, Marx wrote, "the society of this estranged person is a caricature of the real community. . . ." (1975, II, 217)

Marx's distinction between society and community in this context is significant. "Since human nature is the *true community* of persons," he said, "by manifesting their nature people create, produce, the human community, the social entity, which is no abstract universal power opposed to the single individual, but is the essential nature of each individual, [her/]his own activity, [her/]his own life, [her/]his own spirit, [her/]his own wealth." (1975, II, 217) Marx distinguished between social relations that sustain the antagonistic separation of humans from each other—exchange relations of the "society" of capitalism—and social relations that express the organization of the world in a human way; that is, in terms of the self-conscious recognition of social relations as the only form adequate to human existence and the organization of production in a correspondingly "human" form. In the latter sense, recognition of the other is not mediated by objects but is the direct result of one's own particular activity. If we carried out production in the fully human sense, instead of as limited by the laws of capital accumulation, then, Marx argued, the *specific* character of my activity would have been objectified; instead of being viewed as a matter of indifference, as a mere means to subsistence, my activity would be a direct manifestation of the particularity of my life itself. Because my activity would be immediately "useful"—instead of being valued only insofar as it could be exchanged for equivalent objects—then my work could be said to have satisfied a human need, since the "objects" I produce correspond to real human needs, not needs fabricated to facilitate the circulation of capital. Because my activity fulfills a human need, understood as necessarily social, I would become the "mediator between you and the species, and therefore would be recognized and felt by you yourself as a completion of your own essential nature and as a necessary part of yourself, and consequently would know myself to be confirmed in your thoughts and your love." (1975, II, 228)

Marx's description in this passage of nonalienated labor and his characterization of human activity as intersubjective and as nurturant, loving caretaking is remarkable because of the extent to which it is so close to what feminists have argued defines "women's" modes of knowing and producing. Patricia Hill Collins's distinction between an "epistemology of separation based on impersonal procedures for establishing truth and . . . an epistemology of connection in which truth emerges through care," and her identification of an Afrocentric feminist epistemology with the latter, is only one example of feminist literature that connects an ethic of care to an alternative feminist epistemology. (*Black Feminist Thought,* 217) Yet Marx's category of productive activity has much more in common than previously acknowledged with the ethic of care and with understanding human action as the action of particular, embodied beings that feminists have made central to their arguments.

For Marx human knowledge is the product of human acting in the world; it is necessarily intersubjective. The "all round development of individuals" was "not possible without community. Only within the community has each individual the means of cultivating [her/] his gifts in all directions; hence personal freedom becomes possible only within community." (1975, V, 78) Under capitalism, Marx argued, human activity became reduced to "labor pure and simple, abstract labor." (1972, 296) Under capitalist conditions of production, "products," or the developed essential powers of the subject and object as well as of activity itself, became mere economic relations, devoid of specifically human characteristics. "This economic relation," Marx wrote,

> therefore develops more purely and adequately in proportion as labor loses all the characteristics of art; as its particular skill be-

comes something more and more abstract and irrelevant, and as it becomes more and more a purely mechanical activity, hence indifferent to its particular form; a merely *formal* activity, activity pure and simple, regardless of its form. (1972, 297)

Labor understood in the purely abstract sense of labor power, calculable and measurable in terms of discrete units of time, labor whose particularity is ignored, is labor understood from the perspective of instrumental rationality, the logic of capitalist accumulation, and of bourgeois manhood.

Marx's use of the categories of political economy against political economy was intended to explode the understanding of labor as mere instrumentality, returning to productive activity some of its characteristic as "art." Linda Nicholson argued recently that there is a fundamental "ambiguity in Marx's use of 'production'." She contended that "Marx and many of his followers do not make clear which of [the various meanings] they are employing when they use ["labor," "production"] and related words." (in Benhabib and Cornell 1987, 18) My argument with this interpretation of Marx is its failure to contextualize Marx's analysis within the framework of his own ironic critique of the primacy of production. The "ambiguities in the meaning of key words in Marx's theory . . . make possible certain serious problems within his theory"—such as the alleged projection of the primacy of the economic across cultures and times—only if we forget that the purpose of Marx's theory was to break with the hegemony of a particularly narrow understanding of productive activity as abstract labor.

For Marx understanding the artfulness of labor was the result of understanding labor not as abstract labor power, but as the particular actions of specific individuals. Such an understanding of labor was masked by bourgeois relations of production based on exchange. Yet, Marx wrote, "when the limited bourgeois form is stripped away, what is wealth other than the universality of individual needs, capacities, pleasures, productive forces, etc., created through universal exchange?" Deconstructing the commodity form within which human activity is hidden, wealth can then be seen as

the absolute working out of [the individual's] creative potentialities, with no presupposition other than the previous historic development, which makes this totality of development; i.e., *the development of all human powers as such an end in itself.* . . . In bourgeois economics—and in the epoch of production to which it corresponds— this complete working-out of the human content appears as a complete emptying-out . . . as sacrifice of the human end-in-itself to an entirely external end. (1972, 488, emphasis added)

Marx wrote that "[w]ork cannot become play." (1972, 611–12) Yet for him the artfulness of labor lay in the fact that, despite being a practice of necessity, despite being mundane, labor was the "overcoming of obstacles . . . in itself a liberating activity." Once "external aims become stripped of merely external natural urgencies, and become posited as aims which the individual [her]self posits," labor becomes "self-realization, objectification of the subject, hence real freedom, whose action is, precisely, labor." (1972, 611) The artfulness of labor is its expressiveness of this particular individual's life, even when its purpose is survival.

The definition of labor as an artful, whole bodied, and compassionate activity with attention to the particularity of its focus and the specificity of its process has been used by a number of feminist theorists to characterize feminist alternatives to instrumental rationality. This reconceptualization of labor permits us to grasp the possibility that even the most onerous or taken-for-granted work can become the source of resistance and individual expressiveness. For example, Patricia Hill Collins speaks about African-American women's traditions of resistance to and struggle with the norms imposed by the dominant culture, which would otherwise have reduced them to being defenseless victims. (*Black Feminist Thought,* 92) Sara Ruddick's analysis of the work of mothering describes the "cognitive capacities" involved in exercising "protective control."

As she practices her understanding of a child's mind, a mother comes to develop the cognitive capacity for 'concrete' thinking, which is called forth by and enables the work of fostering growth. Concreteness is opposed to 'abstraction'—a cluster of interrelated dispositions to simplify, generalize, and sharply define. To look and speak concretely is to relish the complexity, to tolerate ambiguity, to multiply options rather than accepting the terms of a problem. (1989, 93)

Collins and Ruddick's reconstructions of caring labor and definitions of knowledge derived from women's experiences, as non-instrumental, or aesthetic, concrete knowledge, share the characteristics that Marx had identified with nonalienated productive activity.

Knowledge developed in the context of caring labor differs from instrumental knowledge in the sense that it resists the substitution of techniques of interaction for the real practice of connectedness; it resists "the invasion of the cult of rationality into personal life." (Ferguson 1984, 53) Authority practiced as the process of nurturant caretaking would certainly provide an alternative to authority practiced as the abstract application of rules to diverse situations. Yet if it is necessary to resist the overrationalization of private life, it is equally necessary to acknowledge the limits of nurturant connectedness, derived from traditionally female practices, for founding authority and constructing a public life adequate to solve the complex dilemmas of modern life. It may be that, as Kathy Ferguson has argued, "it puts too great a burden on the private virtues of attentive love and holding to expect them to constitute the entire basis of public life." (1984, 172)

The problem is to consider the extent to which knowledge of nurturant, caretaking practices fostered in the context of intimate relations can be translated into the public realm. Stephen White has argued for a conceptualization of attentive love as "lighter care," which would "share the mood and measure of more intense care; but its distinctiveness and palpability would not be directly anchored in the needs and motivations of intimate relations, but rather in the needs and motivations that are forming in the context of our frustrations and dissatisfactions with modernity." (1991, 105) In the next chapter we will consider the relevance of compassion to judgment, and the possibility for a transformed practice of authoritative decision-making derived from a materialist account of caretaking and reciprocity in the context of the "more equal and reciprocal relations of friendship." (Ferguson 1984, 173)

Notes

1. Emphasis on analysis of the rules, norms, and standards for assigning meaning to events is to be found in Evelyn Fox Keller, *Reflections on Gender and Science* (1985). For a critique of the conflation of the "gender and science" project with a "women and science" project see Keller's article, "Feminist Perspectives on Science Studies" (1988).

2. I have altered the translation of "Mensch" to "human" because it is more consistent with the German meaning and to avoid the reading of it as "male" alone.

4

"What Is Authority?": Toward a Feminist Response

JUDGMENT AND THE DISCIPLINARY GAZE OF AUTHORITY

In the Western liberal tradition, a political authority is supposed to be a neutral, disinterested, and impartial judge, one who issues or interprets rules that are meant to be applied to all members of the polity equally. Of course exceptions to the rules are recognized in law. But these exceptions are grounded in a system of excuses that are themselves defined according to generalizable or universal criteria, as opposed to personalizable or particularized criteria. (Fletcher 1978 and 1974; Jones 1982) Uninfluenced by any particularized connection to or feelings about specific citizens/subjects, all of whom have consented, either explicitly or implicitly, to being ruled and therefore are equally obligated to comply with the rules, an authority makes judgments that, in the political arena, become binding because they are issued by those who have entitlement to judge.

Determinations of entitlement vary constitutionally, but the effect of being entitled to rule in the tradition of positive law is to create an office of command whose purpose is to construct a unity of will out of the diversity of wills consenting to being ruled in the first place. By conferring the power to judge on one person or assembly of persons, as Hobbes wrote, we authorize their judgments as if they were our own. (1962, 134) There is wide debate about the extent of "surrender of judgment" involved in the act of recognizing authority in the first place. (Flathman 1980; Raz 1975; Friedman 1973) I will not engage with this debate except to point out that one of the purposes of authority in the traditional deontological view is to create unity out of diversity; hence the "problem" that authority is meant to solve is the problem of conflict among different, even mutually exclusive, wills. In the strongest version of this view, for authority to work its effects, the will of the subject of authority, necessary

142

at the moment of recognition of authority, disappears immediately thereafter. (Oakeshott 1975)

To judge authoritatively, to make legitimate decisions within this framework means, among other things, to be able to treat persons as fungible objects, where their peculiar characteristics, their specific identity, their irreducible distinctiveness, becomes irrelevant to the practice of authority. To judge authoritatively means to judge impartially, from a position outside and above the conflict itself. As Iris Young has put it:

> Impartiality names a point of view of reason that stands apart from any interests and desires. Not to be partial means being able to see the whole, how all the particular perspectives and interests in a given moral situation relate to one another in a way that, because of its partiality, each perspective cannot see itself. The impartial moral reasoner thus stands outside of and above the situation about which he or she reasons, with no stake in it, or is supposed to adopt an attitude toward a situation as though he or she were outside and above it. (in Benhabib and Cornell 1987, 60)

From this position "outside and above," political authorities promulgate and enforce laws that are themselves assumed to be universal and impartial. Thus, one of the signs of being in authority is the ability to articulate universal and impartial rules, rules that replace disorder with order.

This discourse on rule making normalizes authority as a distant, dispassionate, and disciplinary gaze. (Foucault, *Power/Knowledge;* Kaplan 1983) Such a discourse secures authority by opposing it to emotive connectedness or compassion. Within this discourse authorities order existence through general rules. Actors and actions are defined by these rules. Compassion cuts through this orderly universe with feelings that connect us to the specificity and particularity of actors and actions. Compassionate authority's "rules" are defined by the particularity of actors and actions; to that extent, compassion seems anarchical, even ruleless. Rational-legal authority's rules distance us from the person and the personal. Its rules treat everyone as anyone, not someone in particular. Compassionate authority pulls us into a face-to-face encounter with a specific, concrete other. Rational-legal authority subjugates and domesticates desire, affect, and "those aspects of life associated with the body." (Young in Benhabib and Cornell 1987, 64) Compassionate authority subverts the universal point of view by a refusal of the totalizing and dehumanizing effects of a transcendent rationality in favor of desire's "going public" by joining forces with "reason."

The modern normalization of authority as a disciplinary gaze represents, in classical psychoanalytic terms, the masculinization of this aspect of being in authority; it normalizes an androcentric view of authority. Although it comes to be associated with systems of rule that are themselves genderless, this form of ordering social behavior is at least arguably "masculine." Authority enables groups of individuals, necessarily in conflict with one another, to resolve their conflicts by appealing to the rules that specify priorities of rights. The rules of authority provide sanctuary from the dangers of social intercourse, or from what Hannah Arendt called the uncertainty of action in a world of plural agents. The modern instrumental view of human community and the identification of authority with hierarchy may be based on peculiarities of masculine need.

"Male hegemony in the culture," writes Jessica Benjamin, "is expressed by the generalization of rationality and the exclusion of nurturing, the triumph of individualistic instrumental values in all forms of social interaction." (Benjamin 1983, 295) Following Thomas Hobbes, the standard view of authority is of a mode of discourse that gives expression to rank, order, definition, and distinction and hides ambiguous dimensions of human reality that disorient and disturb. As we have seen, modern authority is constituted so that "female" bodies, gestures, and behaviors are either hidden or fetishized by authority's gaze.

Both the omniscient watchfulness and apparently threatening nature of authority produce passive and compliant subjects. Michel Foucault has contributed significantly to the study of the complex ways that modern discourses and technologies of power—technologies which permit power to "gain access to the bodies of individuals, to their acts, attitudes and modes of everyday behavior" (*Power/Knowledge,* 125)—create the subjugation of the subject through processes which "subject our bodies, govern our gestures, dictate our behaviors etc." (*Power/Knowledge*, 97) The subject of modern discourses of power is produced as a subject *to-be-looked-at,* to-be-watched. As Martin Jay has observed, "vision has been accorded a special role in Western epistemology, and has had an especially powerful role in the modern era." Although there have been a number of contemporary theorists of modernity, Foucault has contributed a highly specific, albeit ambiguous, body of work to what Jay has called an "anti-visual discourse." Perhaps more than any other contemporary thinker on the subject, Foucault has stressed the "sinister implications of ocularcentrism." (5, 7)

Foucault's research on the rise of Panopticism as the "permanent exercise of indefinite discipline" (1979, 217) has amply documented the ways that modern subjectivity as subjugation is produced through the self-policing of the body, the complex ways that we comport ourselves, regulate our gestures and our behaviors before the always assumed-to-be-present gaze of the "absolute eye that cadaverizes life and rediscovers in the corpse the frail broken nerve of life." (1973, 166). Yet he did not always emphasize the peculiar effects of this posing of the body as a problem to be solved in ways that addressed the "specificity of women's situation with respect to secrecy and truth." (Martin in Diamond and Quinby 1988, 14; cf. Bartky 1988) Nor did he always make clear the gendered nature of the subject-position produced by this discourse of power as domination and authority as the "sovereignty" of surveillance: the masculinization of authority follows from the feminization of subjects, subjects whose being disciplined through their bodies represents their "feminization."

In *Discipline and Punish,* Foucault suggested that the localization of power in monarchical sovereignty was superseded by the multiplication of power in what he called a "society of surveillance." The fact of power's dispersal seemed to undermine the existence of structured dimensions to power. "It [power] had to become a faceless gaze that transformed the whole social body into a field of perception: thousands of eyes, posted everywhere, mobile attentions ever on the alert, a long, hierarchized network. . . ." (1979, 214) Yet if sovereignty lost its apparent indivisibility in the context of a "disciplinary modality of power," this is not, as Foucault himself recognized, because the internalization of the gaze has replaced all the other, older forms of power, "but because it has infiltrated the others, sometimes undermining them, but serving as an intermediary between them, linking them together, extending them and above all making it possible to bring the effects of power to the most minute and distant elements." (1979, 216) The subject of disciplinary power takes the sovereign into herself making the existence of external controls appear redundant. It's all done with mirrors.

Laura Mulvey has written that:

in a world ordered by sexual imbalance, pleasure in looking has been split between active/male and passive/female. The determining male gaze projects its fantasy on to the female figure which is styled accordingly. In their traditional exhibitionist role women are simultaneously looked at and displayed, with their appearance coded for strong visual and erotic impact so that they can be said to connote *to-be-looked-at-ness*." (Mulvey 1988, 62)

Since the construction of "to-be-looked-at-ness" is precisely the way that disciplinary power works its effects on all its subjects, it would be more accurate to claim that the "citizen" in the disciplinary state becomes femininized; correspondingly, judgment as the operation of the gaze becomes a masculinized, ocularcentric practice.

To judge outside and above, as if one were an unsituated, disembodied, and disinterested actor, has become the hallmark of rational decision making. Modern theories of judgment postulate the autonomous individual as moral agent, responding to the world in a moral way by applying universal, abstract rules to concrete, yet generalizable, situations. Moreover, to judge impartially is to treat others as if they were just like us, "entitled to the same rights and duties we would want to ascribe to ourselves." (Benhabib in Benhabib and Cornell 1987, 87) To judge is to apply neutral rules to abstracted persons.

This standard of judgment establishes justice as fairness—a formal, public practice of the granting of appropriate rights to and the demanding of corresponding obligations from isolated, undifferentiated subjects by impartial umpires who remain indifferent to the particularity of the subjects in question. The sphere of justice as this sort of practice is structured in opposition to the sphere of personal, intimate, caring relations. In the latter sphere, human relations are "governed by norms of *equity* and *complementary reciprocity:* each is entitled to expect and to assume from the other forms of behavior through which the other feels recognized and confirmed as a concrete, individual being with specific needs, talents, and capacities." (Benhabib in Benhabib and Cornell 1987, 87) Insofar as the dominant model of judgment remains impartiality, then practices of judgment that attempt to judge from within, instead of only from without, are delegitimated as practices of justice and consigned to the private sphere.

Feminists have criticized the representation of judgment as the practice of neutral observers indifferently applying general rules to abstract persons. First, feminists have argued that the idea of the impartial observer is a fiction. All judgments are the judgments of particular persons. All knowledge is situated knowledge. Second, and more important, feminists have argued that the Rawlsian concept of deciding moral questions from behind the "veil of ignorance" is not only incoherent but also incompatible with the notion of fairness implicit in so much of moral theory. If judgment requires moral reciprocity—taking the standpoint of the other, or putting oneself imaginatively in the place of the other—then judgment becomes impossible the moment that the "veil of ignorance" is assumed. As Seyla Benhabib has argued, "under conditions of the 'veil of ignorance,' the *other as different from the self,* disappears. . . . Differences are not denied, they become irrelevant." (in Benhabib and Cornell 1987, 89) To know what it would mean to judge in a situation like X or what it would mean for you to be in a situation like Y requires being able to identify the relevant characteristics of any situation that make it "like" another. To be able to take up the standpoint of the other requires knowledge of the situation *from the perspective of the other.* This means having access to knowledge of concrete, not abstracted, others, to "knowledge of the agents involved in these situations, of their histories, attitudes, characters, and desires." (Benhabib in Benhabib and Cornell 1987, 90)

From another quarter Michael Walzer argued, against Rawls, that the choice of a singular standard for distributing social goods is highly unlikely to result from the actions of "ordinary people." Ordinary people have particular histories, cultures, and memberships or identities, "or they wouldn't be men and women in any recognizable sense." (1983, 8) For ordinary people,

> even if they are committed to impartiality, the question most likely to arise . . . is not, What would rational individuals choose under universalizing conditions of such-and-such a sort? But rather, What would *individuals like us* choose, who are *situated as we are,* who share a culture and are determined to go on sharing it? And this is a question that is readily transformed into, What choices have we already made in the course of our common life? What understandings do we (really) share? (5)

Benhabib's notion of "moral reciprocity," along with the understanding of judgment in the work of other feminist writers on ethics such as Tronto, Young, and Held, requires a de-centering of the "like us" strategy that Walzer here invokes and the taking up imaginatively of the perspective and position of the other. I will argue that this imaginative taking up of the position of the other is what is at work in the concept of "compassionate authority."

In contrast to the distanced stance of judgment, feminist moral theorists have defended a practice of judgment that is derived from the standpoint of the "concrete other." Elisabeth Spelman has called this practice of judgment the moral practice of treating a person as the person one is. Instead of seeing a person exclusively as the universal bearer of rights, this alternative practice of judgment responds "to the person someone is or, more exactly, the person whom someone takes himself or herself to be." (1978, 151) In fact, Benhabib has argued, adding this specific dimension to moral judgment renders the project of universalistic moral reasoning more coherent. For her it is not a question of choosing between the position of the "generalized" or the "concrete" other; rather, we "recognize the dignity of the generalized other through an acknowledgement of the moral identity of the concrete other." (in Benhabib and Cornell 1987, 92)

If recognizing the concrete other requires being able to understand accurately who the other is *as the other sees herself or himself,* then how do we arrive at this position? Spelman has contended that the "concept of treating someone as a person implies that you have a certain authority about who you are, about the features of yourself which are central to the person you are." (1978, 152) We begin to arrive at the perspective of the other from which we should judge an action, or the appropriateness of the application of a rule, by ceding to the other some minimal sense that she is an important source of knowledge about herself. Yet Spelman also cautioned against claiming that a person's authority about who she is, or her control over her standpoint, is unimpeachable. Both the possibility that we may be deceived about the persons we think we are, and the idea that knowledge of the self is constructed in the context of communicative interactions, require us to see identity as socially constituted and, hence, subject to different interpretations. Our identity is not whatever we declare it to be. Instead it is bound up with our own specific individual histories, as well as with the complex web of cultural practices that we share with those with whom we most closely identify. These cultural practices, in turn, are structured by institutions, ideologies, and practices that exceed the boundaries or the origins of the immediate group to which we claim to belong.

Having access to knowledge of the other from the perspective of the other becomes central to the project of building a feminist process of adjudication. Seyla Benhabib has argued that what is characteristic of feminist efforts to conjoin justice with care suggests a model of "communicative need interpretations." This model moves away from understanding judgment as the imposition of rules from outside and above a situation, calling instead for *dialogic* inquiry into "not only rights but needs, not only justice but possible modes of the good life." The emphasis on the dialogic characteristics of the practice of justice as communicative need interpretations has the advantage of supplanting the gaze of impartiality with the discourse of public speech. Unfolding in a space "created by commonality and uniqueness," this sort of ideal role taking—being able to enter into the world of the other, imaginatively taking on the other's view—presupposes the transformation of the condition and content of public speech and action so as to permit an openness to diversity that could enable "moral and political agents to define their own concrete identities on the basis of recognizing each other's dignity as generalized others." (Benhabib in Benhabib and Cornell 1987, 92, 93; cf. White 1991)

Patricia Hill Collins has identified an alternative perspective on judgment that she calls the "outsider-within" stance. "For African-American women, the knowledge gained at the intersection of race, gender, and class oppression provides the stimulus for crafting and passing on the subjugated knowledge of a Black women's culture of resistance." Characterizing the outsider-within stance as a peculiarity of Black women's standpoint, Collins argued that outsiders-within "have a distinct view of the contradictions between the dominant group's actions and ideologies." (Collins *Black Feminist Thought,* 10, 11) In terms of power, their marginalized location situates them on the periphery of the dominant culture. Yet at the same time, as the nurturers and caretakers of the children and families of their masters, or as the producers of surplus for the plantation economy, Black women have been located at the core of the dominant culture and are able to affirm themselves by "seeing white power demystified." Outsiders-within can judge from within and without at the same time; their unusual social location provides them with a perspective from which to critique the dominant culture.

Does this judgment of the outsider-within permit the development of the model of communicative need interpretations that Benhabib identified as an alternative to the dominant understanding of judgment as disinterested reasoning? Marginality may provide a distinctive angle of vision on the social system, but marginality alone does not guarantee the kind of reciprocal "taking up of the position of the other" precisely because the perspective of the marginalized is formulated within the context of subjugation. It seems important to stress the distinction between *being* an "outsider-within" and having the *critical consciousness* of that sociopolitical position. The outsider-within's strategy of resistance is a survival mechanism that *can* lead to critical consciousness or empowerment and, potentially, to the struggle against oppressive institutions. Whether it *automatically* permits the kind of "ideal role-taking" that Benhabib envisions as carried out in an "*actual* dialogic situation in which moral agents communicate with one another" (in Benhabib and Cornell 1987, 93) seems to me highly questionable precisely because the structure of power in the situations that Collins describes remains so skewed in favor of the dominant group.

Besides imagining the location from within as an alternative to the distanced, impartial practice of judgment, feminists have argued in favor of care and sympathy as dynamic practices of judgment, often drawing on the sphere of mothering as an arena within which alternative ethical practices develop. For instance, instead of viewing the problem of judgment as the reconciliation of competing claims of isolated selves, Virginia Held has suggested that we consider the relevance of "moral aspects of the concern and sympathy which people actually feel for particular others" to a theory of judgment. (1990, 338) The need for recognition and the need to understand the other, "created in the context of mother-child interaction, and . . . satisfied in a mutually empathetic relationship" are considered by Held and others to be relevant to an alternative theory of judgment. (1990, 341; cf. Ruddick 1989) Joan Tronto has argued that a broader scope of situations than the mother-child relation be included in the logic of the ethic of care. Patricia Collins has specifically connected the ethic of care to an "Afrocentric feminist epistemology." (*Black Feminist Thought,* 206–12, 215–17)

The norms of judgment implicit in caring for the concrete other, who is seen as a specific person with specific needs and interests, are the norms that Seyla Benhabib has identified as "friendship, love and care." (in Benhabib and Cornell 1987, 87) The practice of judgment developed within the context of caring labor is distinctive:

> These norms require in various ways that I exhibit more than the simple assertion of my rights and duties in the face of your needs. In treating you in accordance with the norms of friendship, love, and care, I confirm *not only your humanity but your human individuality*. The moral categories that accompany such interactions are those of responsibility, bonding, and sharing. The corresponding moral feelings are those of love, care and sympathy and solidarity. (Benhabib in Benhabib and Cornell, 1987, 87, emphasis added)

The central dilemma here is this: how far can we extend these moral categories, derived from intimate relationships, into the arena of political discourse and public action?

My query here is the opposite of what recently engaged Jean Elshtain. In "The Family and Civic Life," Elshtain considered the extent to which family life could be modeled on democratic principles, or the degree to which the development of an ethos of self-governance necessary for the existence of a democratic polity required "perfect congruence between political and familial modes." She argued in favor of both maintaining boundaries between the private, intimate sphere of family and the public, relatively impersonal sphere of civic life, and sustaining "natural" authority in the family. Only in this way could the family be preserved as a sphere within which parents, and not the state, could inculcate "special obligations and duties to special familial others." In Elshtain's view the "special, limited, and particular" authority of parents in the family is necessary for the "capacity to give ethical allegiance" to develop in the first place. (1990, 51, 48, 54) "It is only through identification with concrete others that the child can later identify with nonfamilial human beings and come to see herself as a member of a wider community." (1990, 56) I am concerned here with the extent to which the sort of ethical commitment that we learn through what Sara Ruddick has called "maternal stories" can be extended beyond the horizon of intimate, interpersonal relations. I am less convinced than Elshtain that such an extension does not require reworking both the structure and the ethos of intimate relations, including "the family."

We may be capable of caring far more than we do at present about the sufferings of those who are more distant from us than our immediate circle of family and friends. But we need to consider, as part of the feminist project of rethinking authority and the means by which to establish a polity that is friendly to women, exactly how we can encourage the development of these caretaking enterprises in ways that neither overburden women, who have been disproportionately burdened with the demands of caretaking, nor require us to reduce the feminist concern with caretaking as a model of judgment to what Kathy Ferguson has called the advocacy of a "warm, mushy, and wholly impossible politics of universal love." (Ferguson 1984, 172)

The norms of empathetic caretaking can become criteria for different practices of judgment only if they are reformulated within the context of voluntary, relatively egalitarian relationships of "reciprocity of generosity and trust." (Ferguson 1984, 173; cf. Acklesberg in Bookman and Morgan 1988; Jones 1990; and Jones 1991) The adaptability of "maternal practices" to the exigencies of civic responsibility is limited for several reasons. One limit to the adaptation of mothering practices to the political realm is that the structure of mothering is hardly, especially from the point of view of the child, a voluntary or relatively egalitarian relationship. It, therefore, seems flawed as a model for Held's idea of a "mutually empathetic relationship." Indeed, as Freud implied in *Civilization and its Discontents,* we desire to deny strongly the extent to which the "comfort" of our mother's embrace is something she could choose not to give. Recognizing that the realization of our needs depends upon her will— the will of another—is a necessary step in the process of human individuation, but one tinged with no small amount of anger directed towards the women who have forced us to discover that the object to which we have cathected is a subject. Even from the "mother's" point of view, the voluntary aspect of mothering may be diminished by the culture's desiderata regarding female roles. (Emechita, 1979 Ruddick, 1989).

The judgment of empathetic caretaking depends upon reciprocal generosity and trust, yet trust often develops only as the result of adequate caretaking rather than being its presumed foundation. We cannot be said to trust those on whom we have no choice but to be dependent. Hobbes recognized this. We learn to trust those who protect us *when* they protect us. Yet we are also subject to the danger that those whom we think that we can trust may be deceiving us. Since they often also control the discursive terrain within which we learn to identify trustworthiness in the first place, our ability not to trust them is limited. As Claus Mueller has written about the psychodynamic effects of communication patterns in families which tend to reinforce compliance, those who have never been taught to articulate their interests, those whose silence has been reinforced by one-way patterns of communication in families, "accept the definitions of political reality as offered by dominant groups, classes or government institutions." (1973, 9) The high incidence of violence in families demonstrates further how trust can be precluded or undermined by the exercise of force.

Finally, the practices of empathic judgment frequently associated with mothering in the ideal type would have to be separated from the proprietary dimensions of mothering in order to meet the criterion of reciprocal generosity identified as essential to the political practice of empathic judgment. We cannot be empathic judges of what is needed in the world of global politics if we judge exclusively from the perspective of what is good for "me and mine," if we judge, in other words, as citizens of nations embroiled in conflicts with one another.

Judith McDaniel's concept of "sanctuary" provides one way of constructing alternative practices of judgment that meet the criteria of empathetic caretaking while avoiding the limitations of translating the ethical criteria of "traditional" maternal practices into the political arena. Hers is an ironic strategy that interrogates the concept of sanctuary by connecting it rhetorically to that against which it has been frequently contrasted—danger. "Sanctuary is about living dangerously. Sanctuary is about taking risks beyond the ordinary. Risks of class security or race security. Risks of the heart. Physical risks." (1987, 147) The ability to cross the borders that bound the safe environs of one's own home, one's identity, one's nation, moving in the world "as if" through other people's minds, hearts, and bodies and seeing the world from others' perspectives, as much as that is possible, suggests the connection of empathetic judging to an inclusive theory of justice consistent with feminist critiques of inequality. McDaniel writes that her understanding of justice from a feminist perspective led her to the judgment that she "as a white middle class woman . . . could not fight for access to the white male power elite for [her]self and others" without violating basic feminist principles: "that equality for some and not others is not equality, just as justice that is exclusionary is not justice." (1987, 69) Her understanding of sanctuary implies a vision of judgment that applies generalizable rules about sanctuary to particular others.

Similarly, Sara Ruddick has argued that translating maternal practices into feminist political discourse requires extending maternal thinking through "knowledge . . . motivated and tested by a sympathetic apprehension of others' suffering as 'intolerable, to be rejected in behalf of a transforming project for the future.' " (*Maternal Thinking* 239) The kind of judgment that would found authority in feminist terms, then, depends upon an "ideal of identifying with women's struggles quite different from one's own" that does not reduce these other struggles to instances reflecting one's own view of the priorities of struggle, but responds "to women in particular situations of struggle." (*Maternal Thinking* 240) Barbara Smith expressed this need for solidarity with her notion of "trying to make coalitions with people who are different from you." (in Moraga and Anzaldúa, 126.)

The dilemma, of course, is how to respond to the particular while remaining committed to some vision of a feminist future that subscribes to generalizable criteria for determining the signs of progress measured in terms of greater equality and dignity for women and men. Should we embrace every culture's definition of women's roles as acceptable, even if they are grossly different from "our" own, or should be judge certain practices of subordination as negatively related to human dignity? "When," in the words of Ruth Rosen, "can we call a custom, a crime?" (1991) In addition, we still need to consider whether it is possible and under what conditions, to expand the logic of care-taking to those who are quite distant from us.

Michael Walzer, for instance, has argued that any effort to apply Kohlberg's "rule of prescriptive altruism" universally, that is, not to defend special obligations to kinfolk or friends, will run afoul on the shoals of what mere mortals can manage to do.

> The highest form of ethical life [the universal application of pre-scriptive altruism] is available only to a few strong-minded philoso-phers or to monks, hermits, and platonic guardians. The rest of us must settle for something less, which we are likely to think of as something better: we draw the best line that we can between the family and the community and live with the unequal intensities of love. (1983, 231)

If it is difficult for most of us to apply Kohlbergian moral reasoning, to distance ourselves from the intense feelings that we have about those who are closest to us, how much more difficult and fraught with controversy will it be to attempt to develop this intensity of feeling about and obligation to those who are distant from us that we now develop (at best) only for those in our most intimate circle?

Yet this kind of solidarity with the struggles of others is precisely what seems to be implied by feminist caretaking's "going public." Moreover, the stress in recent feminist theory has been on developing theories and practices which refuse to make the familiar, in every sense of that term, the center of concern. bell hooks, for example, has written that the politics of sisterhood and solidarity that was the promise of feminism would be realized when "white feminist activists have begun to confront racism in a serious and revolutionary manner [that is,] when they are not simply acknowledging racism in feminist movement or calling attention to personal prejudices, but are ac-tively struggling to resist racism oppression in our society." (hooks 1984, 55) In another context Martin and Mohanty have used Minnie Bruce Pratt's "Identity: Skin Blood Heart" as the basis for their interrogation of the limited purchase of concepts such as "home" to building an inclusive feminist theory. They contend that Pratt's autobiographical narrative, by calling into question the security of any home built like a fortress to keep others out, "unsettles not only any notion of feminism as an all-encompassing home but also the assumption that there are discrete, coherent, and absolutely separate identities—homes within feminism, so to speak—based on absolute divisions between various sexual, racial, or ethnic identities." (in de Lauretis 1986, 192) Can any "homely" practices, derived as they are from concerns about those with whom one feels closest, be translated into the public arena?

Patricia Hill Collins has argued in favor of a connection between all struggles for particularized recognition, such as Black women's struggles, and the "wider struggle for human dignity and empowerment." (*Black Feminist Thought,* 37) Through dialogue with others, solidarity and coalition can result, the kind of solidarity that Sara Ruddick has contended "undercuts military loyalty to states." Perhaps the kind of judgment of authorities that I have been describing as the judgment of empathetic caretaking, or the dynamics of compassionate authority, requires becoming "disloyal to civilization"—including one's own civilization—to the extent that any "civilization" has been structured on the basis of separatism and exclusivity. This practice of judgment necessitates turning a scrutinizing eye toward all situated knowledges, even those of the most concrete, particularized kind. Judgment engages through dialogue and intersubjective exchange, since the "reflectiveness of concreteness must be developed through disciplined attentiveness and then expanded and tested through critical conversational challenge." (Ruddick, *Maternal Thinking,* cf. Collins, 236, 212–15)

The extension of empathetic caretaking through the taking up of the position of another often has been linked to the idea of compassion for the suffering of another. It was precisely this linkage that led Hannah Arendt to argue that it was impossible to found authority on such a sentiment. Arendt feared that rather than being reconstitutive of a public realm in which action in concert was facilitated, the "immediacy of suffering" which compassion sought to excite led ultimately to the kind of boundlessness of violence that she associated with the errors of the French Revolution. Ironically, for Arendt compassion, through its inevitable deterioration into pity, was much more likely to lead to domination and the imposition of the will of leaders intent on restructuring society by whatever means, than it ever could lead to the sort of deliberative reflections that were emblematic for her of political life. "Because compassion abolishes the distance, the worldly space between men where political matters, the whole realm of human affairs, are located, it remains, politically speaking, irrelevant." (1963, 81) Before I engage directly with Arendt's critique, I want to explore in more detail the willful dimension of traditional understandings of authority.

THE WILLFULNESS OF AUTHORITIES

The final characteristic of being in authority defined in the extant literature addresses the question of authority's connection to power, or the ability of an authority to *command* obedience. The power of authority, in Hobbes's view, extended to the sovereign's possessing "right and force sufficient to compel performance." (1962, 108). Whether we agree with Hobbes that the absence of the sword, or the "terror of some power [that can] cause [the laws] to be obeyed" (1962, 129) marks the absence of authority itself, or with some weaker version of the idea that authority is marked by its ability to get people to obey, most theories of authority assume the connection between authority and political obligation that follows from the willfulness of those in authority.

Will is perhaps the dimension of being in authority that most directly links the practice of authority to the practice of domination. For this reason, it is the dimension least readily connected to representations of women's actions. If will is evidenced through the unambiguous imposition of my desires on another, and if being willful is the practice of autonomous agents, conceptualized as what Catherine Keller has called "separative selves," (Keller 1986, 4; cf. Nedelsky 1990, 162–89) then women seem to be the ones least likely to be understood as willful. The representation of the separative self as paradigmatic of the willful, autonomous agent rests on its fundamental opposition to the conceptualization of self as integrative or connected. Such a paradigm rests, in turn, on representations of selfhood that are connected symbolically and historically, not necessarily or naturally, to males and the masculine. As Keller argues, "[fear] of merger and self-dispersion motivates all insistence on separate selfhood. But let me suggest that in such a fear of self-loss lurks a profound fear of women." (1986, 3)

The logic of defining authority as a system of "conflict resolution" constructs decision making less as consensus building and more as a process of adjudicating competing private claims of self-interest and then executing decisions in a way that requires compliance. Recall that, in conventional rule-oriented definitions of authority, the need for authority is made identical with the need for some hierarchical system of decision making that defines social cooperation within the context of necessarily stratified relations. To institutionalize authority is to institutionalize vertical hierarchies of differential rights, privileges, and duties in order to facilitate the accomplishment of some "common" project. This conception of authority depends upon an instrumentalist view of political life and public action. Less valued in and of itself, public life—the realm of what Arendt called power, or action in concert—becomes reduced to a mechanism for achieving private ends. Authority, in this perspective, stabilizes social interaction, marking human action by tolerable, rule-governed levels of sociality. Authority, in this view, enables groups of individuals, necessarily in conflict with one another, to resolve their conflicts by appealing to the rules that specify priorities of rights. The rules of authority systems provide sanctuary from the dangers of social intercourse. Authority is understood not, as in the original sense of the word, as an augmentation of our common life, but, rather, as the process by which we can reduce our interaction with others to tolerable limits. Ironically, authority in this construction becomes the very means by which we avoid public life.

If the fear of self-loss and the desire for a protected and bounded self undergird the search for authority as the system that secures obedience, and if, as Keller has argued, a profound fear of women serves as the foundation for the unidirectional willfulness that guarantees obedience, then what are the gendered implications of a conceptualization of authority that privileges the ability of authority to work its effects—to compel obedience? On the symbolic level, the instrumental view of human community and the identification of authority with hierarchy may signal peculiarly masculine representations of the human condition—a denial of the fact that, in Arendt's words, "no human life, not even the life of the hermit in nature's wilderness, is possible without a world which directly or indirectly testifies to the presence of other human beings." (1958, 22)

As I argued in chapter 1, Dinnerstein contended that the psychological effect of the sexual division of labor in the family—the monopolization of mothering by women—explained the identification of authority with male-dominated systems of rule in terms of the retreat to paternal authority as a sanctuary from a maternal authority that is perceived, by the infant, to be overwhelming. Chodorow built upon this paradigm to contend that this system of child-rearing structures gender differentiated affective patterns. The consequence, she claimed, is that for women, intimacy and relations to others become part of the development of the "female" self. For men the self is defined in isolation from others, with the result that intimacy is more frequently threatening to the male. (1978, 180–81)[1]

Both of these accounts point to the importance of the meaning of the memory of the mother—the recognition of "female" bodies and gestures through the remembered fear of rejection—to the reading of the signs of authority. Why authority means rules may be connected to the sense of instability, impermanence and discontinuity "most intimately related to our bodies and our everyday behavior." (Foucault, *Power/Knowledge*, 80) But because this sense of instability is structured differently for women than for men, given the historical structuring of women's lives and the culturally defined experience of embodiment, acceptance of the idea of authority as rules may be more consonant with a masculine orientation to the world.[2]

Carol Gilligan's work on moral development offers some suggestive, although underdeveloped, and certainly controversial, hypotheses about the gendered codes of the representation of authority as the rule-governed imposition of one will on another. Commenting on her interpretation of the ways that the females in her study reached decisions about complex moral dilemmas compared with the study's males, and on the prevalence of images of relationship in girls' fantasies about dangerous situations, Gilligan remarked that women appear to perceive the fracturing of human connections as violent, whereas men see connection itself as threatening. Since women seem to tie the rupturing of relationships to aggression, "then the activities of care, as their fantasies suggest, are the activities that make the world safe, by avoiding isolation and preventing aggression rather than by seeking rules to limit its extent." (1982, 43) For men, by contrast, rule-bound situations, with clear boundaries and limits to aggressiveness, are safe; whereas for women, it is precisely the inability to connect, or to affiliate, that represents the dominance of aggressive willfulness. If we now accept the idea, indicated earlier, that authority is opposed to power and domination, then it would appear that what constitutes authority, for women, is exactly what is feared most by men: sustained connections, or what Freud called the altruistic urge for union in relationship to others.

Sophocles' *Antigone* can be read as a commentary critical of authority conceptualized as the exercise of will to elicit obedience. Upon hearing of Antigone's defiance of his edict forbidding the burial of Polyneices, her brother, King Creon explains his condemnation of her to Haemon, his son: "The man the state has put in place must have obedient hearing to his least command when it is right, and even when it's not." (in Green and Lattimore 204) Haemon replies that the community speaks its discontent with Creon's judgment, though Creon's "presence frightens any common man from saying things [Creon] would not care to hear." Creon denies that he should be moved either by the speech of his subjects or his son: "At my age I'm to school my mind by his? . . . This boy instructor is my master, then? . . . Is the town to tell me how I ought to rule? . . . Am I to rule by other mind than mine?" (in Green and Lattimore, 206) But Haemon replies that "no city is the property of a single man," and warns that Creon wishes to speak but never wants to hear. (in Green and Lattimore, 206) Creon's insistence that his commands be heard is countered by Haemon's insistence that speech is communicative dialogue, not monologue. Antigone's actions speak compellingly to the community because they remain connected to the fabric of its life. Her being silenced by the authority of the state serves as a reminder of what connections are lost in Creon's (male) view of authority: Antigone was burying her dead brother.

By invoking Antigone as an alternative image, I am neither representing her as a "maternal" thinker nor as a rebellious individual. Following Luce Irigaray, Linda Zerilli has argued convincingly that Antigone stands outside the patriarchally defined "maternal ideal," since she lives and dies as a virgin. Yet Antigone's action—burying her dead brother's body—evokes the memory of her own dead mother's body: the body of Jocasta. Honoring her dead brother's body, she simultaneously honors her mother's body—even that body, a body that violated the patriarchal incest taboo, brought forth a life that deserves to be respected. Antigone's action remains loyal to "maternal relations of blood rather than to the paternal fiction of a name." (Zerilli 1991, 256) Creon believes that he alone can issue commands; yet Antigone's refusal to acknowledge his legitimacy mocks the idea that the authority of the king rests on nothing more than itself. Her action is the action of a daughter remembering the mother without whom even Creon could not be. It is a reminder of natality as the sacred beginning of authority. (Irigaray 1985, Feral 1979)

Contrary to the restricted understanding of authority as contingent on conflicting individual and, primarily, male wills, authority is here seen as the construction of a meaningful world. Apart from the problem solving that authority permits, its essence is the vitalizing of community itself. As Hannah Arendt reminds us, authority is derived, etymologically, from the verb *augere,* "to augment." (1968, 121) Authority adds meaning to human action by connecting that action to a realm of value and to justifications for acting beyond the instrumental criteria of efficiency or feasibility. If we define authority as expressing and enabling political action among equals in community, then authority would be represented as a horizontal rather than a vertical relationship and as male/female rather than primarily male.

This alternative view accepts that authority is an essential feature of human social behavior because that behavior is a type of interaction that involves "speech, communication, and mutual understanding." (Friedman 1973, 98–99) Since, within this view, being in community is given ontological priority, then authority as a system of rules for securing private rights, structuring individual obligations, or protecting autonomy through reciprocal duties gives way to authority understood as a way of cohering and sustaining connectedness. Much of the fabric of communal connectedness is lost in the male-rule, instrumental model. In this "female" perspective, the quest for authority becomes the search for contexts of care that do not deteriorate into mechanisms of blind loyalty.

Gilligan notes that female caring traces a path of "deprivation followed by enhancement in which connection, though leading through separation, is in the end maintained or restored." The female self in connection with others "appears neither stranded in isolation screaming for help nor lost in fusion with the entire world as a whole, but bound in an indissoluble mode of relationship that is observably different but hard to describe." (1982, 48, 47) For example, this pattern emerges clearly in the Demeter-Persephone myth. Persephone, daughter of Demeter, while playing in the fields one day, admires the narcissus. As she picks it the earth opens, and Persephone disappears into the underworld. Angered at the loss of her daughter, Demeter, goddess of agriculture, refuses to allow the fields to grow until she is returned. The earth lies fallow until Zeus agrees to release Persephone from his brother Hades's control. Once Persephone is reunited with Demeter, the fields again are productive. But Persephone is required, as part of the agreement between Zeus and Demeter, to return annually to the underworld. And so, in Greek myth, is the origin of the seasons explained.

In interpreting this myth, David McClelland argues that it suggests an alternate interpretation of power, and I would add, of authority. Whereas power is often conceptualized as the willful assertion of control over another—the power of taking—this "female" myth, which invokes "interdependence, building up resources, and giving," contains different understandings of the resources of power. (1975, 96–99.) Demeter's authority seems to stand in a more literal relationship to the activity of augmenting that authority connoted originally.

Her augmentation of the life of the world is born of the restoration, albeit on a constantly changing basis, of her intimate connection with her daughter.

What remains troubling about the idea of authority as an augmentation is that we are aware that every search for harmonious connectedness contains choices and, therefore, losses and limits. In Nietzsche's phrase, "If a temple is to be built, another must be destroyed . . . ." Antigone loses her life, Demeter loses her original relationship to her daughter, and Persephone is limited by the requirement that she regularly return to the underworld. We perceive these limits as threats to the self and fear the authority that constructs them. In part this is because the dominant notion of autonomy is a disembodied one that abstracts human will and agency from the meaning of living as mortals in a world filled with those who are different from us. The refusal to consider the internal connection between authority and caring leads us to search for a spaceless and timeless order through rules and, paradoxically, to the embrace of domination and bondage to those authorities whom we most want to reject. (Sennett 1981)

The inability to reconcile authority's willfulness with human agency in a democratic community is the result, in part, of a conception of self in isolation from others as opposed to a self in connection with others. Authority does not have to be conceptualized as a willfulness opposed to personal autonomy so long as autonomy does not deny the critical function of nurturance and its relation to the humanization of authority. Richard Sennett has noted that the dominant forms of authority in modern life are destructive precisely because they lack the capacity for nurturance and compassion. These emotions are what enable us to "express a full awareness of one another" and, consequently, "to express the moral and human meaning of the institutions in which we live." (6) It is out of this emotive connectedness to others that genuine authority as an augmentation of the texture of daily life emerges.

MODERNITY AND THE CRISIS OF AUTHORITY: HANNAH ARENDT'S CRITIQUE OF DOMINATION

We have seen that the traditional understanding of authority in Western political theory has defined authority as the rightful governance of human action by means other than coercion or persuasion. Having identified rightful control as the basic feature of authority, many contemporary theorists across the political spectrum have argued accordingly that conditions of modernity have undermined the foundation of authority. Theorists as different as John Schaar and William Connolly have asserted that authority has been shattered particularly by those aspects of modernity that have destabilized the fixity and certainty of truth, custom, and leadership. (Schaar 1981; Connolly 1987) Theories of modern subjectivity that make the autonomous individual will central to the concept of personhood and corollary ideas about government derived from consent appear to create an irreconcilable tension between individual liberty and public order, between personal autonomy and political authority. The concept of the autonomy of the self requires, logically that persons rule themselves, yet the concept of authority demands the submission of individual wills to its legitimate commands.

The response of modern theorists to the crisis of authority has been varied. Some, such as Richard Sennett, have claimed that the peculiar nature of contemporary social life in the West—a social world where custom and tradition give way to convention and bureaucracy, even to whim—makes authority more necessary now than ever. A few, such as Christopher Lasch and Allan Bloom, urge returning to the customs and practices of an earlier, more ordered time, strengthening the commanding force of rulers with the engines of contemporary disciplinary strategies. (Sennett 1981; Lasch 1978; Bloom 1987) Others, such as Alisdair MacIntyre and Jurgen Habermas, stop short of this more authoritarian imagery, wishing instead to reinfuse *telos* into our public life. (MacIntyre 1981; Habermas 1983) John Schaar, for his part, has suggested that we rethink the epistemological foundations of authority and reassess the "kind of knowledge that can properly be accepted as constituting a claim to authority in the human realm." (1981, 40)

Hannah Arendt, however, argued that despite their differences, "those who counsel a return to authority because they think only a reintroduction of the order-obedience relationship can master the problems of a mass society, and those who believe that a mass society can rule itself, like any social body . . . agree on one essential point: authority is what makes people obey." (1968, 103) Her distinctive voice about theorizing authority has been in the background of much of my reading of this literature. I will now foreground Arendt's analysis and argue that her effort to create an alternative practice of authority, distinct from the discourse of domination and obedience that has come to infect our understanding of authority in modernity, is relevant to my concern to reconstruct authority in terms consistent with the development of a woman-friendly democracy.

Again, my approach will be ironic. I will deploy Arendt's arguments in ways that are consistent with her central claims but advance in directions that Arendt probably would have been unwilling to go. Nevertheless I justify this approach for two reasons. Following my understanding of authority and authorship—practices more connected than we realize—strong misreadings of an author's work are exactly what a reader of texts is invited to do. If meanings are not controlled by the intentions of an author/speaker, then texts permit the creation of democratic dialogue, the kind of public speech in public space that Arendt so admired. For Arendt authority facilitates political action, a kind of beginning again. Authority invites the practice of translation, an interpretive reworking of a text that fulfills the promise of dialogue that the text represents. As Bonnie Honig has noted, comparing Arendt's and Derrida's readings of the Declaration of Independence:

> translation augments necessarily. It does not merely copy or reproduce; it is a new linguistic event, it produces 'new textual bodies.' It does not simply preserve an original in a practice of mere repetition. ... And this augmentation is, in one sense, arguably like Arendt's practice of authority, which responds to the text or document that seeks to preserve and refer to the past moment of founding by augmenting it with another event, another speech act or, in this case, by an act of translation. (1991, 85)

Second, unlike all other political theorists, Arendt's work is alone because she considered the fact of our plurality, or our relationship to difference, central to the problem of authority—how do we construct a meaningful world in which we are at home with difference? In this sense, "she offers a powerful account of a practice of authority for modernity." (Honig 1991, 97) By resisting the temptation to anchor authority in an absolute, an absolute that would suffocate the freedom of political action that authority promises to call into being, Arendt's theory provides a way of thinking about and constructing authority that promotes the repoliticization of public life. (Honig 1991, 109) More than this, Arendt's specific reflections on the "human condition" as a condition of plurality, or, of what she called "the paradoxical plurality of unique beings," sharply distinguished this concept of plurality from "otherness." In this sense, her work has significant purchase in feminist theory. *Despite* aspects of her theory that would be inconsistent with feminist concerns—in particular, her apparent derogation of the domestic sphere, and her claim that the realm of necessity, as the realm of survival, coupled with the irresistability of the need to survive, make it a politically irrelevant realm—her stress on a model of authority as the process of augmentation that facilitates our living in a secular world of equality and uniqueness provides a particularly appropriate way to think about reconstructing authority consistent with feminist concerns.

Arendt wanted to defend an alternative concept of authority that would not preclude a vigorous and active citizenship, one that would extend, not constrict, the political space for human action. She began by tracing the historical precedents for the contemporary misunderstanding of authority back to Plato and Aristotle. In her view the Greeks were unable to develop an appropriately political notion of authority because all their models for authority were drawn from "politically irrelevant spheres." Faced with the political problem of introducing order into the public sphere, and lacking any immediately political experiences that would not hopelessly compromise the peculiar nature of the polis as a community of free and equal citizens, Arendt argued that Plato and Aristotle, "albeit in different ways," resorted to examples of authority culled from the "naturally" ordered private realm. The only way to introduce "rule" legitimately into the handling of public affairs was to depend upon examples of "natural" relations of superordination-subordination and to make this domination over nature the precondition to political freedom.

Hence, in Plato, the reliance on analogies between ruling and fabrication or between ruling and the command of "expertise" ultimately entailed reliance on the "natural" inequality prevailing between ruler and ruled. Only this could allow Plato to claim that rule would be exerted without the seizure of power or the possession of the means of violence. "What he was looking for," Arendt wrote, "was a relationship in which the compelling element lies in the relationship itself and is prior to the actual issuance of commands. . . ." In Aristotle the necessity of "domination and subjection, command and obedience, ruling and being ruled"—in the household and the slave economy—"are [made the] preconditions for establishing the political realm precisely because they are not its content." (1968, 109, 118)

For Arendt this meant that Plato and Aristotle were led to hopelessly contradictory positions. Having collapsed the distinction between the public and the private realms and having universalized the characteristics of ruling in the prepolitical sphere, the only model of authority which they could articulate was a barely obscured structure of domination which sacrificed the very freedom that the polis was meant to embody. The confusion of authority with tyranny and of legitimate power with violence resulted, in Arendt's assessment, from the Greeks' dependence on the natural despotism of the private realm for their models of authority. The ultimate consequence of this confusion not only undermined authority but also rendered citizenship itself obsolete because, by allowing thought to rule over action, the genuinely political public space which facilitates the development of freedom was destroyed.

Arendt's reason for considering the household (the sphere of reproduction, the sphere of *animal laborans*) and the economy (the sphere of production, the sphere of *homo faber*) politically irrelevant modes of social interaction remains indebted to the classical Greek understanding that the realm of necessity was an essentially private (not to be shown) sphere and that the forms of authority in it were "naturally" dominational. As she put it in *The Human Condition:*

> The distinctive trait of the household sphere was that in it men lived together because they were driven by their wants and needs ... necessity ruled over all activities performed in it. The realm of the polis, on the contrary, was the sphere of freedom. What all Greek philosophers ... took for granted is that freedom is exclusively located in the political realm, that necessity is primarily a pre-political phenomenon, characteristic of the private household organization, and that force and violence are justified in this sphere because they are the only means to master necessity. (1958, 30–31)

For Arendt, what makes the domination of necessity a politically meaningless model for authority is precisely its presumption of the distinction between ruler and ruled—a distinction that has no bearing in the community of equals which is the public sphere.

Yet Arendt's critique stops short of considering the degree to which this kind of authority as domination of necessity is irrelevant in the private sphere as well. Indeed, she goes so far as to suggest that questioning the plausibility of authoritarian relations in child rearing and in education is itself symptomatic of the crisis of authority in the modern world. We have become so confused by our identification of authority with domination that we no longer can distinguish between when subordination is naturally and politically necessary and when it is repressive. By "politically necessary" Arendt means the political necessity of introducing children into a pre-established world in order to maintain the continuity of what she called an "established civilization." (1968, 92) Arendt does not take up the question of whether this kind of indoctrination might undermine the possibility for the sort of political action that she idealizes. Nor does she explore the question of whether every "civilization" should be maintained merely because it is already established. By holding to a radical separation between socialization in the private sphere and activity in the public arena, participation in an authority structure becomes, even in Arendt's theory, limited to participation in authority in order to protect the social and sexual divisions that prevail in the "established civilization."

Clearly, Arendt's critique of the confusion of authority with domination is not derived from any explicitly feminist concerns. In fact her argument with Plato and Aristotle for having collapsed the distinction between the public and private realms of experience is at odds with much of the feminist canon's profoundly different reading of the boundaries of "politics" and the "public sphere." The important connections between the structure of "private" life and the structure of the public world have, as we have seen, led some feminist theorists to explore the ways that the patterns of socialization must be altered in order to facilitate women's greater integration into public life. Arendt saw no reason to transform coercive structures within the "realm of necessity." In fact she argued that this would disrupt the effort to maintain the continuity of an established civilization. Just such a disruption was a central feature of the feminist project.

Similarly, Arendt's sharp distinction between the social and the political, a distinction that leads her to argue that there are limits to what we can accomplish through public debate, might be subject to feminist criticism. "Public debate can only deal with things—if we want to put it negatively—we cannot figure out with certainty." Social problems are those things about which there should be no debate. "With every one of these questions [such as education, or health, or urban problems] there is a double face. And one of these faces should not be subject to debate. There shouldn't be any debate that everybody should have adequate housing." (in Hill 1979, 318) Much of contemporary feminist politics has to do precisely with how we decide which dimensions of the good life are beyond debate—such as certain familial arrangements, sexuality, bodily integrity—and which are subject to public scrutiny, as well as who decides.

Nevertheless Arendt's suspicion of conceptualizing authority as domination, or hierarchical control over others, remains invaluable to feminist theorists' efforts to redefine authority. The move away from authority as domination to authority as meaningful, mutually constructed communal bonds depends upon an exploration of the thesis that the discourse of authority as domination is a gendered one. This means engaging in a reading of that gendered discourse which is prompted by Arendt's critique but which moves beyond Arendt's critical horizon.

AUTHORITY, SACRED BEGINNINGS, AND THE CONCEPT OF NATALITY

If authority is not a command/obedience relationship, then what is it? Arendt begins with her assessment of what authority "never was." It was neither persuasion nor violence. (1968, 92) Here Arendt seems to be on familiar terrain with those other modern theorists who, as we have seen, also distinguish between authority and persuasion, or between authority and brute force. Yet what is at work in Arendt's argument is something much more distinctive. That we have different "key words" [such] as " 'power', 'strength,' 'force,' 'authority,' and finally, 'violence,' " she argues, should alert us to the fact that they "refer to distinct, different phenomena and would hardly exist unless they did." Contemporary political theorists often use these terms as synonyms for one another, in part because of their "conviction that the most crucial political issue is, and always has been, the question of Who rules Whom?" (1963, 43) All discussions of authority ultimately reduce to inquiries into the dynamics, responsibilities, privileges, and duties entailed in relationships of command and obedience. It is only when we cease to "reduce public affairs to the business of dominion that the original data in the realm of human affairs will appear, or, rather, reappear, in their authentic diversity." (1963, 44)

The peculiar need for order above all else is a variable condition expressing the interests and desires of some over others. In *The Human Condition,* Arendt argued that the "concept of rule" was the hallmark of all attempts to escape "from the frailty of human affairs into the solidity of quiet and order." (222) The concept of rule embodied the idea that "men can lawfully and politically live together only when some are entitled to command and the others are forced to obey." (222) The concept of rule as mastery, which led to the reduction of public life to the business of dominion, undercut the concept of action, *archein,* as a beginning.

Arendt argued that in the original linguistic sense, the Greek concept of "rule" (*archein*) connected it to the idea of a beginning that did not yet imply mastery or, at least, still distinguished between beginning and achieving (*archein* and *prattein*). A ruler (*archon*) was one who began an action but did not necessarily "remain the complete master of what he had done"; he still needed "the help of others to carry it through." Ruling was intersubjective, not the "isolated mastership" of experts who use others to execute orders. (1958, 222) Yet in the Platonic tradition,

> this original, linguistically predetermined identity of ruling and beginning had the consequences that all beginning was understood as the legitimation for rulership, until, finally, the element of beginning disappeared altogether from the concept of rulership. With it the most elementary and authentic understanding of human freedom disappeared from political action. . . . The Platonic identification of knowledge with command and rulership and of action with obedience and execution overruled all earlier experiences and articulation in the political realm and became authoritative for the whole tradition of political thought. (1958, 222, 224–25)

Rhetorically, this passage is quite brilliant. Arendt's use of the terms "overrule" and "authoritative" to construct her argument calls attention to the fact that we read into the meanings of these words their "masterful" connotation. Arendt demonstrates her point ironically: we lack a linguistically nuanced theory that would begin getting us again to think our way out of collapsing the meaning of authority with rule, and of the authoritative with masterful knowledge.

In Arendt's view the search for stability and order over political action in freedom transmuted the concept of authority into a command-obedience relationship. Arendt understood the meaning of authority as an augmentation, the "binding of every act back to the sacred beginning . . . of the past." (1968, 123) Authority enacts a looking backwards; it connects actions in the present, actions which Arendt understood as "beginnings," back toward the past, "into the depth of an earthly past." (1968, 123, 124) Authority is not a command, but a connection, a making of the present meaningful through memory. Following Arendt one might say that authority is a creative remembering of the past in the present; it is a remembering of our beginnings that nonetheless enables events in the present to become unique. (Honig 1991) It reminds us of the others who preceded our existence, without whose actions we would not be; it has the humbling effect of reminding us that we did not give birth to ourselves.

Action for Arendt is the "founding and preserving" of political bodies. It creates the "conditions for remembrance, that is, for history" and it is rooted in "natality." Labor and work also are "rooted in natality in so far as they have the task to provide and preserve the world." Yet

> action has the closest connection with the human condition of natality; the new beginning inherent in birth can make itself felt in the world only when the newcomer possesses the capacity of beginning something anew, that is, of acting. . . . Natality, and not mortality, may be the central category of political, as distinguished from metaphysical, thought. (1958, 8–9)

Authority's collapse into the concept of rule as mastery is an effect of forgetting the rootedness of authority in the concept of natality, the idea of beginnings, or of foundations. Recovering this original meaning suggests, following Arendt, returning to the earth-boundedness and birth-boundedness of human political action.

For Arendt, then, the desire for order stems from the desire to "escape the haphazardness and moral irresponsibility inherent in a plurality of agents." (1958, 220) It is a wish that in renouncing the capacity for action, "with its futility, boundlessness, and uncertainty of outcome," by having someone else act for us, "there could be a remedy for the frailty of human affairs." (1958, 195) Modern science has been captivated by the same dreams and fantasies: its desire to escape the earth is the mirror image of the desire to escape the fragility of human life that led to the confusion of authority with permanent order.

The dreams of modern science rest on the "repudiation of an Earth who was the Mother of all living creatures under the sky," a repudiation that Arendt considered even more fateful than the repudiation of "a god who was the Father of men in heaven." (1958, 2) Renouncing the capacity for action by retreating into the "solidity of quiet and order" and repudiating the earth-boundedness of the human condition, both the search for order and the project of artificially creating "life itself" reflect the same "wish to escape the human condition," a condition Arendt argues is marked by our natality, our embodiment, our plurality and the fact that we "live on the earth and inhabit the world." (1958, 7) As a scarcely veiled desire to return to the womb, as a wish to be reincorporated by making the many into one, this renunciation of action, and the exchange of authority as augmentation for authority as command both mark a kind of *resentment* that we were ever "of woman born." Why couldn't we be protected forever from life's futility and the haphazardness of living in the world of plurality, of difference?

I want to extend Arendt's insights and to argue that this confusion of authority with the sovereign power to command is based as well, although not intentionally, on what Carol Gilligan has called a peculiarly masculine approach to conflict: the willingness to sacrifice relations to others in the face of established rules, or to put it another way, to exchange the uncertainty of human relationships and the risk taking of human speech and action for the certainty of rules. It will be intriguing to explore the ways that what has been called a "female" stress on relationships over rules or abstract rights modifies how authority is constituted and practiced.[3] At this juncture I will be making a clear departure from Arendt's argument because I will contend that it is possible to develop a model of compassionate authority that avoids the pitfalls that she had identified with any effort to extend the "sentiments of the heart" into the public world.

COMPASSION, VIOLENCE, AND THE DESIRE FOR SELF-MASTERY

In *On Revolution* Arendt argued that it was the substitution of compassion, or more precisely the confusion of pity for the masses with solidarity, that accounted for the destructiveness and violence of revolutionary authority. She had in mind here the excesses of the French Revolution and the Terror. Virtue, Arendt contends, can be embodied in lasting institutions; compassion cannot. Virtue facilitates political action. It operates in the sphere of choice and knows the limits of human existence. Pity as the "passion of compassion" cannot focus on specific persons in their specific suffering; it comprehends the masses in their boundless suffering. It sees "a multitude—the factual plurality of a nation or a people or society—in the image of one supernatural body driven by one superhuman, irresistible 'general will.' " (1963, 54) More than this, pity, as the sentimental perversion of compassion, undermines solidarity. Solidarity enables the deliberate and dispassionate establishment of "a community of interest with the oppressed and exploited." Arendt calls solidarity a "principle that can inspire and guide action." Although it may be

> aroused by suffering, [it] is not guided by it, and it comprehends the strong and the rich no less than the weak and the poor; compared with the sentiment of pity, it may appear cold and abstract, for it

remains committed to 'ideas'—to greatness, or honor, or dignity— rather than to any "love" of men. (1963, 84)

The problem with compassion for Arendt is that it soon deteriorates into pity; as such it is unable to distinguish among the masses and can only comprehend suffering in its sheer numbers.

The evil of Robespierre's "virtue" of having compassion for mankind was, Arendt wrote, that he could accept no limitations to his own willfulness; his political interventions became transmuted into responses to the "urgency of the life process itself." "It was necessity, the urgent needs of the people, that unleashed the terror and sent the Revolution to its doom. " (1963, 55) Robespierre had "lost the capacity to establish and hold fast to rapports with persons in their singularity." (1963, 85) Moreover his virtue was disingenuous, masking the power relations he wanted to sustain behind his show of emotion. Without the "presence of misfortune, pity could not exist, and it has therefore just as much vested interest in the existence of the unhappy as thirst for power has a vested interest in the existence of the weak." (1963, 84) The limitations Arendt has in mind are the inevitable limitations of ourselves as "organic bodies, subject to necessary and irresistible processes." (1963, 110) For her, the limitations of necessity meant that any effort to end forever the "suffering" or the unhappiness of humankind by political means is not only doomed to failure but always threatens to erupt into a stream of violence, a "raging force . . . nourished by the necessity of biological life itself . . . as irresistible as the motion of the stars, a torrent rushing forward with elemental force engulfing a whole world." (1963, 108–09) In Arendt's view once the "men of the French Revolution raised compassion to the rank of the supreme political passion and of the highest political virtue," the logic of the Terror was set in motion.

We may wish to escape our bodies and the suffering and pain that being embodied entails. Yet Arendt feared the implications of this wish if it is attached, as a "principle," to the public realm. The history of the struggle to end suffering by political means was, for Arendt, the history of the deterioration of authority into "rulership":

All rulership has its original and its most legitimate source in man's wish to emancipate himself from life's necessity, and men achieved such liberation by means of violence, by forcing others to bear the burden of life for them. This was the core of slavery, and it is only the rise of technology, and not the rise of political ideas, which has refuted the old and terrible truth that only violence and rule over others could make some men free. Nothing could be more obsolete than to attempt to liberate mankind from poverty by political means; nothing could be more futile and more dangerous. (1963, 110)

Some applauded the inventions of science because they saw in technology the means to end human suffering. But for Arendt the "rise of technology" was not the harbinger of an age or a world that enhanced freedom. Freedom could only come from engaged political action in the public realm. Instead, for Arendt the modern age of science, with its promise to create "artificial" life, thereby "cutting the last tie through which even man belongs among the children of nature," and the modern world "born with the first atomic explosions," were interrelated. Each had contributed to "modern world alienation, [with] its twofold flight from the earth into the universe and from the world into the self." (1958, 2, 6)

The modern self, floating, freed from being earthbound, like a detached observer in space, no longer sees the earth as home and retreats into the fantasy of omnipotence and the wish for autogenesis.

The future man, whom the scientists tell us they will produce in no more than a hundred years, seems to be possessed by a rebellion against human existence as it has been given, a free gift from nowhere (secularly speaking), which he wishes to exchange, as it were, for something he has made himself. (1958, 2–3)

The danger, Arendt warned, is that this wish may be fulfilled. Mystified by the boundless abundance created through labor, distracted from political action by the never-ending process of consumption, human action would be reduced to

the devouring character of biological life until a mankind altogether "liberated" from the shackles of pain and effort would be free to 'consume' the whole world and to reproduce daily all things it wished to consume. How many things would appear and disappear daily and hourly in the life process of such a society would at best be immaterial for the world, if the world and its thing-character could withstand the reckless dynamism of a wholly motorized life process. ... All human reproductivity would be sucked into an enormously intensified life process and would follow automatically, without pain or effort, its ever-recurrent natural cycle. The rhythm of machines would magnify and intensify the natural rhythm of life enormously, but it would not change, only make more deadly, life's chief character with respect to the world, which is to wear down durability. (1958, 132)

Here Arendt's imagery for our modern rebellion against the knowledge that human existence is a gift powerfully evokes the narcissism that becomes rampant in a world without authority—without, in other words, a sense of "sacred beginnings." This imagery is reflected in the modern fantasy that one could create one's self and find happiness in devouring the whole world, a world one could simply "reproduce daily." What is suggestive about Arendt's critique is the centrality that she gives to the memory of natality. Natality, of course, is not a gift from "nowhere," but from somewhere very particular: we are "of woman born." Arendt's critique, in my reconstruction of it, returns us to consider how the denial of natality may be at the basis of theories of authority as rulership or "control over."

Evelyn Fox Keller has noted that

the knowledge that we are of woman born . . . fuels our dreams of transcendence as it fuels our dreams of immanence. Indeed, being of woman born could be said to provide the subtheme, or wellspring, of both the twin innocences of science and romance: two mirror-image spirits that both drive and constrain each other. More specifically, for the last three hundred years at least, the fact of being of woman born has provided the traditional point of final and indissoluble resistance to the total mechanization of mankind. (1990, 30)

Such resistance is transgressed when authority is postulated as mastery. I would add, following Arendt, that the theory of authority as masterful sovereignty has rested on the appropriation of birth by the ruler who transmutes the promise of birth, as the promise of the capacity to act anew, into the deadening obligation of obedience to an authority who protects paternally. Demanding access to this kind of authority represents an ironic move for feminist theory to make—arguably, it might depend upon an erasure of the symbolic significance of female bodies, a masculinized desire to escape natality into fantasies of sovereignty.

COMPASSIONATE AUTHORITY AND WORLD PRESERVATION: ON BEING AT HOME IN THE WORLD

Is it possible to reconcile freedom and rational discourse with compassion and remain able to distinguish political authority from compulsion, or the demand for blind obedience? What Arendt translates as the "barbarian vice of effeminacy" and rejects as a principle of authority may yet provide an important way to make authority more compatible with agency. Arendt rejected compassion as a political principle because, she argued, by overwhelming the political world with the "cares and worries which actually [belong] to the household," compassion makes a lawful civil society impossible. Compassion substitutes power as force for authority, and will—the force of the multitude—for consent, or the considered opinion of several particular interests. If virtue is rational and its mode of expression is argumentative speech and the doing of the great deed by "particular men," compassion, springing from the "sentiments of the heart," (1963, 87) speaks only the language of emotive gestures. To Arendt the presence of compassion in the public realm triggers the release of the "force of delirious rage." (1963, 86, 107) To base authority on compassion would permit an "irresistable and anonymous stream of violence [to replace] the free and deliberate action of men." (1963, 99)

In Arendt's terms, human understanding is understanding the limitedness of human action in the world. It means living in a world in which one has to make choices and suffer the consequences. Action is earthbound. Yet authority seems to lift one beyond one's emotions, beyond "merely" private, "merely" personal feelings. Authority is embodied in the judge who orders the sentence of death despite sympathy for the accused. Arendt's interpretation of Captain Vere's actions in Herman Melville's *Billy Budd* best represents her view here. She argues that Vere must condemn Budd for the crime of murder, even though he knows Budd is innocent in some larger sense of the term. Authority cannot be modified by compassion in this instance. To allow compassion to rule would be to allow unreflective immediate action to be substituted for the processes of persuasion, negotiation, and compromise. It would be to substitute faith for reason.

Budd cannot defend himself. He lacks the capacity for argumentative speech. Compassion, says Arendt, "speaks only to the extent that it has to reply directly to the sheer expressionist sound and gesture through which suffering becomes audible and visible in the world." (1963, 82) And it is the very directness of the compassionate response, according to Arendt, that removes it, or ought to remove it, from the realm of politics and hence the realm of lasting institutions, of practices that will endure.

Yet Vere's response to Budd is not unmediated, as Arendt claims.

Nor is his compassion for Budd the result merely of the "belief" in Budd's innocence. Both he and his officers know that Budd is innocent since Budd "purposed neither mutiny nor homicide." (Melville 1961, 70; cf. Schaar 1981) Most important, Vere's response to Budd is mediated by his understanding that his relationship to Budd is like that of a father to a son. Arendt contends that this sort of connection, born of compassion and caring, is particularized and that, if brought into the open, into the public realm, it would deteriorate, like Robespierre's concern, into the "boundlessness of an emotion that . . . [would] respond only too well to the boundless suffering of the multitude in their sheer overwhelming numbers . . . drown[ing] all special considerations, the considerations of friendship, no less than considerations of statecraft and principle." (1963, 85)

Compassion and caring are not without their own rules, their own principles and rational interests. Vere's caring for Billy Budd provides him with the knowledge that the law he is required to apply is more barbaric than the act that it punishes. The discourse of authority as orderliness subjugates this knowledge through the privileging of a disinterested, imperious gaze, focusing attention on disembodied agents whose intentions are read by the effects of their acts. As an ironic commentary on Arendt's interpretation that following the rule of law secures the public space for rational, persuasive discourse, Vere declares that among his reasons for condemning Budd is that the people, "long molded by arbitrary discipline, have not the kind of intelligent responsiveness that might qualify them to comprehend and discriminate." (Melville 1961, 68–69) Finally, too, the death of Billy Budd, while ostensibly carrying out the "measured forms" of politics, achieves no positive, augmenting, political value. It does not facilitate action but conformity.

The importance of connecting compassion and authority is that it reminds us that the order that authority as sovereignty imposes can never represent the world in all its complexity. (Connolly 1987, 23) Compassion can respond to the gesture of those who are inarticulate, thereby helping, in William Connolly's words, "that which is subordinate to find its own voice and, perhaps, to expand the space in which [the subordinate] can be for itself rather than only for the order." (1987, 24) In the compassionate view, Budd's last words are not mere gestures, as Arendt characterizes them. They, like Jesus's embrace of the Grand Inquisitor in *Brothers Karamazov*, represent acts of resistance to repression because they are a response outside the terms of repression. (Sennett 1981, 198; Jones 1984)

Without consideration of the meanings of words and gestures outside the realm of the publicly expressible permitted by the dominant discourse, the logic of any theory of authority as the rational practice of freedom become dubious. Many voices speak to us from different perspectives. This does not make what they communicate "mere" gesture. The "rational" modes of speech taken to be constitutive of authority exclude certain critical human dimensions, voices, and "interests" from the discourse of rationality and prevent their circulation in the public realm. Indeed the structure of authority as commanding sovereignty in the public realm is connected internally to this exclusion. These dimensions, voices, and interests cannot be translated simply into the language of dispassionate, discursive speech. Nevertheless their expressiveness is essential to understanding nuances of meaning and to recognizing what has been silenced by modes of political speech that know only the imperative mood and the future tense.

For example, Sara Ruddick describes the ways that the "mother's" interest in the growth and preservation of her child—an interest oriented toward the particularity of each child as a person—leads her to a dramatically different orientation to the child's needs and, potentially, to a critical stance toward the world within which her actions are framed. It is an orientation distinct from the disciplinary orientation toward the child and the more passive orientation toward the world required of the mother by the culture's imperative to train a child in the ways of social "acceptability." This cultural imperative can constrain the mother's concern for the child—a particularized "attentive love" that is structured by a set of flexible rules—and can lead to the mother's regimentation of the child to fit the culture's desiderata. From the perspective of "maternal thinking," the raising of girls for lives of self-abnegation and the raising boys for military service is irrational. It violates the mother's interest in "plurality," in protecting the child and encouraging the child's growth according to the particular needs of each particular child. The subordination of these maternal interests in favor of governing the development of the child, and the world, according to the "rationality" of social acceptability makes the mother's "knowledge" of her child's particular needs, and her awareness of the world's dangers, appear irrational. (Ruddick 1980)

Attentive love "represents a kind of knowing that takes truthfulness as its aim but makes truth serve lovingly the person known." (Ruddick 1989, 104) It is an attention oriented to the other person's needs that resists translating these specific needs and particular desires into reflections of one's self: a "knowing the other without finding *yourself* in her." (Ruddick 1989, 121) Ruddick sees this kind of compassionate attentiveness as capable of allowing "maternal thinking" to be extended outwards into the public realm. It represents the capacity to attend to another's suffering in a way that preserves the other's suffering in all its particularity. This extension of compassion's scope beyond the "private" sphere from which it emerges into the public realm is enabled through the practice of "solidarity," a practice that recognizes the uniqueness of different women's and men's "particular situations of struggle" and suffering. (1989, 240)

Ironically, precisely because compassion preserves the particularity of the other's suffering, because it is "other-directed," María Lugones and Elizabeth Spelman have argued that this is a strong reason to be suspicious of encouraging compassion as a defining element of a feminist ethos. (in Longino and Miner 1987, 244–46) Because compassion works by identifying "the needs and situations of others *as distinct from* one's own," as neither the same kind nor degree of suffering as one's own, Lugones and Spelman contend that it is not an important virtue for feminism. (in Longino and Miner 1987, 245) They argue that the distancing effect of feeling compassion—compassion is not co-suffering, but what Terence Des Pres has called "an imaginative entrance into the world of another's pain"—leads to an inability to make another's problems and pain my own (in Longino and Miner 1987, 245) For feminist communal projects, they conclude, neither compassion, which distinguishes between one's own projects and the projects of others, nor competition, defined as work against or in opposition to another, are acceptable political virtues.

Yet because another's problems are *distinct* from my own does not mean that I cannot, through compassion, perceive another's suffering *as if* it were my own, and work in solidarity with unique others toward certain goals. Such a discourse of solidarity that respects difference seems to be precisely what feminists have been stressing as necessary to build a world that is friendly to women in all their diversity. The tragedy of the human condition is that, as Arendt recognized, we live in a plural world—a world in which we are all the same—that is, human—and at the same time utterly, isolatingly unique. The promise of the human condition is that our very plurality—being born and beginning again and again—provides the opportunity for our speaking and acting to live together, building a world together, and learning to be at home in this world, whose durability will outlast our immediate actions only if our actions move beyond the range of the useful. (1958, 173; Kateb 1984) Although we can never *be* another person, our capacity for speech enables us to bridge this distance between all of us, to understand one another, to achieve what Nancy Fraser has called an "ethic of solidarity." (1986, 425–29, cf. Nancy Love 1991, 101–22; White 1991)

Lugones and Spelman correctly observe that Arendt's conceptualization of the "desire to excel" as the motive that "makes men love the world and enjoy the company of their peers, and drives them into public business" (1963, 120) is a conceptualization of "competition" that salvages it as a political virtue worthy of feminist reflection. Because the "desire to excel" is not, for Arendt, constructed in a "context of opposition," it avoids the negative, destructive characteristics often associated with competition that have made it such a "taboo" for feminists. Yet they fail to observe that Arendt understood compassion as "co-suffering" precisely because it was motivated by the uniqueness of "what is suffered by one person." She called compassion "to be stricken with the suffering of another as though it were contagious." She saw it as an emotion that "touched one in the flesh." (1963, 80) For Arendt the problem was not compassion itself, which she defined as having the very characteristics that Lugones and Spelman deny it, but whether it could work its effects when the object toward which it was oriented was generalized into "suffering mankind" and when the emotion was expressed for public display. I agree with Arendt's representation of compassion as a physically felt sense of "co-suffering," yet I disagree with her representation of it as a purely private emotion, without political merit.

Arendt argued that it was humanly impossible to establish solidarity by bringing compassion into the public arena:

> Whatever the passions and emotions may be, and whatever their true connection with thought and reason, they certainly are located in the human heart. And not only is the human heart a place of darkness which, with certainty, no human eye can penetrate; the qualities of the human heart need darkness and protection against the light of the public to grow and to remain what they are meant to be, innermost motives which are not meant for public display. (1963, 91)

Carried into the public realm, into the light of the world, Arendt argued that the conflicts which emotions express become "murderous because they [are] insoluble." (1963, 93) But for Sara Ruddick, the reasoning of the emotions can provide a lucid kind of knowledge that not only can withstand, but even requires, "going public" to work its transformative effects. "A clear-sighted apprehension of 'oneself and one's society,' combined with real increases in women's opportunities and self-respect, shifts the balance away from illusion and passivity toward active responsibility and engagement." (1989, 237) For Ruddick compassion does not have to be expressed immediately, like Robespierre's "delirious rage," but can become the motive force behind "active responsibility and engagement." Moreover, the language of compassion, taken into the public realm, can be made the language, not of violence, but of protective peacemaking. Ruddick writes:

> Maternal peacefulness is myth. At its center is the promise of birth. To threaten bodies—to starve, terrorize, mutilate, or deliberately injure them—is to violate that promise. Every body counts, every body is a testament to hope. The hope of the world—of birthing woman, mothers, friends, and kin—rests in the newborn infant. (1989, 217)

Ironically, these words echo Hannah Arendt's assessment that

> the miracle that saves the world, the realm of human affairs, from its normal, "natural" ruin is ultimately the fact of natality, in which the faculty of action is ontologically rooted. It is, in other words, the birth of new men and the new beginning, the action they are capable of by virtue of being born. Only the full experience of this capacity can bestow upon human affairs faith and hope. (1958, 110)

Acting on the promise of natality requires compassionate, attentive love toward the world. Ruddick argued that the appreciation of the "full experience of this capacity" for action facilitated by our being of women born required the inclusion of the knowledge of the fact of natality not only from the child's point of view—the child may, in fact, want to deny it—but also from the mother's point of view—the mother may, in fact, be prevented or prevent herself from knowing it. World-protection could follow from the mother's point of view. Although Arendt endorsed the action of world-protection, and complained most vehemently about those human endeavors that seemed rooted in the denial of birth and the rejection of the earth as our home, she distrusted the modelling of political relationships on the household. Yet it is an ironic commentary on Arendt's work that someone who so radically distinguished between the social and the political, and between the private and the public, nonetheless wrote about understanding the "world" as the "man-made home erected on earth" and eloquently contended that "without being at home in the midst of things whose durability makes them fit for use and for erecting a world whose very permanence stands in direct contrast to life, this life would never be human." (1963, 135)

Recently, William Connolly expressed specific fears about the dangers lurking at home. "Any authoritative set of norms and standards is, at its best, an ambiguous achievement; it excludes and denigrates that which does not fit into its confines." (1987, 21) He argued that "an established practice of authority is most *dangerous* when it expresses the urge *to treat society as a home* because its exercise then functions to repress, exclude, and deny that which is discordant with the harmony pursued." (1987, 22, emphasis added) The metaphor of "home" employed here unwittingly alludes to underlying gendered dimensions of both the fear of home and of the compassionate defenses often issued in its name. Women, of course, represent "home" in a figurative sense, and not only in Western cultures. Women are the ones also associated with the parochial and the everyday, and with the protective energies nurturing the familiar and the mundane; women have been associated with homemaking. Yet women themselves often are the ones who are sacrificed, who are at risk and endangered when at home. (Emechita 1979) Is it possible to acknowledge the exclusionary dimensions of the ambiguous harmony that authority seeks to establish and still engage a practice of authority as political "home"-building? In other words, can authority provide us with a way of "being at home in the world" which might alleviate the modern anxiety about chaos and our search for security without excluding "others" from this home and without requiring that women do the overwhelming portion of the homemaking and caretaking alone?

Perhaps it is not "home" but our modern proprietary relationship to it and its residents that creates the problem of the exclusionary dimension of authority as homemaking. (Moraga 1983; Pratt 1984; Lourde 1984) Maybe it is possessiveness—the reification of home as a "thing" that one owns and locks others out of—that precludes a different way of "being at home in the world." What would it mean to shift our perspective and see our earthly home and the authority through which it is founded as a coherent, connected "living thing?" What would be the effect of seeing the public world not as an "object" in the ordinary sense of the term but as being "alive"?

This protective attitude toward the world is precisely what Arendt suggests is the capacity of human action in concert, a capacity that will enable us to avoid devouring the world in an endless act of wasteful consumption. It is the capacity that she specifically connects to our natality, to the ability, by being born, to begin again. And it is this capacity which authority augments by connecting us to the past without being straight jacketed by it. As Arendt put it:

> The life span of man running toward death would inevitably carry everything human to ruin and destruction if it were not for the faculty of interrupting it and beginning something new, a faculty which is inherent in action like an ever-present reminder that men, though they must die, are not born in order to die but in order to begin again. (1958, 246)

In a recent essay in the *New York Times*, Lewis Thomas suggested the radical shift in perspective implied. The photographs taken of Earth from the moon, Thomas argued, revealed a way of seeing Earth as a "love[ly] object":

> as anyone could plainly see in the photograph, it was *alive*. That astonishing round thing, hanging there all alone, totally unlike any of the other numberless glittering but dead-white works of geometry elsewhere in space, was a living thing, a being. . . . The notion that life on Earth resembles, in detail, the sort of coherent, connected life we attribute to an organism is now something more than a notion. . . . (July 15, 1989, p. 15)

Arendt feared that stepping outside the range of our terrestrial habitat would mean that "man [would] only get lost in the immensity of the universe" unless humans could manage to construct a different, but still geocentric and anthropomorphic, world view, one where the "earth . . . is the center and home of mortal men." (1968, 278–79) For her it was important for humans to remain earthbound, homebound. The notion of the aliveness of home warrants reconsideration for its potential to push the analysis of authority away from the sterile discourse by which it has been captured. At the same time, it permits us to break the hold of the dominant gender concepts that infect our understanding of authority.

*"NOBODY IS THE AUTHOR OR PRODUCER OF [HER]
OWN LIFE STORY."* (ARENDT, *THE HUMAN
CONDITION,* 184)

The dominant discourse on authority places strict limits on the publicly expressible, restricting critical reflection about the norms and values that structure "private" life and affecting the rhythms of public speech. This discourse reduces the meaning of human communication to its ability to transmit information. By rejecting the ambiguities that our feelings introduce, we reject a mode of compassionate authority that would remind us that the construction of an harmonious world is always an "ambiguous achievement: it excludes and denigrates that which does not fit into its confines." (Connolly 1987, 21) Nevertheless accepting the concept of compassionate authority does not permit one to so overbroaden the concept of authority as to render it meaningless. The difficult task of distinguishing authority in this more ambiguous sense from other types of political action remains vexing.

Compassion has the potential for humanizing authority. If women do not represent those who speak authoritatively, in a commanding voice, perhaps the hesitancy of this different kind of speech reveals the ambiguity, and the choices, behind all systems of rule. By reminding us of this ambiguity, the voice and gesture of compassion shocks us into a memory of what has been hidden by the ordered discourse of authority: the utter contingency of our being born and our original dependency upon the body of a woman for the possibility of our acting at all.

It is of course possible to go too far in the other direction. Refusing to engage in any political judgment because all judgment smacks of discipline and assumed mastery is dangerous because it leaves untouched the "immediate plight of women" or of anyone suffering under the weight of existing injustices and constraints. Rejecting the idea of Enlightenment truth as a final, fixed point does not necessarily require that we repudiate any efforts aimed at "progress" in human rights, liberatory practices, or the pursuit of a more just, less authoritarian order. We may criticize the limits of certain strategies of resistance—the fact that choices close down other options, close off certain ways of living—but we cannot afford to choose not to choose. In Stephen White's words, we have the responsibility to otherness and the responsibility to act. (White 1991)

We are now confronted with the stultifying combination of the lived reality of poverty, homelessness, racial and sexual oppressions on an enormous scale in the world, *and* the ideological power of a genealogical discourse cautioning us to consider the dangers and the violence of every helpful move we make. Choosing to be identified with a political praxis oriented toward facilitating the development of democratic political practices in the world, feminists need to resist inertia and re-found political authority on this contested terrain. We may refuse the foundational stance of Enlightenment notions of Truth, but we cannot talk at all if we do not accept that statements such as "women are exploited" are at least provisionally true. Our efforts should be spent introducing nuance into these statements, not reducing them to absurdities.

If an aesthetic attitude toward authority is to replace an ascetic order, the result should be, as Nietzsche wrote long ago in *The Geneaology of Morals,* an acceptance of responsibility for the choices we make, which includes responsibility for having closed off certain options. Arendt, too, recognized this. Her strong critique of the confusion of violence with power, and of domination with authority, led her to formulate the practices of promising and forgiving as alternatives to the assumption that we can escape the human world of contingency through mastery, or sovereignty. The riskiness of acting in the public realm is the combined result of the fact that all human action is performed in a space "where everything and everybody are seen and heard by others," (1958, 77) and that action is ultimately unpredictable and irreversible. There can be no false assurance, either for Arendt or for Nietzsche, that we will not do more violence than we intend when we aim for the "good."

My defense of compassionate authority provides no more *certainty* that the "good" feminist community will result, if what we mean by "good" acknowledges, following Arendt, the impossibility for goodness to *be* in the world. Being good requires either a retreat from the world or self-deception about the pain that one's "good works" are inevitably causing another. To think that we are only doing good is, in fact, the height of arrogance. What my defense does is provide a way of thinking about Arendt's practices of "promising" and "forgiving" through specifically feminist lenses. I have argued that compassion can have public resonance because it suggests a way toward establishing a *dialogue* of solidarity about one another's needs. But this ethic of solidarity requires creating what Arendt called "islands of security" in the "ocean of uncertainty, which the future is by definition." (1958, 237) And every effort to secure something, to make certain that it is stable, means that other choices, other decisions, will not be made.

Engaging in feminist promising and forgiving through perspectives on the world that are born of compassion, or attentive love toward the world, requires that we approach even our own identities and experiences, and the stories that we tell about them, with a little more humility. Arendt reminds us of the important social dimension to promising and forgiving:

> Without being forgiven, released from the consequences of what we have done, our capacity to act would, as it were, be confined to one single deed from which we could never recover; we would remain the victims of its consequences forever, not unlike the sorcerer's apprentice who lacked the magic formula to break the spell. Without being bound to the fulfillment of promises, we would never be able to keep our identities; we would be condemned to wander helplessly and without direction in the darkness of each man's lonely heart, caught in its contradictions and equivocalities—a darkness which only the light shed over the public realm through the presence of others, who confirm the identity between the one who promises and the one who fulfills, can dispel. Both faculties, therefore, depend on plurality, on the presence and acting of others, for no one can forgive himself and no one can feel bound by a promise made only to himself; forgiving and promising enacted in solitude or isolation remain without a reality and can signify no more than a role played before one's self. (1958, 237)

Having accepted responsibility for acting does *not* annihilate the imperative to act; instead it serves as its foundation. We should locate differently the imperative to act. The imperative to act becomes a lived, heartfelt need for the individual in solidarity with others, an individual who now acts in conformity with some *political* imperative to begin anew which is no longer sugar-coated with transcendentally moral flavors. (Kristeva 1990–91; Brown 1991) The promising and forgiving individual judges and acts without the protection of an armament of frozen, canonized, moral principles; hence she is subject to the painful knowledge that the chosen action may not be right, or may not be right forever. What is gone in the modern world is the security of self-righteousness and the certainty of authority. But if security and certainty have disappeared, the need for authority as meaningful order has not. Its achievement may be made more ambiguous and humbled by the dynamics of modernity. It nonetheless can and must be re-grounded. Can it be re-grounded through the subjugated knowledge of "women's experiences?"

Notes

1. Chodorow has a tendency in this work to reduce the category of the unconscious to an effect of the social. She also tends to regard the white, middle-class family as paradigmatic of all child-rearing contexts. For criticisms, see Collins *Black Feminist Thought* and hooks (1984). For my purposes, the relevance of Chodorow's and Dinnerstein's argument to understanding the representation of authority as a system of order is that, on the symbolic level, order comes to be defined as a retreat from the lack of control perceived in infancy. The extent to which this defensive retreat is effective at mitigating the unconscious terror of living in a world of difference, especially a world of sexual difference, will vary for different individuals in different cultural contexts; yet the importance of sexual difference should not be underestimated.

2. By calling this orientation "masculine," I do not want to imply the reason is that men necessarily embody this experience—they may or may not, depending on personal and cultural histories. Rather, I want to point to the meaning and signification of this kind of experience. Its connection, historically, in Western political discourse to maleness has developed because the structure of society has facilitated this kind of identity formation as normatively male.

3. Gilligan, *In a Different Voice* (1982). For an assessment of Gilligan's work, see the Kerber, Greeno, Maccoby, Luria, Stack, and Gilligan articles in "On *In A Different Voice:* An Interdisciplinary Forum." See also Bookman and Morgan, "Introduction," in Bookman and Morgan; and Sapiro (1987).

5

The Authoritativeness of Women's Experiences: The Politics of Interpretation

As women, we have been taught to either ignore our differences or to view them as causes for separation and suspicion rather than as forces for change. Without community, there is no liberation, only the most vulnerable and temporary armistice between an individual and her oppressor. But community must not mean a shedding of our differences, nor the pathetic pretense that they do not exist. (Lourde 1984, 112)

SCENE 1

You are seated in an audience at a conference on Reassessing Colonialism in Africa. The panel is called "Diasporic Linkages in African-American and African Caribbean Cultures." The first speaker, a well-known Caribbean novelist, has ended her presentation with several provocative questions: Does Africa exist? Shouldn't we be getting beyond the Black versus White opposition to begin real dialogue on our lives together? The following speaker, a young African-American woman, a graduate student, presents her analysis of the significance of Afrocentric myths in Toni Morrison's recent fiction. She talks so long that there is little time left for the last speaker's presentation. Yet the audience turns its attention to the next, and last, speaker, a young white woman, another graduate student, whose paper is entitled "Dashiki Redux." She begins by

186

playing an excerpt from the contemporary rap songs of X, a group of young Black male rappers known for their aggressive lyrics. Her paper is about the contribution of African-American women rappers who, she argues, provide an internal critique of the sexism of rap music: "Just as Black women spoke out in the Sixties about the sexist assumptions of their brothers, so too Black women in rap music today provide an important critical and feminist edge to its cultural critique. . . . This is the *real* political music. Listen." She plays an excerpt from Lady x.

You're nervous. You see what's coming. At the end of her enthusiastic, if somewhat naive, talk, the room is thick with tension. The first hand raised with a question is a Black woman's. She's angry: "Who do you think you are, telling us about what our music means! We don't need your interpretations. How do you know about this music anyway! I know because I have teenagers who practice this music in my house all the time. Your presentation is just another example of colonialism." And you're in the middle of a particularly acerbic exchange about whether one's color determines one's ability to speak at all and about what: if you're not me/like me, you can't speak for, or even about, me or those like me. I alone have the authority to do that. Your speaking has silenced me for too long.

> You need to learn to become unintrusive, unimportant, patient to the point of tears, while at the same time open to learning any possible lessons. You will have to come to terms with the sense of alienation, of not belonging, of having your world thoroughly disrupted, having it criticized and scrutinized from the point of view of those who have been harmed by it, having important concepts central to it dismissed, being viewed with mistrust. . . . (Lugones and Spelman 1983, 58)

SCENE 2

You're teaching a large class on Women and Politics to an especially diverse group of students, diverse in terms of race and class as well as number of years in the university. You've talked about stereotypes of race, class, and gender and how they structure the American Political System. And how they're used by American capitalism to sell a racist and sexist and classist status quo.

You pass out a copy of an advertisement for the Four Seasons Hotel in Chicago from the *New York Times Sunday Magazine*. It depicts a smiling woman, a woman from a "small Chinese village," the ad says. She works now for the hotel as a maid. She is cheerful, crisply uniformed, and holds two enormous, clean fluffy towels like gifts in her arms. The text reads: "Marlene is the very soul of concern. She cannot sleep well at night unless she is certain that you will." Below "Marlene's" feet the ad continues:

> In the small Chinese village where she was born, a unique love of orderliness was a way of life. So for Marlene, there can be no rest until the rooms in her care are as graciously turned out as those in your own home. From the plush robes she hangs by the bath, to the extra large pillows she lovingly fluffs, guests in Marlene's rooms truly experience the quiet indulgence that is the Four Seasons Hotel Chicago.

You ask the class to respond to this ad. Many have already gasped or snickered in shock. A vigorous discussion ensues, with people who have never spoken before in class offering their analyses. Then, one young Asian-American woman raises her hand.

> My mother is like this woman. She would have felt like Marlene. She would not have been able to sleep unless she knew that everyone else was happy. I understand the point you're trying to make, but in my culture, much as I myself am now critical of it, this image is not derogatory.

You respond by calling attention to who is "owning" the image—the Asian-American population or American capitalism?—but you wonder whether, by using this ad to illustrate a point about the politics of gender images, you have assumed an ethnocentric interpretation of exploitation.

> My mother was apparent to me mostly as a victim of arrogant perception. I was loyal to the arrogant perceiver's construction of her and thus disloyal to her in assuming that she was exhausted by the construction. I was unwilling to be like her and thought that identifying with her, seeing myself in her necessitated that I become like her. I was wrong. I came to realize through travelling to her "world" that she is not foldable and pliable, that she is not exhausted by the mainstream argentinian patriarchal construction of her. I came to realize that there are "worlds" in which she shines as a creative being. (Lugones in Anzaldúa 1990, 402)

TROUBLED BY AUTHORITY

These scenes, real or imagined, reenact the drama of contemporary feminist political theory, but in parodic form. Feminists have challenged the authoritativeness of the great works of the "fathers." "We"[1] have complained that in these canonical works, descriptions of women's experiences often have been either ignored or distorted by the biased frame of the researcher whose objectivist approach to knowledge constructed women's lives in terms of a male-centered perspective. Lacking was what women themselves experienced, expressed in their own terms. Yet as we have set ourselves the task of correcting for this bias by placing women's experiences at the center of our epistemological enterprise, we have continued to insist on the authoritativeness of our own subversive texts. Now the legitimacy of such a claim has been challenged with renewed vigor: postmodernism has undercut the foundation of both authority and the authoritative, and critiques of feminists of color, both those influenced by postmodernism and those not, have deconstructed the category Woman into women so that even the category "women's experiences" seems to have lost its coherence.

The influence of postmodernist perspectives in nearly every subdiscipline of feminist theory has made authority, as concept and practice, central to these debates about recognizing difference, about rendering multiple voices articulate, and about the concept of gender itself as a unifying, but disciplinary, focus for political strategy. Authority has become our totem and taboo: we consider those who claim authority to be powerful and controlling and, simultaneously, we regard them with the deepest suspicion. Shudders go down the feminist spine when someone accuses her of making definitive statements or arrogating to herself the power to speak in declarative sentences about anyone except herself . . . maybe even about herself. Ironically, given the Foucaultian reading of confessions as disciplinary narratives, feminist theory lately seems rife with apologias and mea culpas.

We notice that even the scripts of feminist theory move toward the climax of exploitation and the denouement of liberation. Telling the stories of women's lives was intended to uncover the gendered patterns of oppression and resistance that framed those lives. Now we have warned ourselves about the disciplinary effects of giving authoritative readings of others' lives. Western feminist scholarship, Chandra Mohanty has argued, has analyzed the meaning of sexual difference from a position that privileges "feminist interests as they have been articulated in the United States and Western Europe." The homogenization of women's experiences resulting from ethnocentric definitions of gender "erases all marginal and resistant modes of experience." (Mohanty 1984, 337–38, 352) Can we still employ categories such as "oppression" if we are wary about the bias and abstraction involved in all "emancipatory metanarratives" such as feminism? Can we sustain critiques of patriarchy, of inequality, of subordination without some "master narrative" that plots the story of these "villains" and their "victims"?

"Whose story is to be told? Whose voice is to be heard?" These questions remind us of the political agenda that motivated the turn to "women's experience" as an epistemologically privileged standpoint from which to construct theory: feminists sought new sources and methods in order to discover ways to tell the "true story" of women's reality and to change that reality for the better. When confronted with the criticism, from several quarters at once, that feminist texts can claim to be authoritative interpretations of female experiences only if they ignore some women's voices, or misread them, as in the above scenes, we begin to suspect that our dialogue may have been a series of soliloquies and that we had been mesmerized by our own incantations, not understanding what the words really meant. We are troubled by authority.

The specter of authority haunts debates about who can claim to speak legitimately to or about, and act for, whom. Yet the anti-foundationalism of the post-modern critique appears to undercut the theoretical coherence of authority itself. Consequently feminists are confronted with a paradox: claiming that authority is the practice most necessary for all women—and all "others" who have been marginalized by the dominant discourse—to acquire, while simultaneously deferring the question of writing authoritative texts in favor of a theoretical position supporting a veritable cacophony of self-signifying voices.

This paradox must be confronted directly by considering what feminists have assumed authority to be. I have contended that we remain trapped in and immobilized politically by a peculiar discourse on authority. We have accepted unquestioningly that authority must be understood as a form of social control. This has led to two basic feminist positions: either we have argued that authority must become *accessible* to different women, and to all those currently excluded, so that we can each control our own lives and the texts of those lives; or we have argued that feminists should avoid merely reversing the sexual identity of controller and controllee (which would simply reproduce relations of domination) and should therefore *resist authority* as a tainted, disciplinary practice antithetical to feminist principles. Instead of this either-orism, I urge a reconceptualization of authority itself.

Both the demand to have access to authority and the desire to avoid authority as a practice too corrupt for feminists as "Beautiful Souls" (Elshtain 1987) rest on the same conceptualization of authority: in both cases authority is understood as some kind of legitimate sovereign control exercised by someone over others, as a type of social coordination that occupies a space between coercion and persuasion. In the political sense, as we have seen, authority has been most often understood as what makes people obey; in the interpretive sense, the authoritative has been understood as the discoverable and determinant meaning of events or texts.

Authority and the authoritative act, in this sense, as disciplinary devices. They construct order; they enforce obedience, conformity and acceptance; they silence opposition. Authority constructs rules with which to organize behavior, to master and control it, to fix it in its (proper) place. The authoritative, as an interpretative reading of values and practices, "locate[s] the unruly meanings of a text in a single, coherent intention." (Clifford 1983, 132) Conceptualized in this sense, both authority and the authoritative establish boundaries. What are the consequences of conceptualizing authority as the practice of establishing boundaries?

"The images the concept of boundary invites . . . ," Jennifer Nedelsky has written, "focus the mind on barriers, rules, and separateness, perhaps even oppositional separateness. . . . Boundary imagery teaches . . . that security lies in walls. . . . Boundaries structure relationships, but they do not help us to understand or evaluate those structures, and often the structures are undesirable." (1990, 175) In this sense appeals to authority close down inquiry into the nature of relationships that authority stabilizes. In a very strong sense, that is precisely what traditional notions of authority are intended to do: suspend the process of judgment and decision making as an ongoing, conflicted, collective process and locate it in one ultimate, sovereign point.

The fascination with the idea of authority as sovereignty has a long tradition in political theory, yet the conceptualization of authority in this way has spilled over into most humanistic discourses and social practices, including into feminist theory. In modern political theory, from about the sixteenth century the idea of absolute sovereignty began to be modified by arguments that the sovereign was him/

herself subject to the law (which became the site of sovereignty) and was established as sovereign through the social contract. Despite the rise of republican forms of authority, and the decline of patriarchal models for authority, authority remained connected to sovereignty and sovereignty remained a gendered practice.

As we saw in Hobbes, social contract theorists weakened the basis for supporting patriarchy on the grounds of biological or natural arguments. Yet the ironic result of their construction of consensually founded patriarchy was the identification of authority more completely with masculinity itself. As Carole Pateman has argued, the structure of modern patriarchy became largely conjugal, a "part of masculine sex-right, the power that men exercise as men, not as fathers." (Pateman 1988, 22; cf. Landes 1988) Because authority, as sovereignty, became and remained associated more completely with masculinity, contemporary feminist efforts to include diverse women as "authorizers" of the readings of the "texts" of their lives have confronted their limits in the dominant conceptualization of authority itself.

If the incorporation of different women as authorities increases the *number* of possible rulers (as implied by Fraser's "democratization of access") but otherwise leaves undisturbed the practice of authority itself, then how is feminism different from a form of liberal individualism that so many feminists have argued is inadequate to feminism's radical vision of what constitutes a more fully democratic life? The ontology of liberal individualism treats the autonomous subject as a self-possessed, self-sufficient sovereign, at least within the state-erected walls of personal freedom it constructs via private rights. Perhaps the feminist demand for women's inclusion really amounts to nothing more than an effort to vindicate women as sovereigns, regardless of whether women's practice of sovereignty would be different in design and effect from men's.

My contention is that feminists have been unaware of this continued connection between authority as sovereignty and masculinity.[2] Consequently, our struggles over who should practice authority in feminism are locked in debates about "redistribut[ing] and democratiz[ing] access to and control over the means of interpretation and communication." (Fraser in Cornell and Benabib 1987, 53) Yet we cannot continue to struggle for "collective control over the *means* of interpretation and communication" without also working to transform radically the *mode* of interpretation and communication, that is, the *mode of authority* itself. Only if we engage directly in this transformative practice will we be able to move beyond the politically stultifying arguments about whose voice is controlling, whose voice is authoritative, whose voice is sovereign, whose voice must be heard. Feminist theory must disturb this practice of authority, dislodge its grip on our current understandings of authority through a different staging of the authorial project. This means breaking with the search for sovereign control over representations of women's experiences. It means risking misreadings and engaging in the dangerous practice of "hav[ing] *public* conversations with each other." (Brown 1991, 80)

FEMINIST EPISTEMOLOGY AND THE SOVEREIGNTY OF EXPERIENCE

Feminist efforts to establish women as sovereign rulers over the representation of our own lives derive from feminist criticism of mainstream social and political analysis that is now several decades old. In political theory, feminist theory has been disturbing the canon of Western discourse and decentering its readings of politics. The predominant understanding of politics, feminists have argued, has been "constructed according to specific notions, practices, and institutions of masculinity." (Brown 1990, 12) In place of sets framing the agonistic struggles of a few militaristic heroes or the machinations of infamous political men, feminists have crafted spectacles of ordinary women and men's everyday struggles to survive. We have tried to provide "words, emotions, and an imaginative structure for others to inhabit and create anew onstage." (Wandor 1986, 128) And we have broadened the proscenium of the stage of politics so that the activities of reproduction and the maintenance of life—activities historically and symbolically, though not essentially, connected to women's lives—can become as visible as those activities of production and heroism—activities historically and symbolically, though not essentially, connected to men's lives—which traditionally have been represented in public life.

Feminists have insisted that these words, emotions, and imaginative structures should come from different women's experiences of the political instead of on the basis of mythical constructions of those experiences legion in mainstream political studies. Feminist standpoint epistemologies and its variations have rested on the claim that knowledge about women and politics must be constructed from women's "actual" experiences in women's "own" words and spoken in women's "own" voices because other's (men's) words about women have silenced women or have put words into our mouths. These theorists have claimed, in sum, that women must become "authors of their own lives," telling personal stories of political reality in their own authentic voices without translation into the dominant vocabulary or syntax of what has been called "masculinity." Some have criticized translation as a form of interpretation, since all interpretations are necessarily disciplinary. "The very act of interpretation requires us to choose among the multiple identities and associations shaping a life." (Personal Narratives Group 1989, 19) In place of the ebb and flow of a life's "natural" language and meaning, interpretation forces life's being-lived into straight-jacketing categories. In order to facilitate comparisons, to enable generalizations, interpretation kills life and presents it—"nature morte"—as a mummified artifact locked in the museum of academic knowledge.

Feminists have insisted that authentic knowledge must be grounded in women's experiences; only descriptions rooted in these experiences can claim to provide authoritative readings of women's lives. "Women's experiences" has been invoked as a category that carries epistemic weight in feminist theory. Feminist standpoint theorists, in particular, contend that knowledge is grounded in experience. Hence for standpoint theorists such as Nancy Hartsock, Dorothy Smith, Patricia Collins, and Hilary Rose, "the experiences arising from the activities assigned to women . . . provide a starting point for developing potentially *more complete and less distorted knowledge claims* than do men's experiences." (Harding in Nicholson 1990, 95, emphasis added) Standpoint theorists' efforts have been directed at uncovering, or discovering, knowledge of social reality "from the perspective of women's realities." (Harding in Nicholson 1990, 96) At the same time, standpoint theorists have argued that there is incongruence between women's experiences and the dominant conceptual schemes of most disciplines. Hence their analyses point to a conceptual transformation that would follow from the reconstruction of the social world from the perspectives of different women's (and different men's) experiences.

The invocation of "women's experiences" by feminist critics of the social sciences in the 1970s—a period that was marked by a significant increase in feminist works—was intended to counter the ignorance of women's experiences evidenced by the picture of social, political, economic, and psychological reality painted by mainstream ("malestream") texts. Mainstream analyses tended to assume that women were absent from culture, since they associated women's activities with "natural" or "instinctual" behavior. Yet leaving women's experiences out of the picture came to mean more than simply ignoring historical cases of those women who had in fact participated in culture building as traditionally defined; it became identified with ignoring or derogating "everyday life experiences."

The major impetus behind this version of feminist research has been the search for ways "to correct the partial and distorted accounts [of women, men, and social life] in the traditional analyses." (Harding in Harding 1987, 1) In the early stages of the efforts to correct for sexism in the traditional disciplines, the often unarticulated assumption was made that once what had been excluded, ignored, or distorted was included in the construction of theory, we would reach the plane of objectivity. We would have, in other words, a complete, reliable, unbiased, and accurate, or "real," picture of social reality when women's experiences were included. In this view feminist inquiry would mark a transitional moment in the progress toward better, more authoritative, more truthful science. As Harding has put it in describing these epistemologies' implicit aim, "if women's authority in matters of knowledge were already recognized, that would be because we no longer needed a distinctively feminist social science." (Harding 1987, 187)

The exclusion of women's experiences has been understood to have a profoundly distorting effect on the conceptual paradigms dominant in traditional social and political analysis. For instance, Nancy Hartsock has noted how the centrality of masculine activities structured Western discourse about politics and power.

> The Greek understanding of politics and power rested more directly than ours on the division between men and women, between the household, a private, apolitical space, and the *polis,* a public and political space. ... The result was a theorization of politics and political power that occurred in a masculine arena characterized by freedom from necessary labor, dominance of intellect or soul, and equality among participants, in which political power rested on heroic action defined by courage in war and courage in speech, a world defined exclusively in masculine terms. It rested on, depended on, but at the same time opposed another world ... a world of women.... (Hartsock 1983, 187; cf. Jones in Jones and Jónasdóttir)

In the field of sociology, Dorothy Smith wrote that "the exclusion of women from the 'real' or 'important' world of sociological investigation [arose] because of the more general belief that what women do is trivial and not worthy of scientific enterprise." (cited in Daniels, in Millman and Kanter 1975, 346) And Marilyn Waring has argued that "if women counted," the entire framework for measuring economic value and the national accounting systems derived from these measurements would be altered radically. (Waring 1988)

Feminist social and political theorists have argued for reintegrating women's experiences into the basic paradigms of inquiry. "When we begin our inquiries with women's experiences instead of men's, we quickly encounter phenomena (such as emotional labor or the positive aspects of 'relational' personality structures) that were made invisible by the concepts and categories of these theories," Harding has written. (1986, 646) These theorists have, in effect, called for a broadened epistemological framework to incorporate research on those arenas of social and political action frequently overlooked because formal/institutional structures, or "official" actors and actions, have been privileged as singularly legitimate sources of social and political knowledge. Housework, sexuality, reproduction, personal life, and community networks became some of the important arenas for feminist investigation. Feminists "aimed to broaden analyses by including the *widest possible range of meaningful experience* not all of which . . . is routinely experienced by men." (Levesque-Lopman 1988, 56, emphasis added.) The result would be the transformation of the basic concepts that structure inquiry.

For example in political analysis, a central topic has been the investigation of the characteristics of political action and the study of what motivates citizens to participate in politics. A feminist politicization of "the body" and of everyday, personal reality has increased the range, intensity, and modes of political action which the field of political research needs to explore. Shifting from an exclusive focus on political action framed by governmental institutions to the concept of action as "empowerment . . . connote[s] a spectrum of political activity ranging from acts of individual resistance to mass political mobilizations that challenge the basic power relations in our society." (Bookman and Morgan in Bookman and Morgan 1988, 4) Understanding political action as the process of the empowerment of embodied actors changes the ways that citizenship itself is conceptualized and practiced. (Jones 1990) In place of a theory of citizenship as the rational action of disembodied actors pursuing their private interests through formal interactions with the state, citizenship can be conceptualized as a full-bodied activity in which people are engaged on the level of the concrete, the ordinary, and the everyday as well as through more formal channels such as voting and political parties.

Feminists have contended that this method of analysis can be extended to include other fundamental political concepts such as power, authority, and freedom. What we mean by these "essentially contested concepts" would be transformed if understood from the perspective of different women's experiences. This is because, feminists have argued, different concepts of power, authority, and freedom arise from women's experiences of them, just as a different conceptualization of work arose from women's experiences of housework.

There are interdependent political and epistemological reasons why appeals to experience have had such compelling force in feminist theory. A careful examination of these reasons will enable us to consider, however, some of the less routinely scrutinized political and epistemological quagmires produced by the strategy of invoking experience as the source of knowledge that can best serve feminist purposes. This strategy produces the kinds of scrambling for territorial sovereignty that occurs in feminist theory today, especially in the United States, precisely because it engages with power without admitting that such engagement is what it is all about. It transforms the production of knowledge into the weaving of morality plays that necessarily make us uneasy because we each (secretly) want our own tale to have center stage and to be "authenticated" as the "real thing" by a review in the *New York Times*.

Wendy Brown has explained the "palpable feminist panic" produced by postmodernism's "deconstruction of the subject," and along with it her "experiences," as the result of standpoint epistemologies operating (unintentionally) as *"moral* claims against domination." (1991, 75) She makes a strong case that postmodernism does not erase "the constitutive elements of politics." I agree that it remains possible to "live and work politically without [the] myths" that women's experiences contain hidden truths. Yet I remain less convinced than she that we do not continue to "need" some signposts along the road in order to "map out" the direction feminist political interventions will make, a process which Brown calls for in her essay.

Mapping out the space and direction for collective action will require elaborating the criteria that we will at least provisionally deploy in making the kinds of judgments that we will "need" to make for constructing "democratic political *spaces.*" (1991, 79) Stephen White identifies such criteria with recognition of twin responsibilities—the responsibility to otherness and the responsibility to act. As ethical-political criteria, these responsibilities lead one to favor a commitment to "fostering" diversity, not just "tolerating" it, and to "at least some minimal criteria of normative constraint on what gets fostered." (1991, 127)

If postmodernism should help make us less panicked about politics, it can only do this if it enables us to be unafraid to say that we continue to have "needs." As I argued in the introduction, "feminist vertigo"—reeling from the effects of a depoliticized postmodernism that dances like some whirling dervish in the academy—also requires diagnosis and treatment. Wendy Brown's specifically engaged political reading and political call to "argu[e] from a vision of the common ('what I want for us') rather than from identity ('who I am')" (1991, 80) and Stephen White's defense of articulating minimal constraints on what gets fostered are welcome antidotes to depoliticized postmodernism.

The idea that "experience" is the pure and primordial, prereflective state of being-in-the-world out of which knowledge arises, resulted from feminist efforts to acknowledge and to reconstruct the power relations of knowledge production. It was assumed that by grounding knowledge in women's experiences and privileging women's voices, the hegemony of dominant and dominating readings of women's lives would be broken. Besides broadening the range and scope of experiences considered relevant to social and political inquiry, the feminist strategy of "returning to women themselves" was a political strategy, one that aimed to subvert the claim that the researcher was the uniquely qualified expert, and authoritative reader of experience whose readings were legitimated by their distance from subjects' immediate rendering of their lives. Instead, a standard feminist tenet became the assertion that *the meaning of any experience was best expressed by the subjects themselves, in their own terms.*

Conventionally objectivistic approaches to knowledge were claimed to be approaches antithetical to feminist politics because they tended to negate the ability of subjects, as the powerless "others" being investigated, to be active agents of knowledge. Feminists argued that a more adequate representation of diverse points of view and different voices required a research strategy that permitted "others" to speak for themselves and treated what they said about their lives with the utmost seriousness and respect. By treating what subjects said about their lives as truthful and authoritative, and by structuring the research process as an egalitarian, collaborative event, it was assumed that the power relations of the research process could be transformed. Feminists sought to replace research designs established exclusively in terms of the exigencies, both ideological and professional, of the researcher herself. Feminist research turned away from approaches that privileged the voice-over narrations of investigators toward those that allegedly permitted subjects greater control over research, in terms of its directions, its tactics, and its political intent.

Methodologically, feminists urged women to use their "doubled-consciousness," as women and as researchers, as the avenue to a more direct presentation and more accurate understanding of subjects' lives. "Subjectivistic" or experientially based knowledge was supposed to derive, ultimately, from the "existence of the inner resources for knowing and valuing" that a woman became aware of "as she beg[an] to listen to the voice within her" and "f[ound] an inner source of strength." (Belenky et al. 1986, 54; cf. Mies in Bowles and Klein 1983; Lather 1988) Trusting these inner voices would ostensibly enable feminist researchers to hear subjects' descriptions of their experiences in the subjects' own language rather than translating these descriptions into the language of the dominant discourse—the language in which most feminists' education as professional "experts" had trained them. (Morsy in Altorki and Fawzi 1988)

For example, Joyce Ladner spoke about how her training as a sociologist had prepared her to view the experiences of Blacks from within the perspective of "deviance theory," a perspective that encouraged her to see Blacks as maladaptive and pathology ridden. However, Ladner came to see the years of socialization within her own family and the broader Black community not only as the basis for her own survival in a racist society, but also as the source for a better understanding of Black experiences from a Black perspective:

I *am* sure that the twenty years I spent being socialized by my family and the broader Black community prior to my entering graduate school shaped my perception of life, defined my emotive responses and enhanced my ability to survive in a society that has not made survival for Blacks easy. Therefore, when I decided to engage in research on what approaching womanhood meant to poor Black girls in the city, I brought with me these attitudes, values and beliefs and, in effect, a Black perspective. Because of this cultural sensitivity I had to the life-styles of the over one hundred adolescent, preadolescent and adult females I "studied," I had to mediate tensions that existed day to day between the *reality* and *validity* of their lives *and* the tendency to view it from a *deviant perspective* in accordance with my academic training. (Ladner in Harding 1986, 75)

Altering the research process toward "subject-centered" knowledge also has altered the structure of narratives that feminists have written about people's lives. Feminists have repudiated claims to authorial majesty and have rejected the imperiousness of employing certain classical narrative strategies for describing women's lives. Along with Jean-François Lyotard, some have been engaged in a "war against totality." (1984, 82) Instead of statements with the air of universality about them, some feminists have opted in favor of fragmented, partial, self-reflexive insights that contribute to a "social criticism that is ad hoc, contextual, plural, and limited." (Hartsock 1987, 190)

Following Foucault's annunciation of the death of the author, they have urged the decentering of the researcher's position in the research process. Primary creative responsibility for the production of feminist texts and their meanings should not lie with an "auteur." Instead the call has been for reflexivity in the procedures of inquiry; that is, feminists have contended that the beliefs and behaviors of the researcher should be scrutinized insofar as they contribute to the findings themselves. "Thus the researcher appears not as an *invisible, anonymous voice of authority,* but as a real historical individual with concrete, specific desires and interests." (Harding, 1987, 9, emphasis added) Such reflexivity was promised to facilitate the purging of the researcher's own biases in order to facilitate the production of untainted results. Finally, feminists have urged greater collaboration between the "interpreter" and "narrator" of a life.

> Whose story is to be told? Whose voice is to be heard? . . . None of the authors represented here is comfortable with the traditional scholar's assumption of *the voice of authority* in the creation or interpretation of life stories. They ask instead to consider the implications of a shared ownership and control over various kinds of personal narrative texts. (Personal Narratives Group 1989, 201, emphasis added)

These politically motivated methodological principles proposed changing the hierarchial structure of the research process towards a more egalitarian one that: (1) stressed the "view from below," or in other words, that made the needs and interests of the subjects themselves the starting point of research; (2) rooted science in "living social processes" whose dynamics and meaning are described by the subjects themselves (Mies in Bowles and Klein 1983, 123, 126); and

(3) encouraged empathy, connection, and commitment, or the self-conscious articulation of one's likeness to one's subjects as an avenue to less distorted, less biased analyses. Such principles became canonized as *the* fundamentals of doing feminist research.

Despite the fit between the political intent of feminist research—to empower women as active agents of knowledge production—and these feminist methods, which made experience and women's voices the sovereign locus of truth, what has not adequately been explained is how any alternative conceptual framework for studying politics is necessarily related to the experiences out of which it allegedly "arises." Instead, it has been assumed that experiences produce concepts in some unmediated, self-generating way. We have assumed that the "language" of experience is transparent, nonideological, and that there exist unobtrusive measures to record naked experience and get at the truth.

We need to acknowledge that so-called "unobtrusive measures," such as taped or videotaped interviews, can never fully displace the researcher from the center of the research process or settle the question of interpretation. This is the illusion of transparency, which forgets that the researcher can only be taping a part of a life and that the words spoken are transformed, translated by the process of recording itself. (Derrida 1985) Taping requires a kind of dismemberment of the researcher; there is an investigatory and inquiring hand, a gazing eye, and an eavesdropping ear behind the camera and the recorder. Voyeurism is implicit and unavoidable in the process; looking and listening, even (especially) careful looking and listening, are always intrusions, interventions. No matter how foregrounding of process feminist research aims to be, the framing of these scenes by the researcher, even in collaboration with the subjects, is *always* a framing. The foregrounding of process in a "filmic" approach to feminist research unavoidably calls attention to the fact that the gaze of the researcher/editor is never innocent. What it records has been captured, no matter how much the subjects have collaborated in their own transformation into objects.

Judith Stacey has written that "the research product is ultimately that of the researcher, however modified or influenced by informants." (1988, 23) To the extent that the research process sutures the reader/researcher into the text/life history, by encouraging empathic identification with the subjects, these research methods may be more dangerous than so-called positivistic, distancing methods. Power is displaced, by markers of pseudo-identification and the posture of egalitarianism. Yet, as Stacey argues, the intimacy of the research relationship masks the fact that this particular relationship is situated within a broader "system of relationships that the researcher is much freer than the researcher to leave." (1988, 23)

If the power relations of feminist research settings have been inadequately theorized, neither have we confronted fully the dilemma of how to reconcile a democratic research process with claiming "authenticity" for its findings. Since the idea of authenticity carries within it the implication of norms and standards with which to distinguish between the authentic and the inauthentic, the real and the counterfeit, the genuine and the fake, the question of how to establish those criteria democratically must be considered. The search for "authenticity" in feminist research by means of taking women's words seriously *because* they are the words of women is a highly problematic strategy in the struggle for democracy. Its ramifications extend far beyond the field of feminist research and into the courtrooms of the modern state. We know that women have not been listened to or taken seriously or have been misunderstood, but does this mean that we should always accept women's words as the unmediated source of "truth?"

So far the search for authenticity has been linked to the struggle for sovereignty. Women's words should displace the master's discourse as the sovereign source of the meaning of women's lives. By privileging women's experiences as the unproblematic foundation of authoritative readings of women's lives, we do not automatically challenge the masterfulness of a discourse. Rather, we substitute one sovereign regime of truth for another. We become embroiled in the Anita Hill-Clarence Thomas competition for control over "the truth," a contest that, ironically, deflected attention away from the *politics* of sexual harassment and onto the deeply depoliticized question of who was believable.

THE TRANSPARENCY OF EXPERIENCE?

The recommendation that we "take our directly and spontaneously experienced everyday life as a point of departure" (Levesque-Lopman 1988, 91–92) depends upon the assumption that the meaning of any experience is somehow already present, already constituted and internal to that experience in advance of the articulation of it through language. The assumption seems to be that experience needs only to be "tapped" or "taped" (listened to) in order for it to yield up its secrets (meanings) to its owners (those who "have" it). The researcher needs merely to be there, conveniently, to record (or video-tape) the stories.

Yet ironically, some of the earliest feminist texts about methodol-ogy worked from the opposite premise: that women have not always spoken in their own interests. Instead, having internalized the mas-ter's voice—the mark of oppression—women have been prevented from even being able to articulate their own needs, desires or inter-ests. In these early works, feminists employed the rhetoric of "false consciousness" to describe some women's readings of their own expe-riences. (Mies 1983, 125) Moreover, they characterized the feminist research process itself as a kind of consciousness-raising method that would create the revolutionary context of discovery within which researcher and subject could together uncover the (hidden, alienated) truth of women's oppression, an oppression which ran so deep that many women lacked the vocabulary to name it as such.

This strategy has now been all but jettisoned as we flirt with the postmodernist approach to texts which, eschewing canons as disciplinary, seems to treat all readings as equally valid. (Whether this is an accurate interpretation of postmodernism or a misinterpre-tation will be considered below). We are supposed to resist speaking for others and to avoid expressions of absolute certainty or finality. Rejecting concepts of the truth as a fixed point means deferring to the heteronymity of the meaning of the "same" experience to different women. Impressed by the political appeal of this position, which appears to authorize every one to say anything about herself, to "speak in her own voice," and which seems simultaneously to legiti-mate her studied resistance to counterinterpretations as always he-gemonic and imperializing—a resistance that, ironically, masks its own "will to power" (Brown 1991, 76)—some versions of standpoint theory are now cloaked in postmodernist discourse.

> From the outset, feminist theory has been skeptical of the claim of objectivity. Other critical traditions operating in and on the edges of the academic disciplines share this skepticism. But beyond this, inherent in feminist claims and feminist political strategy, is a positive valuation of the *subjective*. The truths that women's voices express are not regarded as merely subjective, that is, as pertinent only to a single individual; feminists also reject the Truth of the "objective" fact based on the claim that it issues from a standpoint outside individual experience. (*Personal Narratives Group* 1989, 263)

The "Truth" of the " 'objective' fact" may have been rejected, but in its place has moved the unexamined Truth of the subjective, now even more unimpeachably a "fact" than the objective fact precisely because it lies fenced in—inside "individual experience."

Privileging the subjective basis of all knowledge—claiming that authentic knowledge is knowledge *rooted in* experiences that one defines for oneself—inverts the claim that Truth issues from a standpoint outside experience and establishes the claim that Truth issues only from a standpoint inside experience: "If, in fact, feminists hope to dislodge our externally-oriented assumptions about our consciousness in acknowledgement of new conceptions of truth as personal, private, and subjectively known, we need to actively seek *knowledge about all female experiences from the view of the subjective knower.*" (Levesque-Lopman 1988, 98, emphasis added)

Several interrelated theses have served as the foundation for the claim that authoritative readings of women's lives were those that described and explained the meaning of experience from the perspective of, and in the language of, the subjects themselves. Each of these assumptions participates unwittingly in the discourse of sovereignty as the exercise of masterful control. Insofar as experience is cited as the locus of truth *ab origino,* the effort is to establish experience, and the actor's understanding of it, in place of any other source of knowledge. The assertion of "in place of" is a sovereign assertion.

First, feminists have defined *experience* as the unconditional foundation, as the *primordial source or site of truth and meaning.* Those who "have" experiences become the "experts, the authorities, and the sources of knowledge about ourselves. . . . [A] woman knows something to be true because she has lived through it and *has her own feelings and reactions,* not merely the feelings and reactions that she is supposed to have, that she herself expects to have." (Levesque-Lopman 1988, 58, emphasis added) In this case self-defined experience becomes an unadulterated resource. Having escaped the constraints of socially constructed expectations, experience is the residual, albeit potential, source of resistant knowledge. Experience provides the raw material for noncanonical readings of lives: "her own feelings" versus "those she is supposed to have" or those "she herself expects to have." More accurately, experience here provides the basis for other canonical readings of lives: her own feelings *in place of* those she is supposed to have.

Second, feminists have argued that *experience directly produces meanings that are directly accessible to those who have them and should be controlled directly by those who have them.* Ironically, instead of arguing that subjects actively produce meanings, this feminist position seems to be arguing that experiences produce subjects. Subjects have experiences; having experiences produces one's identity as a subject. Thus, it may be more accurate to say that experiences have, beget, subjects. Subjective experience comes to be represented as something one has. It becomes one's private property; it is possessed or owned. Because it is the property of subjects, it should not be forced to disclose its truths without permission. Interpretation, other than self-interpretation, is theft.

The process of consciousness-raising, a process that permits us to "begin to *believe* what our bodies and feelings have been telling us," (Levesque-Lopman 1988, 59, emphasis added; cf. MacKinnon 1982) elicits pure experiential feelings. As a process of collective validation of what could otherwise be seen as bizarre or idiosyncratic, consciousness-raising permits the legitimation of one's own interpretation of experience in the context of the "collective critical reconstitution of the meaning of women's social experience, as women live through it." (MacKinnon 1982, 543) Consciousness-raising often has been represented as a process of authenticating women's self-interpretive strategies. Yet since "women have different life experiences (and experience life differently)," giving rise to "different interpretations that are equally valid for those experiences," (Levesque-Lopman 1988, 59) the problem emerges within consciousness-raising of whether and how to reconcile these competing claims to authoritative interpretation. Moreover, the demand to submit one's experiences to the process of collective validation through consciousness-raising risks the very disciplinary effects that the feminist invocation of experience as possession was intended to preclude.

Third, the language and conceptual framework in the social sciences to which many feminists object are said to mask, that is, to obfuscate or to distort, the reality of subjects' lives as the subjects themselves understand their experience. In contrast, feminists defend a language and a conceptual framework "grounded in the actual experience and language of women." (Levesque-Lopman 1988, 59) Standpoint theorists have drawn contrasts between the definitions of self constructed by narrators in their personal life histories and those "imposed by interpreters of personal narratives and by the narrators' own society." (Personal Narratives Group 1989, 12) Since they have argued that there is a "disjunction between how women experience the world and the concepts and schemes available to think about it"—a disjunction represented by the contrast between "abstract" categories and those constructed from women's concrete, everyday life experiences (Levesque-Lopman 1988, 61, 66)—they have made an effort to articulate paradigms in a *language that is effectively unmediated, transparent.* Listening to women's voices, believing what our bodies and feelings tell us, are construed as methods that permit experience to speak its meanings directly. Such rhetorical strategies, admittedly not always defined as such, are designed to develop ways to express meanings "as is." (Jayaratne 1983, 144)

These three theses about experience—as primordial site of meaning, as directly productive of meaning, and as something expressible in a transparent language by the subjects themselves—are not insights that feminists invented out of whole cloth. A tradition of thinking about how to explain action anteceded feminist incursions into this discourse. The work of Edmund Husserl, Martin Heidegger, Alfred Schutz, and other phenomenologists; that of Peter Winch and a number of anthropologists such as James Clifford, Paul Rabinow, and Clifford Geertz; and even the writing of Max Weber have employed subject-centered modes of interpretation.

Each of these theorists, in different ways, rejected the possibility of scientific or causal, models for explaining human action. They insisted, instead, that since the expression of action is one of "freedom, choice and responsibility, meaning and sense, conventions, norms and rules . . . the explanation of actions must necessarily be in terms of the actors' intentions, motives, reasons, purposes—never in scientific, causal terms." (Pitkin 1972, 242) The relationship between concepts and the actions they are meant to define is different in the natural sciences and in the "human sciences." Although, as Winch noted, the natural sciences employ concepts to explain the world of phenomena that they observe, that world is assumed to have

> an existence independent of those concepts. There existed electrical storms and thunder long before there were human beings to form concepts of them. . . . But it does not make sense to suppose that human beings might have been issuing commands and obeying them before they came to form the concept of command and obedience. For their performance of those acts is the chief manifestation of their possession of those concepts. (cited in Pitkin 1972, p. 244)

One could, of course, argue that although some phenomena that we now call "thunderstorms" existed before the concept "thunderstorm," their existence *as* thunderstorms required human conceptualization.

If performance is the key to understanding, and if only those concepts expressed in terms formulated by or at least intelligible to the actors themselves are relevant, then it is easy to see why feminists would be attracted to arguments which claim that what counts as evidence and what constitutes authoritative readings of reality are those accounts cast in terms of concepts defined by the performers, the subjects, themselves, and from within the action-context being investigated. For a long time, feminists have seen social science as a form of sexist imperialism, as the academic arm of a political process that controls women by imposing men's meanings on women's reality, where those meanings had been derived from (some) men's interests in dominating (some) women. If, as feminists have contended, "the position of women has been overlooked, underrated, and historically distorted" (Levesque-Lopman 1988, 52) in mainstream social science, then any perspective that inverted this process of delegitimation and promised a subject-centered (woman-centered) perspective would be welcomed for its epistemological iconoclasm. And if the context of action must be accessible and knowable in order for an observer to interpret the meaning of actions accurately, then the related postulate that knowers (observers) who are relevantly "like" the "knowable" (performers) would best be able to understand action leads to an additional feminist axiom: that women can best understand other women because they have access to women's experiences. In place of detached observation,

> feminist critique challenges the Weberian definition of rationality for its inability to account for the emotional and psychological complexity of social life. It also suggests that the concept, *verstehen,* is deficient because in a sexist society one must ask who is doing the interpreting. When women are interpreting women, the possibility exists that those concepts will take on new meaning. (Levesque-Lopman 1988, 75)

So feminists should privilege women's experience as the unmediated, direct source of transparent meanings and grant the status of the authoritative to those knowers/performers (women) whose readings are most true because they are most likely to have shared the experience (performed the same actions). This is an attractive position that politically empowers those who have been marginalized by the dominant discourse. It treats women not only as worthy subjects of inquiry but as knowledgeable inquirers. But does it redefine the authoritative in less exclusionary ways? I would argue that it does not. Rather, it substitutes one, frequently limited, set of authoritative readings for another. In place of previously dominant (mis-)readings of women's lives, it substitutes subject-centered (mis-) readings as controlling. It falls again into the sovereignty trap: the search for privileged perspectives *at the expense of others*.

Moreover, by making the social scientist "passively responsive to whatever is in the mind of the observed subjects rather than an active seeker after independent, objective social reality" (Pitkin 1972, 283), it defers inquiry into the nature of the criteria that anyone uses to interpret experience. Instead, it reduces judgments about reality to their face value—to *beliefs* about reality. Ironically, by considering the criteria that anyone uses to judge an experience as exclusively self-legitimating, it reduces those criteria to mere beliefs and dissolves judgment into acceptance or acquiescence. In an effort to privilege those whose views previously have been ignored or distorted, it disconnects the formation of those views and the language expressing them from the historical and social context which shapes them. Wiping out history, politics, and the viewpoints of others, we are left with the sovereign subject as an original and imperious author in the immediate present.

Having implicitly repudiated the existence of an unconscious, since the unconscious represents a seething cauldron of desire which can drive a subject to act in ways unintended, we are left with a grandiose, narcissistic, autonomous subject, clinging to her experiences like a miser to her hoarded treasure. To this anti-social, self-regenerating, self-possessed grandiose ego with full consciousness is added a strongly anti-rational and anti-aesthetic sensibility. It is anti-rational because it privileges a (fantasized) immediacy over critical reflection. It is anti-aesthetic because it forbids the use of the imagination, of fictive and other narrative strategies, as another kind of performative discourse that might enable one who does not (can never) possess another's life (perform another's actions) to take up multiple subject positions, to empathize with another, to travel to another's worlds and feel and understand her joys and pain. At the same time, it opens itself up to the oft-repeated attack that its own "readings," being partial, are no better renderings of the experiences that they (re)present than the dominant ones.

CONCEPTS AND CONTEXTS OF INTERPRETATION

In relation to human action, concepts might be argued to express the very shape of action; there is no independent existence of human action—as this particular sort of action—outside its conceptual framework. Thus it would be difficult to argue that someone was obeying a command unless the concept of "command" was available to the actor in advance of the action. And yet the idea that the meaning of human action depends upon the relevant conceptual framework and social context invoked to describe and explain action creates the very problems that subject-centered explanations were meant to surmount. Even if we recur to actor-centered explanations and to conceptual schemata drawn from within the culture observed, instead of imposed from without, in order to understand action, to discover what actions mean from the inside, how do we address the fact that language, even the subjects' "own" language, preexists the user? "Any field of human endeavor that involves language will present the observer with a pre-articulated interpretation of what is being done, an articulation in terms of which the endeavor is being carried out." (Pitkin 1972, 244)

One solution to the problem of the preexistence of language is to insist on the historicity of language. Language, it is argued, is not fixed; it is fluid. Although the horizon of the social life-world, always already constituted, frames any action, the actor's negotiation of this world provides a way to understand that the meaning of any act may exceed what the concept currently in use to define it permits us to see. If action is conventional, intentional, and purposive, then its "meaning" must be related to those conventions and reasons *as the actors themselves understand them*. In Alfred Schutz's terms, "strictly speaking, the actor and he [sic] alone knows what he does, why he does it, and when and whence his action starts and ends." (cited in Pitkin 1972, 245) Action is not a mere response to a situation, but a purposive negotiation of it. Related to this—although, as Pitkin argues, fundamentally distinct from it—is the Wittgensteinian insight that "meaning and sense depend on context, are incomplete without it." (Pitkin 1972, 93)

The idea of action as purposive negotiation returns us to the performer-centered modes of knowing the meaning of any action in terms of how the subjects see them, or *intend* us to see them. It returns us to the (alleged) sovereignty of the authoritative pronouncements of the speaking subject as a "sovereign self, a center of absolute plenitude and power" (Butler, *Gender Trouble,* 117) whose actions are always more full of meaning than those expressible within the terms of a dominant discourse. But if the subject's/performer's actions are more full of meaning than the dominant discourse permits us to recognize, it is important to acknowledge that they may be more full of meaning than the actor can recognize or control. Certainly the concept of the unconscious suggests that we may not always be fully aware of our desires and motives for behaving in the particular way that we do. And since action always takes place within a context that preexists the actor, a context that can be negotiated but never wished away, then it is possible to imagine action having effects beyond the conscious motives of the actor. When we recognize the effects of language, we do not give up the ability to speak about our experiences. Instead we acknowledge that in speaking about them, as Wendy Brown put it, "our words cannot be legitimately deployed or construed as larger or longer than the moments of the lives they speak from; they cannot be anointed as Authentic or True since the experience that they announce is linguistically contained, socially constructed, discursively mediated, and never just individually 'had.' " (1991, 72)

Even when the performer intentionally acts to subvert the dominant order—that is, self-consciously manipulates a situation so that the excesses of meaning with which it is pregnant can be born— any human endeavor will be represented by the performer, whether intentionally or not, in the terms of an always already existing discourse about what is being done. Even when the performance is a parody of the dominant code, as in the case of transvestism, which is a parodying of the relationship between sex and gender, it can only work as parody insofar as the dominant relationship has not been altogether ruptured. Thus transvestism still depends upon a particular, socially constructed and already articulated meaning of the relationship between sex and gender for the very vocabulary and grammar of its mockery.[2]

Again, as in the previous chapter, Arendt provides an important voice in this controversy. In *The Human Condition,* Arendt wrote that "speech . . . is the actualization of the human condition of plurality, that is, of living as a distinct and unique being among equals." (1958, 178) Living as a "unique being among equals" means that we reveal actively "who" we are by saying and doing specific things. The idea that we "reveal" who we are is not meant here to signal that there is some inner essence that is disclosed, but, rather, that our identity is the socially constructed accomplishment of our speech and action as seen and heard by others who, in fact, have more to do with constituting the "who" that I am than I do. "Disclosure [of one's self]," Arendt wrote, "can almost never be achieved as a willful purpose, as though one possessed and could dispose of this 'who' in the same manner he has and can dispose of his qualities." In fact,

Arendt contended that this "who" "remains hidden from the person himself." (1958, 179) Arendt reverses the implicit assumption made in feminist standpoint epistemologies that the language of experience is transparent and that we are the authors of our own lives.

> Although everybody started his life by inserting himself into the human world through action and speech, nobody is the author or producer of his own life story. In other words, the stories, the results of action and speech, reveal an agent, but this agent is not the author or producer. Somebody began it and is its subject in the twofold sense of the word, its actor and sufferer, but nobody is its author. (1958, 184)

Because our action and speech necessarily engage us with others, they are communicative practices that go on "between" people. And it is this characteristic that gives to political action what Arendt called its "notorious uncertainty." In the "flux and action of speech," which constitutes the "togetherness of men," lies the "frustration" with which action is ridden. But out of this frustration comes the potentiality latent within the human condition: through action and speech "interests," or being together, can be constituted that can "relate and bind [people] together." What results from the action and speech of unique persons, who are also equal, is an "intangible" that Arendt called the " 'web' of human relationships."

We confuse the deeds and words of people, since they can have a sort of permanence and appear to *belong to* someone, with what we mean when we say that persons are unique and distinct. All efforts to get at the "meaning" of action and speech, both in the specific and the general sense, are "reifications," since they are efforts to "fix" something—the "specific revelatory quality of action and speech"— which Arendt contended was "indissolubly tied to the living flux of acting and speaking." (1958, 187) Arendt recognized that all efforts to "talk about" something are distinct from the living practice of "acting and speaking directly *to* one another." Talk about action consists of "stories" we reconstruct after the fact, which are always representations. And as representations they are practices of authority; that is, they augment action by re-telling it.

> It is because of this already existing web of human relationship, with its innumerable, conflicting wills and intentions, that action almost never achieves its purpose; but it is also because of this medium, in which action alone is real, that it "produces" stories with

or without intention as naturally as fabrication produces tangible things. These stories may then be recorded in documents and monuments, they may be visible in use objects or art works, they may be told and retold and worked into all kinds of material. They themselves, *in their living reality, are of an altogether different nature than these reifications.* (1958, 184, emphasis added)

Here Arendt appears to be highlighting the extent to which there is an inevitable "gap" between act and meaning, between word and thing. As Bonnie Honig noted in her discussion of Arendt and Derrida on performative and constative utterances, there is a strong similarity between Arendt and Derrida on this point. (1991, 105; cf. Kateb 1983, 10–14)

The feminist invocation of "experience" as the source of "truth" rests on the assumption that we can learn what actors mean, what their negotiations of a situation intend or reveal, by asking them to tell us about themselves. Feminists have argued that discovering (uncovering) what women mean by what they say and do, as women themselves understand these, depends upon looking at and listening to them carefully, unobtrusively. The assumption is that disinterested looking and listening are possible and will permit the "authentic" person to be seen, the "authentic" voice to be heard. Feminist researchers should not superimpose their desires to find "liberated" sisters onto others' stories. Rather, "we should be asking questions about specific histories, specific texts." (Swindells, 34)

Yet once we are asking questions, we are no longer looking and listening unobtrusively. Nor could we ever be looking and listening unobtrusively, disinterestedly. Neither speaker nor listener are engaged in a locationless, boundaryless, disinterested conversation; you are always speaking from somewhere, I am always listening from somewhere. The conversation, the dialogue, is an effort to bridge the gap between us. Through dialogue it becomes possible to recognize that the sovereignty of the subject as originator of meaning can only be purchased at the expense of the context, including the research process itself, within which it operates. The fiction of an imperious "I" wishing away the world and her body as (merely modernist) fictions replicates the narrative of sovereignty through its fantasy of an unmediated reversal of power relations; taking back inside the "self" what was displaced (or stolen) by those outside, the subject of standpoint epistemologies remains imprisoned by the myth of self-generation.

AUTHENTICITY, SOVEREIGNTY, AND THE PROBLEM OF GENDER AS A CATEGORY OF ANALYSIS

Feminist presence in any discursive field can be represented as a disturbance, an intervention. Yet at the same time, it can be structured as an invitation, an invitation to become part of a collaborative project of documenting women's collective and diverse experiences and exploring the ways that gender has shaped, and distorted, the structure of knowledge in order to prompt inquiry into the possibilities for political change. When seen as an invitation to construct a canon about women's lives, the conflict about who gets to be part of the canon begins immediately. In their introduction to *Conflicts in Feminism,* for example, Marianne Hirsch and Evelyn Fox Keller discuss the effect of such conflicts on the construction and destruction of feminist theory, and call for "restoring dialogue where it had broken down." (1990, 3) Current criticisms of feminist theory have contended that this "invitation" was merely a solicitation to take part in a feast where some people's tastes and some people's interests had already been dismissed.

Ironically, the current emphasis on the "authenticity" of speech and on the masklessness or prediscursiveness of naked, lived experience work together to reestablish seemingly unbridgeable chasms between us. In the name of "difference" we struggle, each of us, to tell our stories at the expense of, in place, of each other's. We want to own meanings. We are caught up in the struggle for scarce resources.

All too frequently the assertion that experience produces knowledge whose meaning is controlled by the experiencer/knower has defined experience in possessive terms. Only I who have an experience can know (own) what it means. Experience, thus, becomes the territory of personal identity, and personal identity becomes the basis for feminist epistemology and politics. The struggle over whose meanings count becomes cast in terms of the discourse of anticolonialism; it becomes a struggle to define the borders of the territory of one's experiences and to assign sovereign control over them to those who live within its newly defined boundaries. This struggle is a reaction to the fact that the dominant groups have, for so long, denied access to such basic dimensions of human survival as space and time to the groups they have ignored or colonized. Patricia Hill Collins, for instance, has written that "the *exclusion* of Black women's ideas from mainstream academic discourse and the *curious placement* of African-American women intellectuals in both feminist and Black social and political thought has meant that Black women intellectuals have remained *outsiders within all three communities.*" (Collins, *Black Feminist Thought,* 12, emphasis added)

Insofar as feminist research praxis is an emancipatory struggle, it seeks to liberate women's experiences from the colonizing effects of master discourses which have so far invalidated them. Like political ideologists of national liberation, feminists have argued that the oppressed should speak for and on behalf of themselves in an indigenous language that is different from the oppressor's. Feminists have gone so far as to claim that the oppressed live in separate worlds, speak a separate language: "It is simple enough to say that the difference between the two groups—the oppressor and the oppressed—prevents the former from adequately comprehending the essence of Black life and culture because of a fundamental difference in perceptions, based upon *separate* histories, life-styles, and purposes for being." (Ladner 1987, 77)

Yet in staking these claims to territorial sovereignty for different women's experiences, we have not always recognized how the discourse of national sovereignty may limit feminist efforts to alter the paradigms of power and authority. Instead we have become caught up in border wars, accusing one another of trespassing on the property of each other's lives; we charge each other with coopting the stories of different women's lives for neocolonialist purposes, purposes masquerading in liberationist garb. Commenting about her skepticism regarding new efforts to talk and write about race by those who hadn't felt the need to talk about race or class before, bell hooks has written:

> My skepticism is shared by many black women who were very active in the struggle to challenge the feminist movement to confront racism politically. We feel that many white women have not considered the issue of accountability for this persecution and racial harassment, nor have they adequately called attention to the process by which their thinking changed. For some, talking about race is merely a way to enhance academic status. (in Hirsch and Keller 1990, 62.)

Feminists of color in particular have contended that feminist theory itself has depended upon the operation of colonizing and totalizing paradigms and textual strategies. Those who make universalistic claims about female experience based on a narrow sample of subjects, or who cite differences between women and "then proceed to negate [those] differences by subsuming women of color into the unitary category woman/women" (Alarcón in Anzaldúa 1990, 358), develop theories that are equally as authoritarian, dominating, and masculine as the patriarchal theories they intended to supplant. Thus bell hooks has argued that "the force that allows white authors to make no reference to racial identity in their books about 'women' that are actually about white women is the same one that would compel any author writing exclusively on black women to refer explicitly to their racial identity." (1982, 138) Gloria Anzaldúa echoes this indictment when she contends that "whites not naming themselves white presume their universality; an unmarked race is a sign of Racism unaware of itself, a 'blanked-out' Racism." (1990, xxi) The color white becomes authoritative in the sense that it does not need to name itself as color. It stands as the name of names, the colorless color. In the texts to which hooks and Anzaldúa are referring, the term "woman" encodes white women with the appearance of universality. (White) woman becomes Woman.

The erasure of race results from what Norma Alarcón has called the "common-denominator" approach that she contends characterizes "Anglo-American feminist theory." This approach constructs the female subject within the terms of "an oppositional discourse (counter-identifying) with some white men, that leaves us unable to explore relationships among women." The recognition that by privileging the centrality of gender as a category of analysis, feminist theory might "distort the representation of many women and/or correspond to that of some men ... gives rise to an anxiety and ambivalence with respect to the future of feminism, especially in Anglo-America." She continues: "In other words, the whole category of woman may also need to be problematized." (Alarcón in Anzaldúa 1990, 360)

These critics take the centrality of gender as a category of analysis in feminist theory as evidence of the quest for sovereignty in feminist theory. To this evidence they add the search for political unity within the feminist movement and related moves to establish sovereign leadership within the movement and within feminist theory, as well as efforts to construct a feminist canon—a set of texts that authoritatively interpret women's experiences—as further proof. Yet ironically, many critics who have noted such tendencies in so-called mainstream feminist theory and practice have not, themselves, escaped from the sovereignty trap. For instance, as Susan Bordo has noted, the search for a more adequate conceptualization of human identity has converted the

> invaluable insight that gender forms only one axis of a complex, heterogeneous construction, constantly interpenetrating, in historically specific ways, with multiple other axes of identity . . . into the authoritative insight, and from there into a privileged, critical framework . . . legislating the appropriate terms of all intellectual efforts, capable of determining who is going astray and who is on the right track. (Bordo 1990, 139)

In other words such critics have worked to delegitimate existing authorities and de-authorize certain readings of women's experiences within feminism while claiming sovereignty for their own maneuvers. They have replaced one set of disciplinary laws with another.

It may be that this was unavoidable. Collins recognizes some of the exclusionary effects of such a strategy of theory building when she writes "the dilemma is that Black women intellectuals must place our own experiences and consciousness at the center of any serious efforts to develop Black feminist thought yet not have that thought become separatist and exclusionary." (35) For her the solution to this dilemma is to build theory like a "collaborative enterprise," structured through "coalitions among autonomous groups . . . each with its own distinctive set of experiences and specialized thought embedded in those experiences." (*Black Feminist Thought,* 36) This solution has a specifically political cast. Feminist theory is to be constructed like a federation or commonwealth of sovereign states, each with its own territory—"distinctive experiences,"—and each with its own history and language—"thought embedded in those experiences." What constitutional mechanisms will be established to deal with the distribution of power among the constituent parties, with "security" issues, with border disputes, with secession, and with miscommunication?

Yet there is another dilemma. The very diversity of experience requires an impossible effort: one cannot reconstruct the "varied experiences of millions of women, much less . . . do so from various perspectives," but "it is equally impossible to claim that any one woman's experience speaks for all women . . . no one can speak for others or judge what others say about their experiences." (Bordo 1990, 139) The alternative to attempting to represent women's experiences in all their diversity or claiming that some women's experiences are universal seems to be a kind of solipsism that courts danger precisely because it wants to avoid political confrontation or even dialogue.

If recognizing the diversity of everyone's experiences and everyone's unmitigated right to own those experiences is supposed to subvert the authoritativeness of the established canon, there is a risk that the political project of feminism—to transform women's lives for the better—also will be lost. If everyone is speaking for and about herself, then how can we articulate, without subverting this practice, any collective goals? At the same time, claiming authoritativeness for any interpretations risks both essentializing women's experiences and silencing those who have not yet had the opportunity to speak for themselves.

Risking unraveling the political project of feminism may be a risk worth taking. This is because the debates internal to feminism about the extent to which the category of women can achieve coherence and stability suggest that the incoherence and instability of the central category of feminist theory—women—is endemic to feminism's peculiar form of representational politics. Since "gender is not always constituted coherently or consistently in different historical contexts, and because gender intersects with racial, class, ethnic, sexual, and regional modalities of discursively constituted identities" so that "it becomes impossible to separate out 'gender' from the political and cultural intersections in which it is invariably produced and maintained," the category of women becomes, for some, a "foundationalist fiction" with which feminist theory should dispense. (Butler, *Gender Trouble*, 3) In this view feminists should search for a different ground for feminist theory and politics other than some notion of "women" as subject. In place of women as subject of feminist theory, Judith Butler offers "practices of parody" as the means whereby "the" critical task for feminism can be re-founded. "*The* critical task is . . . to locate strategies of subversive repetition [of gender] enabled by those constructions [of identity], to affirm the local possibilities of intervention through participating in precisely those practices of repetition that constitute identity and, therefore, present the immanent possibility of contesting them." (147, emphasis added)

Recognition of the hopelessness of feminist theory's effort to refound itself on the grounds of a complex enough theory of human ontology is necessary. Identity politics requires that the construction of the "we" in whose name action is to be taken necessarily depends upon practices of exclusion as it searches for consensus and unity. Ultimately it displaces the questioning of sexual or racial identity itself—the need to be one kind of person or another, to be male or female, to be one racial or ethnic group or another—by the unexamined struggle for territorial sovereignty of sexual (and racial and class) subjectivities. A subject-centered politics cannot critique the foundation of its own strategy: subjectivity.

Yet although it is important to recognize, following Foucault, that subjectivity is an effect of a particular, juridical discourse of power, that, in other words, "the category of sex is constructed in the service of a system of regulatory and reproductive sexuality," and to stress that "the desire to determine sex once and for all . . . seems to issue from the social organization of sexual reproduction through the construction of the clear and unequivocal identities and positions of sexed bodies with respect to each other," (Butler, *Gender Trouble*, 111) the fact that the menstruating body, the pregnant body, the birthing body, the lactating body is (at least for now) a female body will not disintegrate with this analysis. Our birth, our natality, are not merely chimerical effects of a discourse of reproduction.

The assertion that both sex and gender are "phantasmatic constructions" or "fabrications manufactured and sustained through corporeal signs and other discursive means" (Butler, *Gender Trouble*, 146, 136) seems, uncannily, to wish away the body of the mother as a particular woman's body. Not all women's bodies are pregnant bodies. But we would have no bodies at all without women's bodies. As Françoise Vergès puts it:

> for the present, it is a woman's body which is necessary to carry a human being. . . . We were all born of this woman's body. Pregnancy remains the most "visible" sign of sexual difference. With pregnancy, the line of demarcation between masculinity and femininity, which can otherwise be blurred, becomes suddenly "shockingly" present. . . . Pregnancy not only ["enforces"] this line of demarcation between men and women but it also forces us to see sexual difference as a basic difference, i.e. it forces the comparison of men with women. (1991, 5)

Frozen by what Susan Bordo has called a "paralyzing anxiety over falling (from what grace?) into ethnocentrism or 'essentialism' " (1990, 142)—what I refer to as our anxiety about authority—we "dream of being everywhere," refusing to "assume a shape for which [we] must take responsibility." (Bordo 1990, 143, 144) We succumb to fantasies of autogenesis (Vergès 1991, 10). Yet while we are dreaming, the very patterns of sexist, racist, and class privilege which feminists intended to undermine become obscured. "If the postmodernist emphasis on multivocality leads to a denial of the continued existence of a hierarchy of discourse, the material and historical links between cultures can be ignored, with all voices becoming equal, each telling only an individualized story." (Mascia-Lees, Sharpe and Cohen, 29)

The confluence between the feminist invocation of experience and the postmodernist celebration of diversity and "heteroglossia" (Strathern in Mascia-Lees 1989, 22) has contributed to this anxiety about authority. There are ways to dislodge the place of gender as a sovereign analytic category in feminist theory without discarding gender as a relevant category altogether or disintegrating sexual difference as a relevant "fact."

The political impetus that contributed to the development of the categorical sovereignty of gender was the self-conscious effort to write back into history the stories of all those who had been marginalized by the hegemony of its grand narratives. The major methodological contribution of feminist theory has been to expose the gendered nature of dominant forms of historical and social discourse. Initially in political theory, this meant exploring the sexist attitudes about women reflected in mainstream theories. Later this approach was superceded by focusing on the incoherence of the major theories of politics when women were added to them. Yet in both of these cases, gender was conflated with sex; that is, the examination of the gendered nature of political discourse was reduced to an analysis of what was said about women and men directly, or how actual women were located in relation to politics. The extent to which statements about women already reflected gendered assumptions about who counted *as* women, or what was represented *as* feminine often was left uninterrogated. (Spelman 1989)

Yet bringing gender into focus is not the same as studying the actual behavior of women and men, an investigatory strategy that certainly dominated the resurgence of feminist scholarship in the early seventies and an approach that is still making important research contributions. Noticing gender and the difference that it makes to the construction of knowledge should mean noticing the ways that cultural codes of sexual difference structure social relations of human identity and signify relationships of power and status.

Gender is not a synonym for women or for men, although it has been used often enough as if it were. Rather it is a category of representation; it is a linguistic category that refers to social constructions and interpretations. Societies, as Joan W. Scott has observed, "use [gender] to articulate rules of social relationships, or construct the meaning of experience." Gender is both a "social category imposed on a sexed body" and a *cultural code of representation,* a way to categorize and control behaviors and practices that are not necessarily the result of sexual differences *in terms of sexual differences.* (1986, 1063, 1057) Thus in feminist political analysis, to attempt to build theories and practices from the perspective of "women and their interests" has meant to consider the implications for political analysis of those constellations of value and meaning that have been associated with female experience, that have been "feminized"; in other words to investigate self-consciously the political significance of those attributes that have been encoded with culturally defined signs of femininity.

> The radical critical possibility of a feminist perspective on the tradition of political theory thus lies in grasping the ways in which what we know as politics is a politics constructed according to specific notions, practices, and institutions of masculinity. The radical practical possibility emerging from this understanding lies in constructing a politics that is divorced from its historical identification with [particular forms of] manhood. (Brown 1988, 13)

This approach to making gender a central category of analysis avoids some of the tendencies toward sovereignty criticized above.

Critics of the authority of gender as a central category of feminist theory have argued that making gender central flattens out epistemology because it loses "sight of the complex and multiple ways in which a subject and object of possible experience are constituted." (Alarcón in Anzaldúa 1990, 361). Gender tends to be constructed in binary terms—masculine v. feminine—instead of multiple terms— masculines and feminines. Thus in feminist theory one's gender identity has been primarily defined in relation to the *opposite* sex instead of exploring gender also in relation to members of the *same* sex, who are different from one another in terms of class, ethnicity, sexual preference, etc. Elizabeth Spelman has argued that the dominant approach to the analysis of gender has been an additive one: "each part of my identity is separable from every other part, and the significance of each part is unaffected by the other parts." (1989, 36) In contrast, Spelman argues that we cannot talk about gender differences, about women as women, because one's gender identity always is structured in the context of racial and class distinctions. (1989, 148) Thus "if we are going to talk convincingly and clearly about the difference gender makes, we better be [sic] able to isolate it from the difference race and class makes, and we can do this best by talking about *gender relations between men and women of the same race and class.*" (1989, 174, emphasis added)

Such criticism of the sovereign authority of gender as a category in feminist theory has been well-founded. Some of the earliest theorists of women's exploitation, such as Firestone, and even more recent theorists, such as MacKinnon, tended to reduce explanations of different women's situation, to the extent that they even explored *different* situations, to a single causal model. Thus, for Firestone women's biology was the fundamental cause of all women's oppression and for MacKinnon it was the control of women's sexuality by men:

> Socially, femaleness means femininity, which means attractiveness to men, which means sexual attractiveness, which means sexual availability on male terms. What defines woman as such is what turns men on. . . . Gender socialization is the process through which women come to identify themselves as sexual beings, as beings that exist for men. It is that process through which women internalize (make their own) a male image of their sexuality *as* their identity as women. . . . It is sexuality that determines gender, not the other way around. (1982, 531)

Here the reduction of gender to sexuality and the definition of that sexuality in purely binary, oppositional terms—men versus women—is pronounced. Sexuality becomes the sovereign determinant and meaning of gender, men become the sovereign rulers of sexuality, and women become abject victims.

Yet the question remains whether the taxonomic hyphenation of the poles of the binary opposition masculine/feminine into culturally specific, historically contingent variations on a theme of sexual difference, as in Chicana, African-American woman, Anglo-American woman, effectively escapes the binary at the level of the symbolic or more powerfully inscribes it. At the level of the symbolic, the code "woman" attached to or implied by all these terms still figures the marking of bodies within the terms of an as yet unproblematized masculine/feminine binary. If one sets aside the question of disrupting the binary, the proliferation of femininities and masculinities suggested by formulations that qualify the term "woman" or the term "man" permits both difference and coherence under the rubric of sexual difference, promotes political analysis of differences around these poles, and allows for the articulation of political strategies of resistance within the terms of a discourse that accepts, for the time being, that being of woman born is an insistent mark of sexual difference.[4]

Furthermore it remains unclear why, in Spelman's formulation, "finding out about the difference that gender makes," where gender is seen as the residue after race and class are controlled, we can safely assume that race and class are more certainly fixed points that are constitutive of context than gender is. Indeed, as historians and anthropologists have demonstrated, contexts of race and class often have been constructed through gender codes. Gender, as metaphor of difference and classification, and as the representation of the social location and life experience of actual men and women, became central to the way that class belonging has been coded. (Scott 1986; Davidoff and Hall 1987) Gender also has been bound up with the representation of the social location and significance of ethnic groups. Gender is never an accurate or exhaustive descriptor of the actual lives or identities of all women or all men. But theories of gender do establish a dominant discourse about the meaning of sexual difference, a difference that never, of course, exists in quite the way that the ideology defines it. To say that "females become not simply women but particular kinds of women" (Spelman 1989, 13) does not in itself negate the existence of gender as a constellation of meanings around which our lives twist and turn. In fact, such a statement depends upon the relative fixity of gender as a category of representation.

Treating gender as a central category of analysis does not require constructing a hegemonic theory; it does not require making gender sovereign. As a code of meaning, gender may be wedded to a binary structuring of reality, but there is nothing necessarily binary, nor necessarily essentialist, about such a code. If we are careful to distinguish between the *experiences* and behaviors of particular men and women—the experiences of one sex or another—and the *representations* of certain experiences and behaviors, regardless of which sex group has or practices them, as masculine and feminine, then we can avoid treating gender as the sovereign sign of identity.

I argue that gender should be understood as a space whose occupation we negotiate, instead of as an "identity card" we display, as a fixed and determinate identity. (Alcoff 1988) It then becomes possible to understand that those who occupy the space of gender do not experience it in a monolithic way, even though the territorial boundaries of gender can be identified historically. It seems important to continue to stress that the dominant culture encodes gender with a specific set of meanings with which we all struggle. If certain individuals and groups resist the culture's stereotypes of "woman" by struggling to be seen as women even if they do not fit the dominant norm, this does not negate the fact that gender remains a relatively fixed and primary location within which, or against which, "identity" is constructed. Precisely because gender is used to represent status and power, it remains a powerful code of meaning and an important site of resistance. To say that women experience oppression as women does not mean that each woman experiences the same thing. It is one way of understanding the paradox of human existence: we are all unique but equal.

Reading women's and men's lives primarily in terms of what women and men *do* forgets that "women's place in social life is *not in any direct sense* a product of things she does (or even less a function of what biologically she is) but of the meaning her activities acquire through concrete social interactions." (Rosaldo 1980, 399–400) Not all of the experiences *of* women necessarily reflect their experiences *as* women exclusively, although it is probably the case, given the fact that we are embodied persons, that this gendered dimension of consciousness is never wholly absent. Nor, conversely, are those experiences which are not self-consciously and exclusively sexually referent necessarily gender neutral. Even though "if one 'is' a woman, that is surely not all one is," the argument that this is because gender is historically variable and because gender intersects other aspects of identity, such as race, class, sexuality, and ethnicity, seems to me to miss the mark.

The "woman-plus" approach rests on a conceptual distinction between "being" a woman and "being" a particular woman. It focuses again on experience and forgets about language. *Being* female is always a particularized experience that nonetheless intersects the symbolic category "woman" simultaneously. One can never *be* a category, yet categories, as linguistic entities, are essential aspects of constructed, descriptive narratives of experience. Being and fiction intersect, yet one cannot be collapsed into the other. Teresa de Lauretis put it well when she remarked that even the most anti-essentialist theorists would not deny that "feminist theory is all about an essential difference, an irreducible difference, though not a difference inherent in 'woman's nature' (in woman in nature), but a difference in the feminist conception of woman, women, and the world." (in Hirsch and Keller 1990, 255; cf. Jónasdóttir 1991)

Gender may not be negotiated in the same ways, even by the same person, in one period of history, much less across histories and cultures. Yet to speak of gender as a category requires that we regard it as having some identifiable structure, like any other linguistic category, that *can* be negotiated. Having recognized the pervasiveness of gender as a linguistic device for ordering experience, we should remind ourselves of the historicity of language, or else we will fall into the trap of assuming that gender is the sovereign code of meaning, the ultimate sign of power. Even if we understand, as Joan Scott has urged, that gender is both a "constitutive element of social relationships" and "a primary way of signifying relationships of power," (1987, 1067) we need to remember always to ask, "Why?"

WHY? This is the question the sovereign does not want to hear. "WHY?" invites reflection, it evokes memory, it keeps the conversation going. As Linda Gordon has recently noted

> it is arguable that because of the primacy of gender in human acculturation any study attentive to language will notice how gender becomes a trope for all differentiation, alienation, individuation. However, feminist scholarship about gender additionally requires a critical stance, a standpoint that questions the inevitability or desirability of particular gender meanings. (1990, 855)

Strategies of conformity and resistance to a particular culture's definition of gendered identity, in discourse and in practice, are structured around the hierarchically signified values attached to being masculine or being feminine. "Maleness" in Western cultures has represented a panoply of rights, behaviors, and attitudes that has entitled men to be economically, politically, and socially mobile and successful. Not all men have achieved what the masculine gender is permitted because class, color, age, sexual orientation, and a variety of other structures preclude many options for nondominant groups and because some individuals resist conformity. But "success" and "power" have been defined in the dominant system of Western industrial society in ways that are more compatible with being masculine, whereas being feminine has been defined as an intrinsic obstacle to success and power in those same societies. In fact it would not be an exaggeration to say that unsuccessful and nonpowerful men are "feminized" as a way to rationalize their lack of an "equitable" share of status and traditional modes of power.

Of course "feminization" is not the only way to mark a group's or individual's distance from the norm. Sander Gilman has noted the mythic and literary association "between pathology and racial identity." In the antebellum South, this linkage served to

> locate (and thus isolate) the fear and anxiety caused by the black in a source other than the institution of slavery. . . . White southerners needed to project the anxieties felt about potential violence engendered by slavery onto the black. They focused these anxieties through the myth of illness rather than understanding them as stemming from the brutal reality of slavery itself. (1985, 147)

This myth then displaced moral and political conflicts onto a medical arena and translated questions of injustice into the language of medical discourse.[5]

Race, class, and gender are three of a number of terms that mark relationships of power and that locate actual persons within the structure of those relationships. Sometimes they operate as signs in terms of one another. Yet the interdependency of these signs often has been forgotten in the skirmish for territorial sovereignty in the field of theory. Scott has noted how "gender is part of the attempt by contemporary feminists *to stake claim* to a certain definitional ground, *to insist on* the inadequacy of existing bodies of theory for explaining persistent inequalities between women and men." (1986, 1066, emphasis added) As critics increasingly question the legitimacy of staking this claim to the territory of gender and insist on the inadequacy of models constructed in terms of gender, they tend to replicate the very process about which they complain. We are caught again in the sovereignty trap. We accuse each other of trespassing on one another's property—our identities and experiences—of not quite understanding us, of not "getting it," yet without seeing that in doing so we affirm experience as private property; knowledge as total, exclusive control; and understanding as loneliness.

For some, gender is so variegated a phenomenon that constructing any theory in terms of it is fraught with unavoidable dangers. Recently, as Susan Bordo has noted, a dogmatic assertion of difference and diversity has led to the contention that gender generalizations are "*in principle* essentialist or totalizing." (in Nicholson 1990, 139) Instead of some unitary concept of gender identity, such theorists urge the pluralizing of "woman" into "women." Others, such as Butler, urge abandoning "women" as a subject for feminist theory. But is it adequate to resist overgeneralizations by substituting the plural "women" in place of a category which structures sexual difference in more or less binary terms? And what are the political consequences of constructing feminist theory as if women did not exist because all women do not exist *as* women in the same way?

It is true that a "pluralistic" approach to concept building denaturalizes the category of "woman" as well as other unitary concepts such as race, ethnicity, class; and that it thereby undermines "the justifications for patriarchy, colonialism, humanism, positivism, essentialism, scientism, and other unlamented-isms." (Haraway 1985, 74–75). But what also is lost is the conceptual foundation for a critique of those same "isms." If "woman" is merely a myth that deconstructs itself into the plurality "women," and then disappears, then there is no longer any sense to be made of the statement "exploitation of women." This radically deconstructive move transforms the statement "exploitation of women" into the less coherent statement, "exploitation of persons who happen to be women," or worse, into the incoherent statement "random acts of questionable effect performed by unidentifiable, ambiguous agents against, perhaps unintentionally, persons who might be women, maybe unwittingly, and only on occasion." Having so qualified what being a woman means, the category itself is emptied of its contents; it becomes a disposable, ultimately dispensable, label. "Woman" may not be definable. Yet it seems important to stress that powerful institutions and ideologies work daily to constrict and to define women. It is against these that we must continue to struggle, and not just with language games.

Some theorists take a less extreme approach to unseating gender as a sovereign category, insisting on sensitivity to differences among women that pivot along the axes of class, race/ethnicity, sexual preference, etc. Such sensitivity should not mean merely including data on, for instance, women of color, but modifying theories at the level of concepts and methods to reflect the significance of these differences to the production of knowledge itself. (Utall 1990, 42) These important arguments about the need for the transformation of knowledge at the basic categorical level are what feminists have been attempting for years. What we demand of ourselves now seems to be the daunting requirement that feminist theory construct itself only in terms of generalizations that correspond to reality in all its heterogeneity. This is an impossibility. The alternative is to abandon theory building in favor of endorsing local strategies of subversion and local possibilities for disruptive intervention. (Butler, *Gender Trouble,* 147) Yet in the absence of a reasonably coherent category against which one resists, it is difficult to understand how subversion and disruption can be recognized as such in the first place. As Wendy Brown has observed,

> resistance, the practice most widely associated with postmodern political discourse, responds to without fully meeting the normati-

vity challenge of postmodernity. A vital *tactic* in much political work as well as for mere survival, resistance by itself does not contain *a critique, a vision, or grounds for organized collective efforts to enact either.* (1991 79, emphasis added)

If only generalizations not undermined by counterfactuals are permissible, then no generalizations are permissible—except, of course, the sort I have just made. Is this what we really want to do? We have been most willing to dispense with gender generalizations while, at the same time, we have been resistant to applying "the same attentiveness to difference, or the same sensitivity to issues of interpretation and textuality from the analytics of race and class that we do from the analytics of gender." (Bordo 1990, 145) In fact the sovereignty of race and class has been asserted at precisely the same time that the tactfulness of making sovereign claims about gender has been resisted: "Why . . . are we so ready to deconstruct what have historically been the most ubiquitous elements of the gender axis, while so willing to defer to the authority and integrity of race and class axes as fundamentally grounding?" (Bordo 1990, 146)

The answer is political, and it has to do with authority on a number of levels. First, within the U.S. feminist movement and within its academy, the demand for access to traditional positions of privilege has increased, and the search for political allies and supporters has reached a critical stage. There is no question that most feminist networks have been racially, class, and otherwise segregated. Gatekeeping in feminist publications has occurred and has been no less pernicious because we were "supposed to know better." The fallout from Reaganomics has had disproportionate material effects on the lives of people of color—nonwhite people—and the poor(er) not only in the United States, but globally. Those who have never been able to afford to think "purely in feminist terms," as Alice Paul once urged, are now less able or willing to do so. The frustration that Gloria Anzaldúa has expressed about energy drained from feminists of color—that could have been invested in their own literary and political movements—by repeated demands that the same feminists of color work to educate and to build solidarity in the (white) feminist movement is a typical response, more and more frequently heard. (1990, xvi) The possessive tense—"our literary and political movements"—resonates in Anzaldúa's and others' statements in part because the fragmentation precipitated by heightened attacks on the poorer and more marginal have made them acutely aware of what is being lost. Unlearning white privilege is needed now more than ever. The question is how to create the "democratic political space" so that we can "confront as a permanent political condition partiality of understanding and expressions" and work simultaneously to resolve conflicts, to have dialogue. (Brown 1991, 80)

Second, the centers of power have had to confront the reality of increasing numbers of "others" entering the sanctum sanctorum. So with an effortless sleight of hand, power now has been proclaimed dispersed: the Berlin wall comes tumbling down; the call for perestroika is sounded in all quarters; even South Africa moves, however glacially, towards democracy. In the midst of such changes, raising questions about gender and sexual difference seems anticlimactic. Yet both the renewed and vicious attack on reproductive rights in the United States within the context of Bush's "kinder, gentler nation," the inability of newly unified Germany to settle the abortion question, and the concerns expressed by Eastern European women that they will be the ones asked to leave the labor market as their economies struggle with rampant unemployment are recent examples that should remind us of what is at stake in the hasty deconstruction of gender both as a social category and as a code of meaning.

In the writings of feminists of color, a suspicion of the straightjacketing effect of sovereign categories already has been articulated. Race, class, and gender ought to be understood as more than categories into which one is born; they are *political* categories around which movements have coalesced. At the same time, to fit the category ought not to require annihilation of individuality or difference.

> We shun the white-looking Indian, the 'high yellow' Black woman, the Asian with the white lover, the Native woman who brings her white girl friend to the Pow Wow, the Chicana who doesn't speak Spanish, the academic, the uneducated. Her difference makes her a person we can't trust. *Para que sea "legal,"*—she must pass the ethnic legitimacy test we have devised ... woe to anyone who doesn't measure up to our standards of ethnicity. (Anzaldúa 1990, 143)

If gender, race, class, and sexual preference are not to be used as mere "markers to describe the race [etc.] of the respondent" nor as disciplinary devices to police the borders of identity—either by keeping some "outside" or by insisting on the faithful being "inside"—then we must abandon the search for sovereignty through any of them, or even all of them in combination, and work toward solidarity—solidarity based on what Stephen White calls the responsibility to act combined with the responsibility to otherness. We cannot succeed politically to unseat those who have monopolized power and authority, and thus continue to insist on their definitions of these terms, if we play according to the rules of their game; that is, if we continue to insist on territorial sovereignty for our identities. We may not agree on all the issues, but those who watch our vituperation from the wings are, in Ntozake Shange's words, "the same old Men."

FROM SOVEREIGNTY TO COEXISTENCE: "WORLD"-TRAVELING

If we displace sovereignty—the desire to control difference by representing it as unity—what happens to the coherence of the feminist project in theory and practice? Authority, instead of ending discussion, becomes its beginning. Looking for authority means searching for the basis to refound our social relationships. Gender, race, class, and sexuality do not dissolve into endlessly mobile, hence nonexistent, chimeras. Instead, we give these concepts flesh while maintaining analytic distance between them, as heuristic devices, and the lived, material reality in and through which they echo and are refracted. If we remain aware of the existential difference, often rhetorically transgressed, between the *analytic utility* of a concept and the *material reality* which it seeks to express, we can avoid the essentialism that haunts much of the discussion of "differences."

We should set about the important political task of constructing not unity, but political community and solidarity from the vantage point of our differences, "differences that are not only sexual or racial, economic or (sub)cultural, but all of these together, and often at odds with one another," (de Lauretis 1986, 14) but never *only* differences. We can think of authority not as border-patrolling and boundary engendering, but as meaning giving; and as with all gift giving, we should prepare ourselves for the disappointment of possible refusal.

Different accounts of experience, from "rival [sic] disciplines of language regions, need not be mutually incompatible; they can coexist." (Pitkin 1972, 257) At the cross-cultural level of observation, we are most likely to misinterpret, to transpose, to translate the meaning of an event or an utterance into our "own" language. Yet there is no way around the fact that we cannot *be* other than who we are. We can, however, travel to another "world." If we are playful in our traveling, if we are loving and nurturant in our journeying to others' "worlds," we will be moved to "see oneself in other women who are quite different from oneself." (Lugones, 1990, 393). And we should not only "see oneself" but empathize with others.

The question of whose interpretation is "true" has been framed most frequently in terms of inquiring whether understandings "from the outside" are true at the expense of experientially founded ones." Yet this is the wrong question. Different accounts do not have to be at the expense of each other. As long as we relinquish the search for sovereignty—that is, the practice of authorizing or legitimating interpretations by excluding others or by possessing and owning knowledge and experiences by rigidly defining and adhering to the boundaries between you and me—we can begin to construct a political community, a polity that is friendly to women.

If the feminist author declines ownership of her text, she/he should not abdicate responsibility for it. We can replace the voice of the sovereign master not with babble, but with efforts to recognize and admit responsibility for patterns of relationships that sovereign boundaries aim to negate—including the ways that we have internalized what Marilyn Frye called patterns of "arrogant perception," leading to fence building, name-calling, forgetfulness, and political torpor.

On the horizon of the contentious struggles for sovereign authority, theorists have been exploring how to reconfigure "the subject of feminist theory, and her relational position to a multiplicity of others." (Alarcón in Anzaldúa 1990, 359) Existing at the juncture, at the border "where phenomena collide," (Anzaldúa 1987, 79) feminists have argued that her "experience" cannot be represented adequately within the terms of a sexually dimorphic, oppositional discourse. Her *mestiza* subjectively opens "geometric possibilities" because it can be interpreted as a "potent subjectivity synthesized from fusions of outsider identities." (Haraway in Nicholson 1990, 216) Defying singularity as the mode of identity, living on the boundaries, her subjectivity subverts the authority of dimorphous codes to represent or to exhaust experience. She challenges the logic of authority as sovereignty; she upsets the search for an exclusive meaning, for a fixed identity on the basis of which to found politics anew.

As long as the temptation either to define this as the new privileged position or as the exclusive territory of some is resisted, we may discover in it the potential for reconceptualizing authority in a way that takes boundary transgression as fundamental and gives meaning—since an author/*auctor* is one who gives meaning—to it. This new practice of authority will become a practice of founding community not on identity politics but through a politics of diversity; it will mean "embracing the skillful task of reconstructing the boundaries of daily life, in partial connection with others, in communication with all our parts." (Haraway in Nicholson 1990, 223)

SCENE 3

So the stage is set for scene 3. It will be a playful play about what María Lugones has called "world-travelling." " 'World'-travellers have the distinct experience of being different in different 'worlds' and ourselves in them. . . ." (1990, 396)

You are at a picnic, high in the mountains of Isle de Réunion, a tiny, multicultural jewel of a place in the middle of the Indian Ocean. Colonized by the French in the seventeenth century with slave labor imported from neighboring Madagascar and other parts of Africa (there was no indigenous population), Réunion is precisely that: the constant reunion of the peoples and cultures and languages of Asia, Africa, and Europe. This picnic is a cornucopia of unimaginable delight and sadness. There are giant cauldrons of steaming, spicy meats and vegetables, enormous coffers of rice; there's champagne and rum. And a sense of camaraderie, cooperation, and friendship among this political family of friends who work for social change in this small place where identities are so intermixed it seems ridiculous to think in terms of borders. But here, nevertheless, the issues of borders and boundaries will be debated as this bastard country— for that is how she has been represented in the French colonialist literature of a previous era, as the bastard child of a white French man and a woman of color—still attached to her mother France, will become part of the European Community of 1992. (Vergès, "Daughters of Sycorax," 1991)

You are thinking about borders and boundaries as you remember, at this feast, the little girl you met earlier that day, yards away from the apartment where you are a comforted and protected guest. She and her brothers and sisters and nephews and mother are all crammed together in a tiny room, the noise and the heat competing with one another for dominion. One of her sisters is already pregnant, at 16, with her second child. "It's one way to gain a little extra income for the family," a Réuionnaise who has worked as a political organizer in the neighborhood tells you. The little girl, practicing her English, says to you, "I want to be a teacher, like you."

And you think about the meeting you attended earlier in the week, a meeting of the *Parti Communiste de la Réunion,* a party that stresses building roads, public work projects, and improving transportation networks so that people like Maria, who works as a maid in one of the French diplomat's estates on the island, won't have to wait for hours for a bus to take her to and from work, worried about her children's dinner, her children's safety—Maria who is forbidden to eat leftovers from the feast she prepares for the diplomat's friends. She supports the Communists. "Of course," she says. And she will continue to do so, despite the dissolution of the Soviet Union and the changes in Eastern Europe.

When you talked with the women of this island, women of so many different races and classes, about what issues they saw as most important to them today, without hesitation they said: "work and development."

So you have been made different by this traveling, and yet you returned "home." You have a responsibility to remember and to witness: "sanctuary is about crossing lines, about making connections rather than exclusions. If I choose to create my own safe place by closing my eyes and heart, then I will not be safe for long." (McDaniel 1987, 69) In your "home," in feminist theory, people are rushing to put up fences, to keep others out. There can be no safety, no sanctuary in a world of sovereign borders and boundaries. You have to create a new kind of home, a "new culture—*una cultura mestiza*—with [your] own lumber, [your] own bricks and mortar and [your] own feminist architecture." (Anzaldúa 1987, 22) It has to be strong and sturdy, that is why you need the bricks and mortar; but it has to be open to diversity, that is why you need the principles of feminist architecture.

Again you travel. This time, along with your Réunionnaise friend, who is also a feminist scholar, you decide to go to El Salvador to extend your coauthored research project on women's political organizations and to extend yourselves. About a week before you leave, you begin to have nightmares; your friend is troubled by premonitions of an unnameable fear. These are normal fears, you reassure each other. If one hadn't been worried about going to El Salvador, the other would have doubted her friend's ability to react quickly if the fears became reality. But you never imagined the worst would occur.

In this state of mind—watchful, cautious, but not immobilized— the two of you and three companions are stopped by heavily armed governmental troops in a rural province, early on a summer Sunday morning, allegedly for travelling without safe conduct passes. You never make it to the meeting of the rural women's cooperative that had been organized by your companions—another U.S. woman, and two Salvadorans.

With no charges brought against you, you are detained under the surveillance of Salvadoran forces of the Atlacatl brigade. Then they transfer you all into the custody of the infamous Treasury Police. Your Salvadoran companions weep. You refuse to relinquish your passports until your embassies are informed of your incarceration. All demands are ignored. "It will go worse for you if you refuse to cooperate," your captors intone. So you give up your passports, all your personal possessions, your liberty and, you are certain, your life, to the parade of captors who interrogate you with more than thirty hours of pointless, yet terrifying, questions.

Huddled together in a barren cubicle you try to make sense of the insanity you are witnessing. Would these men abuse you? Would you or the Salvadorans be tortured? How would you live, if you lived, with the knowledge of the risk that the two young Salvadorans had taken so that you could witness and recount to North Americans the horror of Salvadorans' daily lives? Would anyone listen? Did anyone know where you were?

And all along you have the nagging sense that Kafka's world was not a metaphor, but a prescient image of a world where "resistance" seems to be as unavailable as a breath of fresh air. And all along, as long as you are thinking, and making jokes, and inventing games, you know you are not dead, yet. You have an incredible sense of victory when you outwit your interrogator, who understands no English, by pretending you understand no Spanish and by sneaking verbal messages to your friend, who is translating only some of your words in between the actual answers to questions. Yet this "victory" is laced with an incredible sense of dread that it may be bootless if there is no more ability to be outside this world.

Men come to look at you. One accuses you of having been there before. "You are a subversive! We have pictures of you in demonstrations! Don't lie!" he shouts at you. For a few minutes you're uncertain—maybe he's right. Your release papers say *sospechosas de ser D/T* (suspected of being a delinquent terrorist).

Although you remain scarred by the journey to a place where truth is whatever the powerful declare it to be in the moment, this is a journey that the Salvadoran people make every day. You visit the University of El Salvador after your release. A psychology professor tells you that she cannot conduct her research on the victims of torture because she has received repeated death threats and has been told to leave the country in 48 hours if she dares to continue her investigations.

One mural in the biological sciences building speaks volumes. It depicts a pregnant woman's body. The fetus inside is grasping a miniature rifle in its hand. The woman is shackled. The lock on the shackles is painted in red, white and blue, with the tiny initials "USA" barely visible.

Now back in the United States, you wonder how this "experience" that is yours, but doesn't belong to you, and which happened to you when you weren't looking, will work into efforts to build the democratic political space needed to discuss the shape of a world that is friendly to women.

"World"-travelers have to become unencumbered, vulnerable selves. And no one can be acting the part of the sovereign.

Notes

1. In this paragraph and elsewhere in this chapter, I use the term "we" self-conscious of its rhetorical power both to invoke an assumed identity or unity and to unmask the politics of exclusion through which it is always constructed. My use of "we" is a device meant to unsettle the reader by calling attention to the fact that we become unsettled when things are said in our name. I want to highlight the territoriality of "we-claims," to problematize the terms of the debate about difference, to speak of the trouble that we have with authority.

2. I am using the concept of masculinity not as synonymous with men but as a signifier of a particular embodied practice defined culturally as masculine regardless of the sex of the person engaging in it.

3. See Judith Butler's discussion of Wittig's arguments about lesbianism: "Whereas Wittig clearly envisions lesbianism to be a full-scale refusal of sexuality, I would argue that even that refusal constitutes an engagement and, ultimately, a radical dependence on the very terms that lesbianism purports to transcend." (*Gender Trouble* 124) Yet the same criticism applies to Butler's work: whereas she envisions transvestism—the discourse of performative sex—as a refusal of the regulative fiction of a true gender identity, I would argue that even that refusal depends upon the (relative) fixity of a

sexually different body—the pregnant body as incontrovertible marker of a female body—that it purports to transcend.

4. I am grateful to Kirstie McClure for helping me clarify my argument on this point.

5. For a related discussion of the effect of the professionalization of medicine on the evolution of social authority within the medical community and American medicine transformation into a "resource for social order," see Starr (1982). I am grateful to Howard Kushner for calling my attention to the relevance of this source for my work. See also the important essay by Valerie Smith, "Split Affinities: The Case of Interracial Rape," where she talks about the theoretical "slippage between sexism and racism." (in Hirsch and Keller 1990, 271–287)

Conclusion: Democracy, Leadership, Augmentation, and the Vernacular

The idea that democracy consists of the equal access of anyone to rule-formulation processes and in the equal application of the rules to anyone has been the hallmark of social contract theory. Embedded in this theory was a particular conception of personhood. Social contract theory, which continues to shape much of the contemporary discussion of authority, treats individuals as abstract entities whose identity as members of groups or classes is inconsequential to their political standing. (Marx, in Marx and Engels, 1975) At least in principle, the concept of the individual as an autonomous self is an abstract, disembodied idea that denies the political significance of all differences—of class and race, as well as sex. Persons are *represented* in authority relations equally. Each is equal to any other before the law since each has equal access to it and since the law is applied equally.

Consequently, even if women are recognized as among those who can authorize, the representational system that liberal contract theory creates excludes from it by definition sexuality and gender and every other particularized aspect of being human, such as race and class. Representation of women in the practice of sovereignty comes to mean representation of persons who happen to be women. Being women is considered politically irrelevant in this view, since it is not representation of women *because* they are women—that is, because, *as women, they embody and signify something particular*—that must be present in politics if the promise of equality is to be fulfilled. Instead, the mere presence of *more* persons in public space is taken as an indication of the increasing equality of representation. The particularity of the activity of being female is rendered inconsequential to the personhood of the citizen who is represented.

Hanna Pitkin has called this idea of representation "descriptive representation" and notes that it has limited purchase for represen-

236

tation as a specifically political practice. In this conceptualization, representing is reduced to resembling, or *"being* like you, not *acting* like you." (1967, 89) This view

> does not allow for an activity of representing. . . . It has no room for any kind of representing as acting for, or on behalf of, others; which means that in the political realm it has no room for the creative activities of a representative legislature, the forging of consensus, the formulating of policy, the activity we roughly designate by "governing. . . ." Representing here can at most mean being typical or resembling. (1967, 90)

In the canonical literature on authority, we have seen that leaders are those whom we recognize as having authority to act because they exhibit certain marks or signs of leadership. Such marks entitle leaders to speak for the community. These may be certain personal characteristics, expert knowledge, the occupation of certain offices or roles, or some combination of all of these. Theorists of authority have generally accepted the argument that communal beliefs, as well as the "objective" requirements of different leadership roles, establish the initial criteria for recognizing authorities. Physiognomy, voice, and physical stature have been among the personal marks believed to signify one's being an authority. We speak, for instance, of a commanding presence, of authoritative voices. Rhythms, nuance, emphasis, and assertiveness in both tone and syntax appear to vary with gender and ethnicity. (Trinh 1988; Gates 1987) Nevertheless, Western discourse defines the masculine mode of self-assured, self-assertive, unqualified declarativeness as the model of authoritative speech. "Female" hesitancy and other-oriented language patterns, considered to be the marks of uncertainty or confusion, are excluded. Authoritative language as the language of the dominant and dominating is monopolized by the masculine voice. The mark of an authority depends upon the leader's distinctiveness from those others who lack its sign, who seem voiceless or silent. Those who are silent become feminized.

Leadership often has been justified through claims that invoke knowledge in order to establish legitimacy. Yet as we have seen, the kinds of knowledge that are thought to constitute a claim to authority also are embedded in a gendered system of signs. In modern Western discourse, knowledge that counts as such comes from the disinterested application of objective rules and techniques of knowing. Rationality is understood as the practice of a disembodied, decontextualized, and detached observer whose aim is to fix the truth, to become more comfortable in the world by exchanging myth for science. Cognition appears to be separated from affection. The epistemological urge then reflects a move "toward abstraction and toward comparison and grouping by common attributes. Abstraction and comparison in turn require measuring tools that will yield comparable units: among the favored ones are money, time, weight, distance, and power." (Schaar, *Legitimacy,* 36) Yet the urge to reduce ineluctably different "objects" to discrete, exchangeable parts betrays a desire to reduce the threat that difference represents: undomesticated difference, difference neither pregnant nor barefoot, neither enslaved nor stooped over a field, neither constructed as a lack nor a deformity, insists on itself as irreducible.

Some contemporary feminist theorists have made strong arguments for the case that objectifying knowledge has been linked to an ontology of hegemonic masculinity. They argue that the desire for certain knowledge, for the destruction of ambiguity, for controlling objects by having them yield up the truth of their nature under the imposing and persistent gaze of an observer who explains their words and actions to them, is a masculine way of knowing. (Keller 1985) Others have extended this criticism and have explored the colonialist ontology of the racial hegemony it also reflects. "We set out here, she and I, to undo an *anonymous,* all-male, and predominantly white collective entity named *he,* and we wish to freeze him once in a while in his hegemonic variants." (Trinh 1988, 48)

The question of what has been excluded from this field of knowledge has been connected by John Schaar and other political theorists to the search for "humanly meaningful authority and leadership." (Schaar, *Legitimacy,* 38) In recent feminist writings, especially by feminists of color, this search has been specifically linked to the development of an epistemology of differences that includes knowledge of differences not in order to make knowledge more complete but, rather, more opaque and heteronomous. Consequently, the ability of authority to found itself on solid ground has been radically called into question.

The literature on authority also includes the criterion of recognizing authorities by virtue of the roles that they occupy. In the political arena these roles most often are associated with governmental positions in the formal institutions of state. Access to the arenas of recruitment for such roles limits some groups' opportunities to be among those having authority. In recent years political science researchers have demonstrated that it is not so much women's lack of qualifications or lack of motivation that leads to their underrepresentation in the formal political systems of Western democracies. More important are the ways that political cultural factors, such as support for general welfare policies, as well as the structures of party and electoral systems, such as machine politics and single-member district systems, preclude women's greater participation.

Yet even if greater numbers of women enter these state systems, the question remains of what those public roles represent. The fact is that the roles most frequently associated with political authority reflect patterns of behavior more frequently associated with masculine than feminine action: government leaders, military rulers, "expert" consultants. We get used to thinking of heads of states as our fathers because, as Locke argued, we have been habituated through the ideology of the family to internalize the identification of paternal roles with authoritative roles. The circuit of political authority flows from fathers to military leaders to heads of state. Although Locke contended that this authority was derived from consent, it becomes questionable whether we can ever escape the logic of the circuit. Locke himself fell back on the assumption that fathers should rule by consent in families since, he claimed, we need one person to make decisions. "The one" should be the father/husband who is "naturally the abler and stronger." (Locke, 1960, 364) The roles of mothers, of wives, of community workers, of nonmilitary protectors become disconnected from the tasks associated with statecraft and leadership.

Even when the traditional bases of male-dominated roles have been eroded, as is the case with both the decline of kinship as the fundamental social link and the later transformation from property based patrimonial systems to symbolically based paternalistic systems, authoritative roles remain connected to the symbolic order of the father:

> In a paternalistic society, males continue to dominate. The domination is based on their roles as fathers: protectors, stern judges, the strong. But this basis is symbolic rather than material as in a patrimonial order. In a paternalistic society no father can guarantee to his children a known place in the world; he can only act protectively. (Sennett 1981, 54)

These roles institutionalize what Judith Stiehm has called the "male protection racket": a system of relationships that secures a woman's protection from any man who threatens her through structuring woman's dependence on the strength and willingness of other men. Leadership as male protection depends, then, on women's absence. The only way to break this cycle of female dependence, according to Stiehm, is for women to have access to force by becoming defenders. (1982, 367–74)

I have argued for broadening the options available for women aspiring to roles of authority without sacrificing the symbolism, familial and nonfamilial, linked with the female. Conditions of (post) modernity, such as the existence of nuclear weapons and the vast threats to ecological balance and the environment, have created the need to shift away from paternalism and the male protection racket as inefficient and heartless forms of social coordination no matter who practices them. Our understanding of authority changes if authoritative roles include female symbolism. Practices of leadership are altered toward a network model, and the relationship between leaders and followers shifts from a command-obedience structure based on fear of loss of protection toward a more consensual, egalitarian model. Leadership and the political action it stimulates move from efforts to destroy alternatives to those celebrating the birth of alternatives as new beginnings. (Elshtain, 1985, 51–55)

The paradigm shift away from authority's interest (purpose) in protection against threats to its interest in nurturant growth and augmented beginnings marks the displacement of the dominant discourse on community, which had conceptualized community as an abstract collectivity, by a communitarian discourse rooted in "concreteness and particularity" and in "the living reality of singularities, differences, and individualities rather than a human mass as objects of possible control or manipulation." (Elshtain 1985, 50, 53) Such a shift calls attention to the gendered, and hence falsely universal, discourse in which the authoritative has declared itself to be so.

In democratic theory, values are accepted as authoritative purposes to the extent that they are universally definable and abstractly applicable. They represent the interests of everyone and anyone, not anyone in particular. Liberty, equality, and justice, for instance, are abstract principles freed from their existential roots. As in Rawls theory, these are the sort of principles that we would arrive at behind "a veil of ignorance," where ignorance means to forget the peculiarly embodied dimensions of our *human* being and the fact that we are all "of woman born." But are the forms in which these values have been articulated truly universal? Is the idea of freedom as the practice of an autonomous self genderless? Is the conceptualization of equality as the ultimate substitutability of anyone for anyone genderless? Is justice as fairness, as the equitable application of *general* rules, a genderless, neutral conceptualization?

Reflecting on the dilemmas of being a woman writer of color who nonetheless wants her work accepted, Trinh Minh-ha explores how the authoritative norms of "good writing" resist the expression of the values of the world seen from her perspective:

> Achieve distance, they keep on saying, as much distance from your own voice as possible. . . . For a woman, such distance easily takes on the face of Alienation. She must *learn* not only to impersonalize the voice she stole or borrowed, but also to internalize gradually the impersonal generic interpretation of masculine pronouns and nouns. She must *learn* to paint her world with colors chosen more often than not by men for men to suit their realities. *She/her* has always conveyed the idea of a personal gender-specific voice. In order to be taken more seriously, she is therefore bound to dye this voice universal, a tint that can only be obtained through words like man, mankind, he-him. . . . Such a convenient way to generalize and to transcend the sex line. (1988, 27)

In this view both the requirement that there be "objective" and dispassionate distance from what is being spoken or written about, and the idea of the author as one who expresses the authoritative, like a God or Priest, participate in a discourse that reproduces a hierarchy which is foreign to interpretations of women's experiences.

An alternative conceptualization of the authoritative, in form and substance, turns on a reconfigured understanding of the language and practice of authorship. In place of the idea of authorship as the revealing of truths (the authoritative) to a passive readership, this counter view interrogates the "modalities of production and reception of meaning." (Trinh 1988, 42) It first calls attention to and then blurs the borders separating the author from the reader and the ruler from the ruled, moving authority away from conceptualization in terms of master-slave discourses and the language of dominance. Yet if authors give meaning to the world, this practice must be different from *noblesse oblige*, from a gift giving that reinforces the relationship of subservience between recipient and giver. We need a practice of authority and authorship that does not always say "I am giving to you so that I can keep you for my own."

Naming the authoritative values or founding principles of order that give guidance to a community within the language of this discourse of particularity and difference is complex. How is it possible to speak coherently about the authoritative within a language that calls attention to differences, that defers meaning, and that resists the hegemony of settled, revealed truths or fixed meanings? The possibility of sustaining coherence depends first upon an awareness of the epistemic, historical location out of which any values emerge. Metaphorically speaking, our perspective is changed from one looking toward the heavens to one that is earthbound. We exchange the vertical for the horizontal, but with an awareness that the earth is not flat and that we are located on it in changing relation to each other's location. Equally important is awareness of who is speaking to and about whom. Maybe "speaking for" is a position we will need to abandon even when the ones we are speaking for are "like" us, at least according to our wishes and needs.

The recent emphasis in feminist theory and in African-American literary theory has been to describe the perspective of the nondominant in ways that do not simply superimpose one set of meanings and signs on another, but develop an enabling discourse which "reshap[es] the critical canon with our own voice and in our own images." (Gates 1987, 35) This emphasis has suggestive, if problematic, implications for reconceptualizing the voice of authority. Growing out of awareness of the emergence of authoritative values from the material, the concrete, and the everyday is a new emphasis on a *vernacular idiom* within which to express such values. To avoid "discursive indenture," (Gates 1987, 41) to resist being enslaved again by having to represent one's self in the language of the dominant in order to be heard, becomes imperative. So the writings of feminist theorists renew the stress on the importance of developing a discourse that is based in the material lives of the subjects it intends to describe and on giving "voice" to "experience." Such theorists draw a sharp distinction between "authentically" vernacular speech and the translation and derogation of this vernacular idiom into the language of "nativism":

> Have you ever attended a white man's presentation (often also ours) on a "native" society, be he a photographer, a filmmaker, a choreographer, a musician, a speaker, or a writer? It is as if, unvaryingly, every single look, gesture, or utterance has been *stained with anthropological discourse,* the only discourse in power when it is a question of the (native) Other. Knowledge belongs to the one who succeeds in mastering a language, and standing closer to the civilized language is, as a matter of fact, coming nearer to equality. (Trinh 1988, 56, emphasis added)

Yet the question of discovering one's *own* "authentic" voice and making incursions into the canon by means of it is profoundly complicated and ironic. Insisting on a voice of difference risks, we have seen, reestablishing the very possessiveness and self-legitimating characteristics of speaking "with authority" that it appears to oppose. Only I who am speaking know (own) what I mean. The challenge is to get others to listen to what "different" voices are saying without negating the participation of the recipient and while simultaneously avoiding having the reader/listener/citizen merely retranslate different voices and visions into the language of the dominant. This is the dilemma reflected in debates about interpretations of the authoritative, about canonicity. If you cannot use the master's tools to dismantle the master's house, (Lourde 1984) then how can you develop different tools to build authority?

I have argued that the extent to which the reconfiguration of authority in the language of the vernacular remains dependent on the discourse of authenticity—the "truly" vernacular, as opposed to the imitative—will limit the extent to which it can escape the kind of representational matrix that constructs a circuit connecting authority with sovereignty. This representational matrix sees the author/speaker/representer as a delegate of the social constituency that she resembles. It carries into the process of meaning-building the very policing of borders that it otherwise opposes.

Recently, Henry Louis Gates discussed the paradox implicit in debates about the constitution of a literary canon or tradition. Once we limit the notion of cultural authenticity to those who are members of the culture, he argued, we necessarily engage in the kinds of paralyzing debates about ethnic, racial, sexual, or class identity that mirror the nineteenth century legal system that "went to absurd lengths to demarcate even octoroons and demi-octoroons from their white brothers and sisters." ("The Lesson of Little Tree," *New York Times Book Review,* November 24, 1991, 26) Instead, Gates called for an approach to literature and authorship that neither reduced ethnic or sexual identity to "mere contingency" nor made it a straight-jacketing determinant of whose interpretations were legitimate. It is true that "our histories, individual and collective, do affect what we wish to write and what we are able to write. But that relation is never one of fixed determinism. No human culture is inaccessible to someone who makes the effort to understand, to learn, to inhabit another world." (1991, 30) "Learning to inhabit another world," "world-travelling," "Being at home in the world." Each of these phrases has been evocative of an often unrecognized and certainly underarticulated connection between authority and the foundation of political community in a world of plurality.

Claude Lefort suggested in a recent work that "the peculiarity of modern democracy . . . is [that it is] the only one to have represented power in such a way as to show that power is an empty place . . . that those who exercise power do not possess it; that they do not embody it." (Lefort 1988, 225) Yet I have argued that those who have been recognized as present in the place of power and authority in modern democracies generally have had to conform to specific forms of presence and modes of action that are both embodied and gendered in order to be recognized as being "there" in the first place. This fact has been masked by liberal democracy's postulation of popular sovereignty as a "pure diversity of individuals, each one of whom is abstracted from the network of social ties within which his existence is determined. . . ." (Lefort 1988, 227). Individuals appear to be abstracted from social ties yet, as Marx noted, the structure of social ties still limits the extent to which some individuals can be more abstracted and, therefore, more present, than others.

The kind of community that liberal democracy constructs is illusory. Feminists have noted that it also is androcentric because of the sorts of claims and connections that have been excluded. Feminists have begun to elaborate an as yet unsynthesized alternative set of *norms of presence and purpose* capable of rendering "women's interests" politically salient and visible. These norms ultimately depend upon a theory of community for clarity—with whom we are together in public space, what our relations with one another are understood to be and mean, and what our responsibilities are. I have argued that these norms of presence and purpose might push us towards a reconceptualization of authority that lessens the hold of the dominant view of it as a practice of rules and modifies this practice by the view of "compassionate authority." But I also have argued that compassion is not ruleless. Thus, compassion does not abandon rules or rights; instead, it seeks to enrich these conceptions by detaching them and itself from private, possessive moorings.

Joan Tronto's discussion of an ethic of care is germane. "An ethic of care," Tronto writes, "constitutes a view of self, relationships, and social order that may not be incompatible with the emphasis of individual rights that is so predominant in Western, liberal, democratic societies." But she warns that "as onerous as rights may seem when viewed from the standpoint of our desires for connected, extended selves, they do serve at least somewhat to protect oppressed individuals." (Tronto 1987, 662) The elaboration of a theory of community that addresses these dilemmas returns us to arguments about authority.

A more fruitful, more humane practice of authority will follow the cues offered by the return to a consideration of authority as the relationship that founds the meaningfulness of a political community not in terms of command-obedience structures of imposed interpretations, but by weaving stories together that invite dialogue across our differences.

This book has explored where this return might take us together.

Bibliography

Alarcón, Norma. "The Theoretical Subject(s) of This Bridge Called My Back and Anglo-American Feminism." In *Making Face, Making Soul: Haciendo Caras, Creative and Critical Perspectives by Women of Color,* edited by Gloria Anzaldúa. San Francisco: Aunt Lute Foundation Books, 1990.

Alcoff, Linda. "Cultural Feminism versus Poststructuralism: The Identity Crisis in Feminist Theory." *Signs* 13 (1988): 405–36.

Allen, Paula Gunn. *The Sacred Hoop: Recovering the Feminine in American Indian Traditions.* Boston: Beacon Press, 1986.

Altorki, Soroyo, and Camillia Fawzi, eds. *Arab Women in the Field: Studying Your Own Society.* Syracuse, NY: Syracuse University Press, 1988.

Anzaldúa, Gloria. *Borderlands/La Frontera: The New Mestiza.* San Francisco: Aunt Lute Foundation Books, 1987.

———. *"En Rapport,* in Opposition: *Cobrano Cuentas a las Nuestras."* In *Making Face, Making Soul: Haciendo Caras, Creative and Critical Perspectives by Women,* edited by Gloria Anzaldúa. San Francisco: Aunt Lute Foundation Books, 1990.

———, ed. *Making Face, Making Soul: Haciendo Caras, Creative and Critical Perspectives by Women.* San Francisco: Aunt Lute Foundation Books, 1990.

Aptheker, Bettina. *Tapestries of Life: Women's Work, Women's Consciousness and the Meaning of Daily Experience.* Amherst, Mass.: University of Massachusetts Press, 1989.

Aquinas, Thomas. "Summa Theologica." In *Selected Political Writings,* edited by A. P. Entreves and translated by J. G. Dawson. Totowa, N.J.: Barnes and Noble Books, 1981.

Arendt, Hannah. *Between Past and Future.* New York: Viking Press, 1968.

———. *The Human Condition.* Chicago: University of Chicago Press, 1958.

———. *On Revolution.* New York: Viking Press, 1963.

———. *On Violence.* New York: Harcourt Brace and Jovanovich, 1970.

Atwood, Margaret. "Paradoxes and Dilemmas: The Woman as Writer." In *Woman as Writer,* edited by Webber and Grumman. Boston: Houghton Mifflin, 1978.

Axton, Marie. *The Queen's Two Bodies: Drama and the Elizabethan Succession.* London: 1977.

Aylmer, John. *An Harborowe for Faithfvll and Trewe Svbiects, Agaynst the Late Blowne Blast, Concerninge the Gouernment of Wemen.* In Phillips.

Barber-Banfield, G. J. *The Horrors of the Half-Known Life: Male Attitudes Toward Women and Sexuality in Nineteenth Century America.* New York: Harper and Row, 1976.

Barry, Brian. "Warrender and His Critics." In *Hobbes and Rousseau,* edited by Cranston and Peters.

246

Bartky, Sandra Lee. "Foucault, Femininity, and Patriarchal Power." In *Feminism and Foucault: Reflections on Resistance,* edited by Diamond and Quinby. Boston: Northeastern University Press, 1988.

Bassnett, Susan. *Elizabeth I: A Feminist Perspective.* New York: St. Martin's Press, 1988.

Bataille, George. *Death and Sensuality.* New York: Arno Press, 1977.

Belenky, Mary Field, Blythe McVicker Linchy, Nancy Rule Goldberger, and Jill Mattuck Tarule. *Women's Ways of Knowing: The Developing of Self, Voice, and Mind.* New York: Basic Books, 1986.

Bell, Wendell, Richard J. Hill, and Charles R. Wright. *Public Leadership.* San Francisco: Chandler Publishing Co., 1961.

Benhabib, Seyla. "The Generalized Other and the Concrete Other: The Kohlberg-Gilligan Controversy and Moral Theory." In *Women and Moral Theory,* edited by Eve Feder Kittay, and Diana T. Meyers. Totowa, NJ: Rowman and Littelfield, 1987.

Benhabib, Selya, and Drucilla Cornell, eds. *Feminism as Critique: On the Politics of Gender.* Minneapolis, MN: University of Minnesota Press, 1987.

Benjamin, Jessica. "Master and Slave." In *Powers of Desire: The Politics of Sexuality,* edited by Ann Snitow, Christine Stansell, and Sharon Thompson. New York: Monthly Review Press, 1983.

Bloom, Alan. *The Closing of the American Mind.* New York: Simon and Schuster, 1987.

Bodin, Jean. *The Six Bookes of the Commonwealth.* Edited by Kenneth McCrae. Cambridge, MA: 1962.

Bookman, Ann and Sandra Morgan, eds. *Women and the Politics of Empowerment.* Philadelphia: Temple University Press, 1989.

Bordo, Susan. "Feminism, Postmodernism and Gender Skepticism." In Linda Nicholson.

Boserup, Esther. *Women's Role in Economic Development.* New York: St. Martin's Press, 1970.

Bowler, Peter J. "Preformation and Pre-Existence in the Seventeenth Century: A Brief Analysis." *Journal of the History of Biology* 4 (1971): 221–44.

Bowles, Gloria, and Renata Dueli Klein. *Theories of Women's Studies.* Routledge and Kegan Paul, 1983.

Boxer, Marilyn. "For and About Women: The Theory and Practice of Women's Studies in the United States." *Signs,* 1982.

Brennan, Teresa, and Carol Pateman. " 'Mere Auxiliaries to the Commonwealth': Women and the Origins of Liberalism." *Political Studies* 27 (1979): 183–200.

Brown, Wendy. *Manhood and Politics: A Feminist Reading in Political Theory.* Totowa, NJ: Rowman and Littlefield, 1988.

———. "Feminist Hesitations, Postmodern Exposures." *differences* 3 (1991): 63–84.

Butler, Judith. *Gender Trouble: Feminism and the Subversion of Identity.* Routledge, 1990.

———. "Gender Trouble, Feminist Theory and Psychoanalytic Discourse." In *Feminism/Postmodernism,* edited by Linda Nicholson. Routledge, 1990.

Calloway, Barbara. "Contrasting Socialization of Igbo and Hausa Women and Political Efficacy." *Women and Politics* 8 (1988): 45–68.

Caraway, Nancy. *Segregated Sisterhood.* Philadelphia: Temple University Press, 1991.

Chodorow, Nancy. *The Reproduction of Mothering.* Berkeley, CA: University of California Press, 1978.

Christian, Barbara. "The Race for Theory." In *Making Face, Making Soul: Haciendo Caras*, edited by Gloria Anzaldúa. San Francisco: Aunt Lute, 1990.

Clark, Stewart. "Inversion, Misrule, and the Meaning of Witchcraft." *Past and Present* 87 (1980): 98–127.

Clark, Suzanne and Kathleen Hulley. "An Interview with Julia Kristeva: Cultural Strangeness and the Subject in Crisis." *Discourse* 13 (1990–91): 149–80.

Clastres, Pierre. *Society Against the State*. Translated by Robert Hurley. Zone Books, 1987.

Clifford, James. "On Ethnographic Authority." *Representations* 1 (1983): 118–46.

Cocks, Joan. *The Oppositional Imagination: Feminism, Critique and Political Theory*. New York: Routledge, 1989.

Collins, Patricia Hill. *Black Feminist Thought*. Unwin and Hyman, 1991.

Connolly, William. "Modern Authority and Ambiguity." *Nomos* xxix: *Authority Revisited*, edited by Rolland Pennock and John W. Chapman. New York: New York University Press, 1987.

Coole, Diana. *Women in Political Theory*. Sussex, England: Wheatsheaf Books, 1988.

Cowan, Ruth Schwartz. *More Work for Mother: The Ironies of Household Technology from the Open Hearth to the Microwave*. New York: Basic Books, 1983.

Cranston, Maurice and Richard S. Peters, eds. *Hobbes and Rousseau*. New York: Anchor, 1972.

Crawford, Patricia. "Attitudes to Menstruation in Seventeenth Century England." *Past and Present* 91 (1981): 47–73.

Darcy, R., Susan Welch and Janet Clark. *Women, Elections, and Representation*. New York: Longman, 1987.

Davidoff, Leonore and Catherine Hall. *Family Fortunes: Men and Women of the English Working Class, 1780–1850*. London, 1987.

Davis, Natalie Zemon. *Society and Culture in Early Modern France*. Stanford, CA: Stanford University Press, 1975.

de Jouvenel, Bertrand. *Sovereignty: An Inquiry into the Political Good*. Chicago: University of Chicago Press, 1957.

de Lauretis, Teresa, ed. *Feminist Studies/Critical Studies*. Bloomington, IN: Indiana University Press, 1986.

de Pisan, Christine. *The Book of the City of Ladies*. New York: Persea, 1982.

Derrida, Jacques. *Dissemination*. Chicago: University of Chicago Press, 1981.

———. *Ear of the Other*. New York: Schocken Books, 1985.

Diamond and Quinby. *Feminism and Foucault: Reflections on Resistance*. Boston: Northeastern University Press, 1988.

Dietz, Mary, ed. *Thomas Hobbes and Political Theory*. Kansas: University of Kansas Press, 1990.

Dinnerstein, Dorothy. *Mermaid and the Minotaur*. New York: Harper and Row, 1976.

Di Stefano, Christine. "Masculinity as Ideology in Political Theory: Hobbesian Man Reconsidered." *Women's Studies International Forum* 6 (1983): 633–44.

———. *Configurations of Masculinity: A Feminist Perspective on Modern Political Theory*. Ithaca, NY, Cornell University Press, 1991.

Dostoevsky, Fyodor. *Brothers Karamazov*. New York: The Modern Library, 1937.

duBois, Page. *Sowing the Body: Psychoanalysis and Ancient Representations of Women*. Chicago: University of Chicago Press, 1988.

Dunham, William Huse, and Charles T. Wood. "The Right to Rule in England: Depositions and the Kingdom's Authority, 1327–1485." *American Historical Review* 81 (1976): 738–61.

Eisenstein, Zillah R. *The Female Body and the Law*. Berkeley, Calif: University of California Press, 1988.

———. *The Radical Future of Liberal Feminism*. New York: Longman, 1981.

Elshtain, Jean Bethke, ed. *Power Trips and Other Journeys: Essays in Feminism as Civic Discourse*. Madison, Wisconsin: University of Wisconsin Press, 1990.

———. *Public Man/Private Woman*. Princeton, N.J.: Princeton University Press, 1981.

———. "Reflections on War and Political Discourse: Realism, Just War and Feminism in the Nuclear Age." *Political Theory* 13 (1985): 39–57.

———. *Women and War*. New York: Basic Books, 1987.

Emichita, Buchi. *The Joys of Motherhood*. New York: Braziller, 1979.

Evans, Sara. *Personal Politics*. New York: Vintage, 1980.

Feral, Josette. "Antigone or the Irony of the Tribe." *Diacritics* 8 (1979).

Ferguson, Kathy. *Feminist Case Against Bureaucracy*. Philadelphia: Temple University Press, 1984.

Flathman, Richard. *The Practice of Political Authority: Authority and the Authoritative*. Chicago: University of Chicago Press, 1980.

Flax, Jane. "Mother-Daughter Relationships: Psychodynamics, Politics, and Philosophy." In *The Future of Difference,* edited by Hester Eisenstein and Alice Jardine. Boston: G. K. Hall, 1980.

Fletcher, George. "The Individualization of Excuse." *Southern California Law Review* 47 (1974): 1269–1304.

———. *Rethinking Criminal Law*. Boston: Little, Brown, 1978.

Foucault, Michel. *The Birth of the Clinic: An Archaeology of Medical Perception*. London, 1973.

———. *Discipline and Punish: The Birth of the Prison*. New York: Vintage, 1979.

———. *Herculine Barbin: Being the Recently Discovered Memoirs of a Nineteenth Century French Hermaphrodite*. New York: Pantheon, 1980.

———. *Power/Knowledge: Selected Interviews and Other Writings, 1972–1977*. New York: Pantheon, 1980.

Fraser, Antonia. *The Warrior Queens*. New York: Knopf, 1989.

Fraser, Nancy. "Toward a Discourse Ethic of Solidarity." *Praxis International* 4 (1984): 425–9.

———. "What's Critical About Critical Theory? The Case of Habermas and Gender." In *Feminism as Critique: On the Politics of Gender,* edited by Selya Benhabib and Drucilla Cornell. Minneapolis, Minn.: University of Minnesota Press, 1987.

Freud, Sigmund. *Civilization and Its Discontents*. Edited by James Strachey. New York: Norton, 1961.

Friedman, Richard. "On the Concept of Authority in Political Philosophy." In *Concepts in Social and Political Philosophy,* edited by Richard Flathman. New York: Macmillan, 1973.

Fuss, Diana. *Essentially Speaking: Feminism, Nature, and Difference*. New York: Routledge, 1989.

Gallop, Jane. "Feminist Criticism and the Pleasure of the Text." In Schor.

Gates, Henry Louis. "Authority, (White) Power, and the (Black) Critic: It's All Greek to Me." *Cultural Critique* 7 (1987): 19–46.

Ghoussaub, Mai. "A Reply to Hammami and Reiker." *New Left Review* 170 (1988): 107–9.

Gilligan, Carol. *In a Different Voice*. Cambridge, MA: Harvard University Press, 1982.

Gilman, Sander. *Difference and Pathology: Stereotypes of Sexuality, Race and Madness*. Ithaca, NY: Cornell University Press, 1985.

Githens, Marianne, and Jewell Prestage. *A Portrait of Marginality: The Political Behavior of the American Woman.* McKay, 1977.

Gordon, Linda. "Review of Joan Scott, *Gender and the Politics of History.*" *Signs* 15 (1990): 853–58.

Green and Lattimore, eds. *Greek Tragedies.* Chicago: University of Chicago Press, 1960.

Habermas, Jurgen. *The Theory of Communicative Action,* vol. 1: *Reason and the Rationalization of Society.* Boston: Beacon Press, 1983.

Hammami, Reza, and Martina Rieker. "Feminist Orientation and Orientalist Marxism." *New Left Review* 170 (1988): 93–106.

Haraway, Donna. "A Manifesto for Cyborgs: Science, Technology and Socialist Feminism in the 1980s." *Socialist Review* 15 (1985): 65–107.

Harding, Sandra. "The Instability of the Analytic Categories in Feminist Theory." *Signs* 11 (1986): 645–64.

———. *The Science Question in Feminism.* Ithaca, N.Y.: Cornell University Press, 1986.

———, ed. *Feminism and Methodology.* Bloomington, IN: Indiana University Press, 1987.

Hartsock, Nancy. *Money, Sex and Power: Toward a Feminist Historical Materialism.* New York: Longman, 1983.

———. "Rethinking Modernism: Minority v. Majority Theories." *Cultural Critique* (1987): 189.

Hawkesworth, Mary. "Feminist Rhetoric: Discourses on the Male Monopoly of Thought." *Political Theory* 16 (1988): 444–67.

Hegel, G. W. F. *Phenomenology.* Oxford, England: Oxford University Press, 1979.

Held, Virginia. "Feminist Transformations of Moral Theory." *Philosophy and Phenomenological Research* 1 (Supplement 1990): 321–344.

Herzog, Don. *Happy Slaves.* Chicago: University of Chicago Press, 1989.

Hirsch, Marianne and Evelyn Fox Keller. *Conflicts in Feminism.* Routledge, 1990.

Hill, Melvyn A. ed. *Hannah Arendt: The Recovery of the Public World.* New York: St. Martin's Press, 1979.

Hobbes, Thomas. *Leviathan: Or the Matter, Forme and Power of a Commonwealth Ecclesiastical and Civil.* Edited by Michael Oakeshott. New York: Collier, 1962.

———. *Man and Citizen: Thomas Hobbes's De Homine and De Cive.* Edited by Bernard Gert. New York: Anchor Books, 1972.

Honig, B. "Declarations of Independence: Arendt and Derrida on the Problem of Founding a Republic." *American Political Science Review* 85 (1991): 97–114.

hooks, bell. *Ain't I a Woman?* Boston: South End Press, 1982.

———. *Feminist Theory: From Margin to Center.* Boston: South End Press, 1984.

———. *Yearnings: Race, Gender, and Cultural Politics.* Boston: South End Press, 1990.

hooks, bell, and Mary Childers. "A Conversation About Race and Sex." In *Conflicts in Feminism,* edited by M. Hirsch and E. Keller. Routledge, 1990.

Illich, Ivan. *Gender.* NY: Hayday Books, 1988.

Irigaray, Luce. *Speculum of the Other Woman.* Translated by Gillian G. Gill. Ithaca, NY: Cornell University Press, 1985.

———. *This Sex Which Is Not the One: The Power of Discourse.* Ithaca, N.Y.: Cornell University Press, 1985.

Jacobus, Mary, Evelyn Fox Keller, and Sally Shuttleworth, eds. *Body/Politics: Women and the Discourses of Science.* New York: Routledge, 1990.

Jay, Martin. "The Empire of the Gaze: Foucault and the Denigration of Vision in Twentieth Century French Thought." In *Foucault: A Critical Reader*, edited by David Couzens Hoy. NY: Blackwell Publishers, 1986.

Jaquette, Jane, ed. *Women in Politics.* New York: John Wiley and Sons, 1974.

Jayaratne, Toby. "The Value of Quantitative Research Methodology for Feminist Research." In *Theories of Women's Studies,* edited by Gloria Bowles and Renate Klein. London: Routledge and Kegan Paul, 1983.

Johnson, Barbara. "Introduction." In *Dissemination,* by Jacques Derrida. Chicago: University of Chicago Press, 1981.

———. *A World of Difference.* Baltimore, Md.: Johns Hopkins University Press, 1987.

Johnston, David. *The Rhetoric of Leviathan: Thomas Hobbes and the Politics of Cultural Transformation.* Princeton, N.J.: Princeton University Press, 1987.

Jónasdóttir, Anna. *Love, Power, and Political Interests: Towards a Political Theory of Patriarchy in Contemporary Western Society.* Göteborg, Sweden: Örebro Studies 7, 1991.

Jones, Kathleen B. "The Articulation of Authority: Women, Nature, and Relations of Domination." Paper Presented at the American Political Science Association-NEH sponsored Seminar, Washington, D.C., 1980.

———. "The Irony of the Insanity Plea: A Theory of Relativity." *Journal of Psychiatry and Law* (Fall 1982): 285–308.

———. "Women, Compassion, and Rationality: Rethinking the Power/Authority Distinction." *Papers in Comparative Studies* 4 (1984): 81–90.

———. "On Authority, or Why Women Are Not Entitled to Speak." *NOMOS XXIX: Authority Revisited,* edited by Rolland Pennock and John Chapman, New York: New York University Press, 1987.

———. "Le Mal des Fleurs: A Feminist Response to the *Closing of the American Mind." Women and Politics* 9 (1989): 1–22.

———. "Citizenship in a Woman-Friendly Polity." *Signs* 15 (1990): 781–812.

———. "Boundaries: Feminist Citizenship and the National Security State. Paper Presented at the Meeting of the International Political Science Association. Buenos Aires, Argentina, 1991.

Jones, Kathleen B., and Anna Jónasdóttir. *The Political Interests of Gender: Developing Theory and Research with a Feminist Face.* London: Sage Publications, 1988.

Jones, Kathleen B., and Françoise Vergès. "Women, Politics and the Paris Commune of 1991." *History of European Ideas* 13 (1991): 711–32.

Jordanova, L. J. *Sexual Visions: Images of Gender in Science and Medicine Between the Eighteenth and Twentieth Centuries.* London: Harvester Wheatsheaf, 1976.

Kahn, R. F. "A Note on the Concept of Authority." In *Leadership and Authority,* edited by Gehan Wijeyewardene. Singapore: University of Malaya Press, 1968.

Kantorowicz, Ernest. *The King's Two Bodies: A Study in Medieval Political Theology.* Princeton, NJ: Princeton University Press, 1957.

Kaplan, E. Ann. *Women and Film: Both Sides of the Camera.* Methuen, 1983.

Kateb, George. *Hannah Arendt: Politics, Conscience, Evil.* Totowa, N.J.: Rowman and Allenheld, 1983.

Keller, Catherine. *From a Broken Web: Separation, Sexism, Self.* Boston: Beacon Press, 1986.

Keller, Evelyn Fox. *Reflections on Gender and Science.* New Haven, CT: Yale University Press, 1985.

———. "Feminist Perspectives on Science Studies." *Barnard Occasional Papers on Women's Issues* 3 (1988): 10–36.

———. "From Secrets of Life to Secrets of Death." In *Body/Politics: Women and the Discourse of Science,* edited by Mary Jacobus, Evelyn Fox Keller, and Sally Shuttleworth. New York. Routledge, 1990.

———. "Feminism, Science, and Postmodernism," *Cultural Critique* 13 (1990): 15–32.

Kelly, Joan. "Early Feminist Theory and the Querelle des Femmes, 1400–1789." *Signs* 8 (1982): 4–28.

Kerber, Linda K., Catherine G. Greeno and Eleanor E. Maccoby, Zella Luria, Carol B. Stack, and Carol Gilligan. "On *In a Different Voice:* An Interdisciplinary Forum." *Signs* 11 (1986): 304–33.

Knox, John. *First Blast of the Trumpet Against the Monstrous Regiment of Women.* [1588] In *The Works of John Knox,* edited by David Laing. Edinburgh, Scotland: James Thin, 1864.

Kuhn, Annette. *Women's Pictures: Feminism and Cinema.* Routledge and Kegan Paul, 1982.

Ladner, Joyce. "Introduction to *Tomorrow's Tomorrow: The Black Woman."* In *Feminism and Methodology,* edited by Sandra Harding. Bloomington, IN: Indiana University Press, 1987.

Laing, David, ed. *The Works of John Knox.* Edinburgh, Scotland: James Thin, 1864.

Landes, Joan B. *Women and the Public Spherre in the Age of the French Revolution.* Ithaca, NY: Cornell University Press, 1988.

Laqueur, Thomas. "The Facts of Fatherhood." In *Conflicts in Feminism,* edited by M. Hirsch and E. Keller. Routledge, 1990.

———. *Making Sex: Body and Gender from the Greeks to Freud.* Cambridge, MA: Harvard University Press, 1990.

Lasch, Christopher. *The Culture of Narcissism: American Life in an Age of Diminishing Expectations.* New York: Norton, 1978.

Laski, Harold. *Authority in the Modern State.* Archon Books, 1968.

Laykoff, Robin Tolmach. *Talking Power: The Politics of Language.* NY: Basic Books, 1990.

Lefort, Claude. *Democracy and Political Theory.* Minneapolis: University of Minnesota Press, 1988.

Lerner, Gerda. *The Majority Finds Its Past.* Oxford, England: Oxford University Press, 1979.

Levesque-Lopman, Louise. *Claiming Reality: Phenomenology and Women's Experiences.* Totowa, NJ: Rowman and Littlefield, 1988.

Levine, Carole. "Queens and Claimants in Sixteenth Century England." In *Gender, Ideology and Action: Historical Perspectives on Women's Public Lives,* edited by Janet Sharistanian. Westport, CT: Greenwood Press, 1986.

Lloyd, Genevieve. "Selfhood, War and Masculinity." In *Feminist Challenges: Social and Political Theory,* edited by Carole Pateman and Elizabeth Gross. Boston: Northeastern University Press, 1987.

Locke, John. *Two Treatises of Government,* edited by Peter Laslett. New York: Mentor Books, 1960.

Lourde, Audre. *Sister Outsider: Essays and Speeches.* Trumansburg: Crossing Press, 1984.

Love, Nancy. "Politics and Voice(s): An Empowerment/Knowledge Regime." *Differences* 3 (1991): 85–103.

Lugones, María. "Playfulness, 'World'-Travelling, and Loving Perception." In *Making Face, Making Soul: Haciendo Caras, Creative and Critical Perspectives by Women of Color,* edited Gloria Anzaldúa. San Francisco: Aunt Lute Foundation Books, 1990.

Lugones, María, and Elizabeth Spelman. "Have We Got a Theory for You! Feminist Theory, Cultural Imperialism and the Demand for 'Woman's Voice.' " *Women's Studies International Forum* 6 (1983): 573–81.

Lyotard, Jean François. *The Postmodern Condition: A Report on Knowledge.* Minneapolis, MN: University of Minnesota Press, 1989.

MacIntyre, Alasdair. *After Virtue.* Notre Dame, IN: University of Notre Dame Press, 1981.

MacKinnon, Catherine. "Feminism, Marxism, Method and the State: An Agenda for Theory." *Signs* 7 (1982): 515–44.

MacKinnon, Catherine. *Feminism Unmodified.* Cambridge, MA: Harvard University Press, 1987.

MacMillan, Carol. *Women, Reason, and Nature.* Princeton, NJ: Princeton University Press, 1982.

Marcuse, Herbert. *One Dimensional Man: Studies in the Ideology of Advanced Industrial Society.* Boston: Beacon Press, 1966.

Martin, Biddy, and Chandra Mohanty. "Feminist Politics: What's Home Got to Do with It?" In *Feminist Studies/Critical Studies,* edited by Teresa de Lauretis. Bloomington, IN: Indiana University Press, 1986.

Marx, Karl. *Economic and Philosophic Manuscripts of 1844.* New York: International Publishers, 1964.

———. *Grundrisse.* Edited by David Mclellan. New York: Harper and Row, 1972.

———. *The German Ideology.* In *The Marx-Engels Reader,* edited by Robert Tucker. New York: Norton, 1987.

Marx, Karl and Friedrich Engels. *Collected Works.* London: Lawrence and Wisehart, 1975.

Mascia-Lees, Frances E., Patricia Sharpe, and Colleen Ballerino Cohen. "The Postmodern Turn in Anthropology: Cautions from a Feminist Perspective." *Signs* 15 (1989): 7–31.

McClelland, David. *Power: The Inner Experience.* New York: Irvington, 1975.

McDaniel, Judith. *Sanctuary: A Journey.* Ithaca, NY: Firebrand Books, 1987.

Meilaender, Gilbert. "A Little Monarchy: Hobbes on the Family." *Thought* 53 (1978): 401–15.

Melville, Herman. *Benito Cereno.* London: Nonesuch Press, 1926.

———. *Billy Budd and Other Tales.* Signet, 1961.

Mies, Maria. "Towards a Methodology for Feminist Research." In *Theories of Women's Studies,* edited by Gloria Bowles and Renata Klein. London: Routledge and Kegan Paul, 1983.

Miles, Sara, Patricia Jones, Sandra Esteves, and Fay Chiang, eds. *Ordinary Women/ Mujeres Comunes.* New York: Ordinary Women, 1978.

Miller, Nancy. "Changing the Subject: Authorship, Writing and the Reader." In *Feminist Studies/Critical Studies,* edited by Teresa de Lauretis. Bloomington, IN: Indiana University Press, 1986.

Millman, Marcia and Rosabeth Moss Kanter. *Another Voice: Feminist Perspectives on Social Life and Social Science.* New York: Doubleday Anchor, 1975.

Miner, Valerie and Helen Longino, eds. *Competition: A Feminist Taboo?* NY: The Feminist Press, 1987.

Modleski, Tania. "Feminism and the Power of Interpretation." In *Feminist Studies/*

Critical Studies, edited by Teresa de Lauretis. Bloomington, IN: Indiana University Press, 1986.

———. *The Women Who Knew Too Much: Hitchcock and Feminist Theory.* New York: Methuen, 1988.

Mohanty, Chandra. "Under Western Eyes: Feminist Scholarship and Colonial Discourse." *boundary* 2 (1984): 337–38.

Montrose, Louis Adrian. "Shaping Fantasies: Figurations of Gender and Power in Elizabethan Culture." *Representations* 1 (1983): 61–94.

Moraga, Cherríe. *Loving in the War Years: lo que nunca pasó por sus labios.* Boston: South End Press, 1983.

Moraga Cherríe and Gloria Anzaldúa, eds. *This Bridge Called My Back: Writings By Radical Women of Color.* San Francisco: Aunt Lute, 1983.

Morgen, Sandra, and Ann Bookman. *Women and the Politics of Empowerment.* Philadelphia: Temple University Press, 1988.

Morsy, Soheir. "Fieldwork in My Egyptian Homeland: Toward the Demise of Anthropology's Distinctive Other Hegemonic Discourse." In *Arab Women in the Field: Studying Your Own Society,* edited by Soroyo Altorki and Camillia Fawzi E1-I1. Syracuse, NY: Syracuse University Press, 1988.

Mulvey, Laura. "Visual Pleasure and Narrative Cinema." In *Feminism and Film Theory,* edited by Constance Penley. Routledge, 1988.

Nedelsky, Jennifer. "Law, Boundaries, and the Bounded Self." *Representations* 30 (1990): 162–89.

Nelson, Cynthia. "Public and Private: Women in the Middle Eastern World." *American Ethnologist* (1974).

New York Times, July 15, 1989, p. 15.

Nicholson, Linda. "Feminism and Marx: Integrating Kinship with the Economic." In *Feminism as Critique: On the Politics of Gender,* edited by Selya Benhabib and Drucilla Cornell. Minneapolis, MN: University of Minnesota Press, 1987.

Nicholson, Linda. ed. *Feminism/Postmodernism.* New York: Routledge, 1990.

Oakeshott, Michael. *On Human Conduct.* Oxford, England: Clarendon Press, 1975.

Oakley, Ann. *The Sociology of Housework.* New York: Pantheon, 1975.

O'Brien, Mary. *The Politics of Reproduction.* Routledge and Kegan Paul, 1981.

Okin, Susan. *Women in Western Political Thought.* Princeton, NJ: Princeton University Press, 1979.

———. *Justice, Gender and the Family.* NY: Basic Books, 1991.

Ong, Aihwa. "Colonialism and Modernity: Feminist Representations of Women in Non-Western Societies." *Inscriptions* 3/4 (1988).

Pateman, Carole. *Participation and Democratic Theory.* Cambridge, England: Cambridge University Press, 1970.

———. *The Problem of Political Obligation: A Critical Analysis of Liberal Theory.* New York: Wiley, 1979.

———. "The Disorder of Women: Women, Love, and the Sense of Justice." *Ethics* 91 (1980): 20–34.

———. "Women and Consent." *Political Theory* 8 (1980): 149–168.

———. *The Sexual Contract.* Stanford, CA: Stanford University Press, 1988.

Penley, Constance, ed. *Feminism and Film Theory.* Routledge, 1988.

Personal Narratives Group, ed. *Interpreting Women's Lives: Feminist Theory and Personal Narratives.* Bloomington, IN: Indiana University Press, 1989.

Peters, R. S. "Authority." In *Political Philosophy*, edited by Anthony Quinton. Oxford, England: Oxford University Press, 1967.

Phillips, James E., Jr. "The Background of Spenser's Attitude Toward Women Rulers." *Huntington Library Quarterly*. 5 (1942): 5–32.

Phillips, James E., Jr. "The Woman Ruler in Spenser's *Faerie Queen*." *Huntington Library Quarterly*. 5 (1942): 211–34.

Pitkin, Hanna. *The Concept of Representation*. Berkeley, CA: University of California Press, 1967.

———. *Wittgenstein and Justice*. Berkeley, CA: University of California Press, 1972.

———. *Fortune Is a Woman*. Berkeley, CA: University of California Press, 1984.

Plowden, Alison. *Two Queens in One Isle: The Deadly Relationship of Elizabeth I and Mary Queen of Scots*. Sussex, England: Harvester Press, 1984.

Plowden, Edmund. *The Commentaries and Reports of Edmund Plowden, Originally Written in French, and Now Faithfully Translated into English*. London: 1779.

Pratt, Minnie Bruce. "Identity: Skin Blood Heart." In *Yours in Struggle: Three Feminist Perspectives on Anti-Semitism and Racism*, edited by Elly Bulkin, Minnie Bruce Pratt, and Barbara Smith, eds. Long Haul Press, 1984.

Raz, Joseph. *Practical Reasons and Norms*. London: Hutchinson, 1975.

———. "Authority and Justification." *Philosophy and Public Affairs* 14 (1985).

Rice, George, ed. *The Public Speaking of Queen Elizabeth: Selections from Her Official Addresses*. New York: AMS Press, 1966.

Rich, Adrienne. *Of Woman Born*. New York: Norton, 1976.

———. *On Lies, Secrets and Silence*. New York, 1979.

Romero, Mary. "Chicanas Modernize Domestic Service." *Qualitative Sociology* 11 (1988): 319–34.

Rorty, Richard. *Contingency, Irony and Solidarity*. Cambridge, England: Cambridge University Press, 1989.

Rosaldo, Michelle. "The Use and Abuse of Anthropology: Reflections of Feminism and Cross-Cultural Understanding." *Signs* 5 (1980): 389–417.

Rosen, Ruth. "Reflections on the Gulf War." Paper Presented at Gulf War Symposium. University of California, Berkeley. Berkeley, CA, April, 1991.

Rousseau, Jean Jacques. *Émile Or, On Education*. Translated by Allan Bloom. New York: Basic Books, 1978.

Rousseau, Jean Jacques. *Politics and the Arts: A Letter to M. d'Almbert on the Theatre*. Ithaca, NY: Cornell University Press, 1968.

Rowbotham, Sheila. "Breaking the Codes." *New Society* 20 (1987): 28.

Ruddick, Sara. "Maternal Thinking." *Feminist Studies* 6 (Summer 1980): 342–67.

———. *Maternal Thinking: Toward a Politics of Peace*. New York: Ballantine Books, 1989.

———. "Thinking about Fathers." In M. Hirsch and E. Keller (1990).

Rule, Wilma. "Why Don't Women Run: The Critical Contextual Factors in Women's Legislative Recruitment." *Western Political Quarterly* 34 (1981) 60–77.

Rustow, Dankwart. *Philosophers and Kings: Studies in Leadership*. New York: Braziller, 1970.

San Francisco Chronicle, May 4, 1991, p. A12.

Sangren, P. Steven. "Rhetoric and the Authority of Ethnography." *Current Anthropology* 29 (1988): 405–35.

Sapiro, Virginia. *The Political Integration of Women: Roles, Socialization and Politics*. University of Illinois Press, 1983.

———. "Reflections on Reflections: Personal Ruminations." *Women and Politics* 7 (1987): 21–28.

Saxonhouse, Arlene. *Women in the History of Western Political Thought: Ancient Greece to Machiavelli*. New York: Praeger, 1985.

Schaar, John. *Legitimacy and the Modern State*. New Brunswick, NJ: Transaction Books, 1981.

Schochet, Gordon. *Patriarchalism in Political Thought*. New York: Basic Books, 1975.

Schor, Naomi. *Reading in Detail*. New York: Methuen, 1982.

———. "Dreaming Dissymmetry: Barthes, Foucault and Sexual Difference." In *Coming to Terms: Feminism, Theory, Politics*, edited by Elizabeth Weed. Routledge, 1989.

Scott, Joan W. "Gender: A Useful Category of Historical Analysis." *American Historical Review* 91 (1986): 1053–75.

Seery, John. *Political Returns: Irony in Politics and Theory, from Plato to the Antinuclear Movement*. Boulder, CO: Westview Press, 1990.

Sennett, Richard. *Authority*. New York: Knopf, 1981.

Shakespeare, William. *Midsummer Night's Dream*. London: Cornmarket, 1969.

Sharistanian, Janet. *Gender Ideology and Action: Historical Perspectives on Women's Political Lives*. Greenwood Press, 1986.

Showalter, Elaine. *Sexual Anarchy: Gender and Culture at the Fin de Siècle*. New York: Viking Press, 1990.

Skinner, Quentin. "The Context of Hobbes's Theory of Obligation." in *Hobbes and Rousseau*, edited by Maurice Cranston and Richard S. Peters. New York: Anchor Books, 1972.

Spelman, Elizabeth. "On Treating Persons as Persons." *Ethics* 88 (1978): 150–61.

———. *Inessential Woman: The Problem of Exclusion in Feminist Theory*. Boston: Beacon Press, 1989.

Spenser, Edmund. *The Fairie Queene*. In *The Poetical Works of Edmund Spenser*, edited by J. C. Smith and E. de Selincourt, Oxford, 1924.

Springborg, Patricia. *Royal Persons*. Allen, Unwin and Hyman, 1991.

Stacey, Judith. "Can There Be a Feminist Ethnography?" *Women's Studies International Forum* 11 (1988): 11–27.

Starr, Paul. *The Social Transformation of American Medicine*. New York: Beacon Books, 1982.

Stiehm, Judith, "The Protector and the Protected." In *Women and Men's Wars*, edited by Judith Stiehm. Pergamon Press, 1982.

———. *Women's Views of the Political World of Men*. Transactional Publishers, 1983.

Thompson, Seth. "Women As Chief Executives: Does Gender Matter?" Paper presented at Annual Meeting of the Western Political Science Association, Seattle, WA, 1991.

Trinh, Minh-Ha. *Woman/Native/Other*. Bloomington, IN: Indiana University Press, 1988.

Tronto, Joan. "Beyond Gender Difference to a Theory of Care." *Signs* 12 (1987): 644–63.

Turgenev, Ivan Sergeevich. *Fathers and Sons*. New York: The Heritage Press, 1941.

Utall, Lynet. "Inclusion Without Influence: The Continuing Tokenism of Women of Color." In *Making Face, Making Soul: Haciendo Caras, Creative and Critical Perspectives by Women*, edited by Gloria Anzaldúa. San Francisco: Aunt Lute Foundation Books, 1990.

Vergès, Françoise. "Memories of Origin." *Reproductive and Genetic Engineering* (1991): 3–15.

———. "Daughters of Sycorax: Islands and the Calvinized Female Subject." Unpublished manuscript, University of California, Berkeley, 1991.

Vicinus, Martha. *Independent Women: Work and Community for Single Women, 1850–1920*. Chicago: University of Chicago Press, 1985.

Vogel, Ursula. "Under Permanent Guardianship." In *The Political Interests of Gender: Developing Theory and Research with a Feminist Face,* edited by Kathleen B. Jones and Anna G. Jónasdóttir. London: Sage Publications, 1988.

Walker, Alice. *In Love and Trouble: Stories of Black Women*. New York: Harcourt Brace Jovanovich, 1973.

———. *In Search of Our Mother's Gardens*. San Diego, Calif.: Harcourt Brace Jovanovich, 1983.

Walzer, Michael. *Spheres of Justice*. New York: Basic Books, 1983.

Wandor, Michelene. *Carry On, Understudies: Theatre and Sexual Politics*. London and New York, Routledge and Kegan Paul, 1986.

Warner, Marina. *Joan of Arc: The Image of Female Heroism*. New York: Knopf, 1981.

Warrender, Howard. *The Political Philosophy of Hobbes*. Oxford, England: Clarendon Press, 1957.

Webber and Grumman, eds. *Woman As Writer*. Boston: Houghton Mifflin, 1978.

Weber, Max. *Theory of Social and Economic Organizations*. Glencoe, Ill.: The Free Press, 1947.

———. *Economy and Society: An Outline of Interpretive Sociology*. Edited by Guenther Roth and Claus Wittich. Berkeley, CA: University of California Press, 1978.

Weed, Elizabeth, ed. *Coming to Terms: Feminism, Theory, Politics*. Routledge, 1989.

Wheelwright, Julie. *Amazons and Military Maids: Women Who Dressed As Men in Pursuit of Life, Liberty and Happiness*. London: Pandora, 1989.

White, Stephen. *Political Theory and Postmodernism*. Cambridge, MA: Cambridge University Press, 1991.

Williams, Patricia. "On Being the Object of Property." *Signs* 14 (1988): 5–24.

Winch, Peter. "Man and Society in Hobbes and Rousseau." In *Hobbes and Rousseau: A Collection of Critical Essays,* edited by Maurice Cranston and Richard S. Peters. Doubleday Anchor Books, 1972.

Wolf, Margery. *Woman and the Family in Rural Taiwan*. Stanford CA: Stanford University Press, 1972.

Wood, Charles T. "Queens, Queans, and Kingship: An Inquiry into Theories of Royal Legitimacy in Late Medieval England and France." In *Order and Innovation in the Middle Ages: Essays in Honor of Joseph R. Strayer,* edited by William Jordan, Bruce McNab, and Teofilio Ruiz. Princeton, NJ: Princeton University Press, 1976.

Young, Iris. *Justice and the Politics of Difference*. Princeton, NJ: Princeton University Press, 1990.

———. *Throwing Like a Girl and Other Essays in Feminist Philosophy and Social Theory*. Bloomington, IN: Indiana University Press, 1990.

Zavarzadeh, Mas'ud. *Seeing Films Politically*. State University of New York Press, 1991.

Zerilli, Linda. "Machiavelli's Sisters: Women and the 'Conversation' of Political Theory." *Political Theory* 19 (May 1991): 252–76.

Index

259

Vogel, Ursula, 67
Voyeurism, 201

Walzer, Michael, 147, 154
Waring, Marilyn, 195–96
Weber, Max, 109–17, 126–31
White, Stephen, 141, 182, 197–98, 229
Whitefeminism, 14–15

Williams, Patricia, 24n.2
Winch, Peter, 47, 50, 206
Women's history, 65
Wright, Charles, 104

Young, Iris, 15, 143

Zavarzadeh, Mas'ud, 10
Zerilli, Linda, 19, 77, 159